Bob Ansett
AN AUTOBIOGRAPHY

Bob Ansett
AN AUTOBIOGRAPHY

WITH ROBERT PULLAN

JOHN KERR

© *Robert G. Ansett and Robert Pullan 1986*

This book is copyright. Apart from fair dealing for the purposes of private study, research, criticism or review, as permitted under the Copyright Act, no part may be reproduced by any process without written permission from John Kerr Pty Ltd.

Mr R. G. Ansett's income from this work has been assigned to various charities.

First published 1986
by John Kerr Pty Ltd
1285 Toorak Road
Hartwell, Victoria 3124

Typeset in 12/13 Baskerville
by Setrite Typesetters Ltd
Wanchai, Hong Kong

Colour separation & plate film-making
by Bookbuilders Ltd
Kowloon, Hong Kong

Printed
by Globe Press Pty Ltd
Melbourne

Distributed in Australia by:
Tower Books, NSW & ACT
Herron Books, Qld
Aaron Books, SA & NT
Book Agencies of Tasmania, Tas
Kingfisher Books, Vic
Pickwick Books, WA
and in New Zealand
by David Bateman Ltd

*National Library of Australia
cataloguing-in-pubication data:*

Ansett, Bob, 1933-
    Bob Ansett.

    Includes index.
    ISBN 0 9588161 0 7.

    1. Ansett, Bob, 1933-   . 2. Businessmen — Australia
    — Biography. I. Pullan, Robert, 1944-   . II. Title.

338.7'092'4

To the memory of my friend Pete Kemmsies

Contents

    Introduction   9

    Prologue   11

1 Childhood and Youth   13

2 Alaska, Japan and Australia   37

3 An Ex-greasemonkey's Luggage   65

4 Uphill and Roadblocks   76

5 Driver's Seat   103

6 The Airport Concession War   110

7 This Image Business...   137

8 The Budget Culture   147

9 In the Air   152

10 Thoughts of an Early-Morning Jogger   171

11 Around the Next Bend   193

12 Soapbox   201

    Acknowledgements   213

    Index   215

Introduction

My wife Josie and I made the decision to write this book on a Qantas flight between Auckland, New Zealand and Melbourne, Victoria, in September 1984.

We were returning home after a week in the High Court of New Zealand giving evidence in an action Budget had taken against Avis. The hearings covered the entire history of the Australian and New Zealand car rental industry and we both thought it should be recorded for posterity.

A few weeks later Josie contacted Rob Pullan, an old friend who had written several books and asked what he thought of the idea. He was a little nonplussed at the beginning, but his enthusiasm grew as we talked about the directions the story could take.

It was not my intention to write an autobiography, but when we pieced together the elements of the story, it simply evolved as one. That was all right with me for two reasons. First, my favourite books are biographies: I'm fascinated by the details of other people's lives. Second, and more important, I think it's good to have a record of what you've achieved. I've always regretted that there's no detailed record of my father's life, and now that he and many of his contemporaries have gone, perhaps there never will be.

I have a certain uneasiness about revealing the intimate facts of my life in a book, but if it is to be an honest account of my life, I know it has to be warts and all. Some things I'm not particularly proud of, but I guess they all played a part in shaping my character.

Writing this book provides me with the opportunity to pay tribute to the thousands of Australians who have worked in the company and contributed to its success over the past 21 years. Their loyalty and commitment has been outstanding. They have demonstrated that given the right circumstances and environment there is nothing Australians cannot achieve. I tip my hat to every one of them.

If this book offers encouragement to just one person, it will have been worth while.

Prologue

The first time I visited my father in his office I read on a wall a framed quotation from Calvin Coolidge, President of the United States from 1923 to 1929:

> Nothing in the world can take the place of persistence. Talent will not; nothing is more common than unsuccessful men with talent. Genius will not; unrewarded genius is almost a proverb. Education will not; the world is full of educated derelicts. Persistence and determination alone are omnipotent. The slogan 'press on' has solved and always will solve the problems of the human race.

Perhaps because I had just returned to Melbourne after 20 years in the United States I was particularly receptive to advice from an American President. I said to Reg Ansett: 'That's the best quotation I've ever seen.' My father agreed, but he wasn't interested in talking about it — in his early pioneering years the quotation had the essence of the way R. M. Ansett conducted his enterprises, but in the later years I think it had little meaning for him. In 1965 I thought it perfectly encapsulated my own philosophy, and 21 years later I still do. Persistence is the essence of success in business or anything else. I think I'm a good example of what Coolidge was talking about: I'm not an extraordinarily talented person, nor am I a genius. As for education, I have not gone beyond high school, and while there I wasn't top of the class. My father wasn't either — the only two pieces of paper he ever had proving he could do something were a knitting machine mechanic's certificate and a pilot's licence. At that meeting my father told me there was no place for Bob Ansett in his business empire, Ansett Transport Industries. The day I returned to Melbourne, NO JOB FOR BOB was the page one headline in the *Melbourne Herald*. (The headline now adorns the stairwell in the Budget headquarters building in North Melbourne.)

When I came back to Melbourne and started with Budget car rentals after my father's rejection, I started with nothing. My job experience was limited to pumping petrol and driving a milk truck in Los Angeles and a bread truck in San Diego. I had three young children and a wife to support. But I had three things to offer. The first was the strong competitive sense I developed playing American football — in sport or in business I wanted to beat the hell out of the other guy. The second was my confidence in myself — I've always believed I have a charmed life and no matter what I do it will work out. The third was persistence, another lesson from football. I wasn't a brilliant footballer — there were lots of faster, bigger guys, guys with safer hands, but I discovered that I could start a game against a bigger, more talented opponent who was on top in the first plays, but if I kept at the task, just kept grinding away, I would get to him in the end. The Budget philosophy, which is the key to our success, evolved from my experience on gridiron fields in California and Japan, from my work on the gas pumps in Southern California, and from thousands of hours on bread and milk delivery runs. But I'm getting ahead of myself...

1
Childhood and Youth

The most important influence on my life, my father Reginald Myles Ansett, was born in Inglewood, 40 kilometres west of Bendigo, central Victoria, on 12 February 1909. His father, Charles John Ansett, listed his occupation on the birth certificate as 'cycle engineer'. His father, my great grandfather, also named Charles John, was a bootmaker. My great great grandfather, the first Charles John Ansett, migrated to Victoria in 1853 with his wife Elizabeth and three children; he was a 'carrier', and perhaps he carried some of the genes that have come down to me, because he seems to have been a combative and litigious character. When the ship sailed without him after he had booked a passage to Victoria early in the 1850s, he sued the shipping company not once but twice — once for breach of contract, and a second time over the costs of the first action. He must have been an adventurer, and I like to think he carried the itch to beat the next guy to Port Melbourne. He certainly wasn't born with a silver spoon in his mouth: his father was a gardener.

The Ansetts have never been a dynasty — we've been too competitive and individualistic for that, and my father was hostile to the very idea. When my brother John showed him the law report involving his great grandfather, he wasn't interested at all. John thought Reg was 'a man without a past — for him the world started with Reg'. But four generations of us, strangely enough, have been involved in the car rental business. Two years ago, the father of one of the Budget staff was sifting through a dusty cardboard box of clippings when he discovered an advertisement in the *Inglewood Advertiser* for a local garage that repaired motorcars and hired cars out. The proprietor of that garage was Charles John Ansett, my father's father. That was in 1915. My grandfather must have run one of the first rent-a-car businesses in Australia: even in the United States at that time Henry Ford's assembly-line Model T was still a novelty and the rent-a-car business didn't start till three years later.

My father left school at 14 like most kids of his generation, then qualified for a knitting machine mechanic's certificate from Swinburne Technical College. He effectively worked two jobs, repairing knitting machines for his employer's customers during the day, then the same thing at night for people who couldn't afford a mechanic on full rates. They were hard times: he was a child of the depression.

In 1929 he caught a boat to Darwin — there was no road then between Alice Springs and Darwin — with the idea of getting into the ground nuts business. On the boat he met a guy setting up a survey party who offered him a job as axeman. This was the raw, hard Northern Territory that Xavier Herbert wrote about in *Capricornia*.

Reg took the job without any experience as an axeman, but in the bush he had to learn quickly. One day, he was chewing into a gum tree, chips flying, making the jagged lines of a beginner. The surveyor approached, looked at the marks on the tree, at Reg sweating it out, and said, 'Every stump you leave stays there forever — they're a memorial to this party.' Reg reckoned that after that he left every stump as smooth as a billiard table, and he became a master axeman — he could swing right or left handed, he knew exactly what weight head to use on what timber, he could cut a V into a redgum as cleanly as a knife cuts butter. When he was an old man he told stories of his days in the Territory bush, of seeing Amy Johnson fly over to become the first woman to fly from Britain to Australia in 1930, and that he, a bloke who never played any sport because he was a driven worker, a workaholic from the age of 14, believed that mastering axemanship was one of the achievements of his life.

CHILDHOOD AND YOUTH 15

Reg loved the Territory and stayed in touch with people there for the rest of his life; but with the great depression bleeding the economy, survey parties were few. Besides, the vast Territory with its tiny population of drifters and outlaws wasn't a promising place for a man with Reg's drive and entrepreneurial instincts. He wanted a place with more people and more money.

He returned to Victoria, and when his parents moved to Maryborough — they opened a bicycle shop outside the town — he started a limousine service to run the Maryborough farmers and their wives into Ballarat, 50 kilometres away. He did everything. He was his own mechanic, driver, schedule planner, promotions man, accountant.

On his trips to Ballarat he quickly got to know people — in those days everybody in country towns knew everybody else — and one of the main weekend obsessions was, of course, Australian Rules Football, the Ballarat League. Reg had formed an acquaintance with the young Maryborough Town Clerk, Stanley Nicol, who was a brilliant ruck-rover soon to interest the talent scouts of the Fitzroy Football Club in the Victorian Football League, the big league. Reg and Stan regularly went halves on bets on Maryborough; their limit was a £5 bet, which was a big plunge — Stan's weekly salary was £6. But Reg did better punting on the football than he did driving the big Studebakers and Buicks into Ballarat. The car rental business wasn't thriving — Maryborough was too small. Even so, in the middle of the depression Reg was moving on.

He bought a Tiger moth; when he took Stan for a flight to show him the new toy, Stan was terrified. 'He almost turned it over, no belts, no nothing, but I couldn't have fallen out — I was frozen stiff.'

Reg was beginning to show form as a businessman. His brother Jack had started Ansett Knitting Mills in the town of Seymour 120 kilometres north of Melbourne, but the business was struggling. Reg went down, ran his eye over it, took a seat on the board, and the industry quickly picked up.

Reg's most important encounter in Maryborough was with Stanley's sister, Grace Nicol. Grace, the second youngest of eight children, was born in Cobden, Victoria,

80 kilometres west of Geelong, where her father ran a cheese factory; the family moved to Carisbrook, a small gold-mining town, then to Maryborough. After a year at the Methodist Ladies College in Ballarat, Grace was in Maryborough 'playing an awful lot of tennis and doing nothing' when she was invited to an evening at a family home — 'it was Sir Henry someone and his wife,' she says. 'They were very English.' Reg Ansett was there. She found him 'very outgoing, very charming. He was fun. He was very much like Robert is now. I just fell in love with him. I used to go up to Kerang to play tennis — we played tennis all day and half the night; Reg used to call me all the time while I was up there.'

Reg and Grace married and moved to Hamilton, the heart of Victoria's Western District. As they started their married life business picked up; Reg started buying extra Studebakers and hiring extra drivers, he started the run from Hamilton to Ballarat. He started Ansett Airways, with Grace doing the bookkeeping. 'I didn't know what I was doing really — but it was a very simple system and it was very neat. It worked. It was accurate. At least we knew who we owed.' But Reg was expanding quickly; when Grace told him the job was getting too big for her he hired her brother Melville, a former poultry farmer who had the family gift for figures and a sound business head.

While Ansett Airways was in its infancy, so was I. I was born on 8 August 1933, and apparently started making a pest of myself immediately. My mother remembers my pulling the freshly glued wallpaper from the hallway walls of their Hamilton home — probably I was curious to see what was underneath it. And I was always trying to find out what was behind the electricity sockets around the house, grabbing a knife or a screwdriver and trying to get those intriguing plates off the skirting boards. (My younger brother John got a dangerous shock from an exposed electric wire — but I don't know if I was to blame.) We lived in a rambling old house with an enormous verandah and a very large garage for the cars; Reg built a small house behind the garage for two of his drivers.

Three images are burnt into my memory of those days in Hamilton and have stayed with me for nearly 50 years. The first is of our red setter, called Tim. When I was three or four I used to ride Tim like a horse; I loved that dog and I've loved red setters ever since. I named my younger son Tim remembering the pet of my childhood. The other two indelible images are of Reg. I often rode in the front seat of the big Studebaker — they could seat eight or nine passengers — and as he drove through the Western District farm country between Hamilton, Ballarat, Maryborough and Bendigo, my dominant impression was of incredible speed. I thought the father who towered beside me on the front seat drove like a racing driver. When he took me for my first ride in an aeroplane, a Fokker Universal, I don't think I had any fear of flying, but I was impressed by the noise of the engine and the wind whistling around us, and the fact that my father was flying it. These images of his skill in control of the Studebaker and the Fokker are vivid to this day: I thought he was a daredevil and wonderfully exciting.

Reg was a bit of a loner all his life, but before Ansett Airways consumed all his time and energy he made a close friend in Hamilton, John Burge, who was dying from tuberculosis. John was a well-read man, and Reg, who had never had time for books, was fascinated to talk over business problems with John and get his advice. Reg visited him every day while he was dying — he never forgot or shirked. My mother thinks that after his friend died, Reg missed him but never grieved. 'I don't think Reg would grieve over anybody. He thought you either survived or you didn't — and it was your tough luck if you didn't.'

In Hamilton when I was three I went to a little pre-school, a Catholic kindergarten, where the idea was to teach kids obedience, and how to use their hands. I don't remember those days — my mother says I was interested in using tools as a youngster, sawing pieces of wood at a carpenter's bench, but I know I failed obedience.

When we came down to Melbourne in 1938 I went to Scotch College while my parents waited to move into Sir Stanley Bruce's old house at Mt Eliza, a seaside town 50 kilometres by road from Melbourne. Stanley Melbourne Bruce led the Nationalist Party and was Prime Minister from 1923 to 1929 with the Country Party in coalition. At Mt Eliza a small exclusive school was established near a golf club for the children of the surrounding estates. I don't remember it, but my mother remembers those wealthy children made a fetish out of not wearing shoes; they would even go barefoot into Melbourne. Grace thought it was peculiar, a bit like the rich college kids of the 1960s wearing dirty T-shirts and jeans as a uniform.

My first memory of school is my arrival at Wesley College as a boarder. I was only seven, pretty young for a boarder. Reg and Grace took me there, and we were surrounded by kids crying because they were being wrenched away from their families. I couldn't understand such emotion — it just seemed logical to me that I'd be living at the school, even though my mother remembers I didn't say much and I looked very stoical. My mother found it a wrench; she felt she was losing me, handing me over to somebody else, particularly when the headmaster did his best to despatch parents immediately. Grace managed to stay for about 20 minutes, with the headmaster ushering her and Reg towards the door.

I enjoyed Wesley — even at seven I was a fairly confident and outgoing kid. My memories are only of playing cricket and football: I don't remember the teachers or the lessons. But when I found I had to spend most weekends at school, I was disappointed. I ended up spending a lot of weekends at a friend's house. Jack Joel's father was a doctor in Williamstown, a bayside western suburb of Melbourne, and I still remember those weekends at his family home. The doctor was very generous with candy — Jack was a spoilt kid, and I was able to join in the spoils. Jack later became the general manager of Kays Rent-a-Car, then coincidentally started his own car leasing company which is now in competition with Budget's leasing division. But I can't remember any of the normal father-and-son things between Reg and me, except that once or twice he gave me a rifle and we went rabbit shooting at Mt Eliza.

By the time I was settled into primary school Reg and Grace's marriage was in trouble. Reg was spending a lot of time away from home and was completely absorbed in expanding Ansett Airways. Grace should tell this part of the story:

'Reg had worked all his life since he was 14 and he never had time to play. He'd never had any women before me. He'd never played. Then about six years after we were married, when we moved to Melbourne, he decided it was time, which was too bad. He had lots of other women, his secretaries, one after another. He'd fire one when he was through with her, and then he would start with the next one. With his time taken up between the company and time away from home and other women, I thought there was something wrong with me, that it was my fault. The airline was a tremendous effort for him, and he changed. He wasn't a loving person, he wasn't a happy person any more, he didn't want me around, nothing seemed enough for him, it was all business. He thought he could do anything, that I should just stay home with the children and accept it. But I couldn't. I felt I was losing my sense of self. I talked to my father about it, and he said he didn't think Reg would change. I didn't either.

'He formed a serious attachment to Joan Adams, an Ansett Airways secretary and wanted a divorce. He got it, and married her in 1944.

'I just couldn't believe it and felt at the time that it had finished me. I was devastated, because I still loved him then and I did for years after. Three years after Reg and I separated I agreed to marry an American, Don Campbell, a Lockheed engineer Reg had brought to Melbourne to service his aircraft. I should never have married Don, but I had to get away, and I didn't have any job experience or training and I thought, "Well, this man loves me — I won't let Reg affect me." But of course, he did — I was still in love with him.'

Naturally, I knew very little of these adult dramas. In the year I spent at Wesley I knew they were pretty much separated — Reg was often away from home for a couple of months, then back for a few days, then gone again. When Grace had had enough, she decided to move from Reg's house at Gunyong Valley, Mt Eliza to a house at North Balwyn. My father was to remain at Gunyong Valley for the rest of his life.

She explained the situation to me, that they were separating and ultimately divorcing. But it wasn't traumatic for me: I wasn't a kid who internalised unhappiness and blamed himself for his parents splitting up. I didn't think

'What have I done wrong?' I was vaguely aware that the American Don Campbell was around. Then Grace and Don married — I wasn't at the wedding. I was just told afterwards that they were married, just before my brother and I left for California with them. I boarded the *Paracoola*, a Swedish freighter, bound for San Francisco with Grace and John in 1943. It was a great trip, a big adventure for me. Because it was wartime, the crew and the 20 adult passengers were very conscious of Japanese submarines; we travelled without lights and it was very quiet. Somewhere in the middle of the Pacific we lost a rudder and everything stopped for several days until they got it up and running again. Later we did sight a submarine, but it was friendly — a U.S. Navy submarine. Nevertheless, the Captain cut the power and drifted for a time until they identified it. John and I were conscious of the adults' fear of submarines, but we were too young to understand anything about torpedoes and death by high explosive, and neither of us, then or later, was inclined to dwell on risks or danger. We were adventurers, and the crew let us, two small boys, ten and eight, have the run of the ship. Once we were on the bridge and saw the signals for the officer of the watch to signal 'Full Speed Ahead,' 'Slow' and 'Stop.' John the urger told me: 'Go on, pull that one,' and like a dope I pulled it — alarm bells rang, everyone thought it was a submarine attack, and we were barred from the bridge for the rest of the voyage.

After six weeks we made it to San Francisco via Vancouver and caught a bus to Los Angeles. I don't know if we were entirely appropriate immigrants — Los Angeles is the city of the angels. But we went to live in Tihunga with Don Campbell's mother.

John and I were the cause of the first serious difference between Grace and her second husband: before they left Melbourne Grace had made Don promise that we could live at home, that he wouldn't send us to boarding school, because she hadn't liked us being away from her when we were boarding at Wesley. 'You might as well not have kids if you're going to send them away to boarding school as young as that,' she told him. But after we got to

Tihunga, Don's mother made it clear she didn't like Grace, she didn't like John and she didn't like me. The only solution was for us to go to boarding school again — this time the Ridgeway Military Academy about 40 kilometres from home. Military academies in the U.S. are the equivalent of the English-style boys' boarding school — the idea is to turn out educated teenagers with a strong sense of what's proper and what isn't, who know how to wear uniforms and tip their hats and say 'Yessir' and 'Yes Ma'am' to their fathers and mothers. We achieved ranks — private first class, corporal and so forth, and we did military training every night. We wore uniforms to classes, had daily rifle drill, shined our shoes each night till they gleamed. Spit-and-polish was the order of the day, every day. I remember one 12-year-old whose hand slipped when he was sitting in his underpants running a cleaning rod through his rifle. It pierced his testicles; we never saw him again. Stories of homosexuality made the rounds of the academy, but I was never exposed to it, and didn't understand what it was.

John, who was a wild kid — even I thought he was headed for a juvenile reformatory — hated it, as I did. Once he wrote a letter to Grace saying he was very unhappy: the Academy authorities intercepted this rebellious letter and read it out to John's class while he squirmed. I don't want to whinge about it, but this was the most unhappy period of my life. I've had some pretty difficult times in a bit more than 50 years, but this was the only time I look back on and think 'Jeez, it was terrible.' Perhaps the free-and-easy years as an Australian country kid had left me ill-prepared for this peculiarly formal existence even by American standards. It's the only time I've really hated the circumstances facing me. The one bright spot was sport: I played American football for the first time, and found I was good at it, and competed in 75-yard sprints.

Eventually I accepted the system and even ended up a sergeant, but for the first year it was very tough. I was a stranger in America, my mother was unhappy with Don Campbell and thinking about taking us back to Australia, and the Military Academy was trying to bully us into premature manhood. I hitch-hiked home to Grace's house several times; both John and I always tried to change things when we were caught in situations we didn't like, but all we could do then was run away — and we did.

After a year Grace rented a house in Monrovia, about 30 kilometres from Tihunga, and found a job as an eye-specialist's receptionist. Don Campbell, who was a strange, highly strung man, took a job with an aerial photography mission, working on a DC3, based in Bogota, the capital of Columbia, a violent, crime-ridden city in the Andes. He was making big money — aircraft engineers were in big demand after the war — but he was away for months at a time. When he came back to Monrovia to stay he set up a woodworking shop — he was clever with his hands — and delivered laundry in the neighbourhood. Then he had a shop making outdoor furniture — all mid-life autonomous job-retraining! — and he was doing pretty well, but he and Grace decided they wanted an avocado ranch. We all drove down in the family car to Vista, 150 kilometres south of L.A., to look at an undeveloped ranch with no house on it. They bought it on the spot, together with a caravan, in which we lived for the following year, the year I started high school.

When we moved in there were about 1500 avocado trees and a thousand bird of paradise plants, those orange flowers that the well-off of Southern California bought for bouquets for their wives and daughters. The flowers are easy to grow, and they're fresh three weeks after picking.

Grace was struggling to survive. When she spoke to one of the early customers for the birds of paradise she had stopped spending on hairdos and makeup and apparently she looked alarmingly different from the well-turned-out Vista wives. The man told her later: 'I thought some kind of wild woman was living on the ranch.'

Don Campbell started building a house, a prefabricated army-type affair, but by then Grace's second marriage was really breaking up and Don was going a bit crazy. He left — Grace didn't know where he had gone — then he returned unexpectedly at night and crawled under the house, hammering on the floorboards. Fairly obviously, it was disturbing and he was equally obviously disturbed. He often stole my mother's car: she was always on the phone to the sheriff. His paper bills, gas bills and grocery bills came to our house. In desperation Grace called a Vista attorney, who in turn called the sheriff to ask for protection, but there was not much the police could do. They divorced.

Once after the divorce one of the six-monthly cheques my old man sent to pay for John's and my clothing disappeared from our mailbox, which was a long way from the house. Don knew when the clothing cheque came, and Grace reckoned it had to have been him. Grace should have found out from Reg if the cheque had been cashed, bu Reg wasn't very friendly to her then. Today she merely says philosophically, 'I didn't make very good choices in men,' but then she was very poor indeed. Another time Don drove up to the ranch and took our dog away in his car. John and I chased him in Grace's car and cornered him in a cul de sac; I grabbed a huge wooden Javanese club from our car, smashed the window and got the dog out. I was 13 — and Don was a pretty big fellow, one or two inches over six feet.

The last time I saw him John and I were pulling the weeds around the bird of paradise flowers and Don drove up with his brother. Don started shaking John; I leapt on his back and started choking him with an arm around his throat till his brother pulled me off.

About two years after we moved to the ranch, Don vanished. He just disappeared and Grace never heard from him again. Not once. She doesn't know if he's alive or dead today, though she did try to find him once because he had run up a lot of bills and they all came to her. The avocado and bird of paradise sales didn't cover the costs of the ranch; within two years of the move, the bank foreclosed, forcing my mother to rent a small house in Vista where she got a sales assistant's job in the town drugstore. Although Vista architecturally had Southern California written all over it and Spanish place and street names, Mexican bars and the fan palm trees let you know immediately you were in San Diego County. In the late 1940s and early 1950s there was a lot to remind an Australian of home, in a town so small it didn't even have a traffic light. In 1890 the Santa Fe Railroad company established forests of gum trees as a source of hardwood for railway sleepers. In the 1930s a Vista family established a passion fruit grove, believing that Southern Californians would learn to love the purple-seeded fruit as much as Australians did, and that a 'passionfruit cocktail' would soon become an essential part of cocktail hour in San Diego County, perhaps even in Hollywood and after that, how could trendy Wall Street stockbrokers resist it when they went home to their apartments on the east side of Manhattan? As it turned out, both these ideas were business disasters: the Eucalyptus hardwood rotted between the iron railroad tracks, and for some reason the passionfruit never caught on in the Californian cocktail circuit. (Perhaps it was a marketing problem: some of the older Vista residents remember that there was some confusion about the name — people thought it had a sexual connotation, although the name actually derives from the passion of Christ because the flower is said to resemble the wounds and the crown of thorns of Jesus.) But the gum trees stayed; a picture of Eucalyptus Avenue in 1950 from a point opposite the Town Hall complex could be springtime in the Australian bush. Golden wattle crowded the street; mixed with the blue-green cactus were a variety of flesh-coloured gums, red bottlebrush and the Australian flame tree. I doubt that this affected me much because I was too young to have established emotional ties to Australia, but it was a pleasing coincidence.

In Vista I established my closest friendships, learned some important lessons and became a man. They were happy years.

They were also high-risk years. Twice I was arrested. I stole avocados — not nicking a handful now and then from the avocado groves, but a car full, 600 pounds (270 kg) at a time. I swiped petrol too, not just milking a parked car when I ran out of gas, but by the 44-gallon drumful. I illegally ran unauthorised Mexican aliens from San Diego to Los Angeles, past Immigration Department checkpoints. Once, in a hare-brained adventure, I broke into a house and stole a toolbox and a set of tyres.

My brother John had a different line of business — he nicked condoms from the local drugstore where he worked and sold them to the high school boys. It wasn't so different from the schoolboy pranks that most kids get up to — except that I pushed it so far that I guess I was lucky not to see the inside of a State home for juvenile delinquents.

It would be hypocritical for me to say now that I regret it — I was having too much fun — but I would have gone white if my kids behaved the way I did, and my mother says she went white 'several times' during my high school years.

California, which then and now had more people, more money and more social problems than existed in the whole of Australia, is famous for setting trends, its movies and the ideas that are generated there. Then and now, the thinkers at the University of California in Los Angeles and San Diego, and in private industry laboratories, were at the cutting edge of world research. Hundreds of high schools were the seeding ground for gifted kids who would one day enter the ranks of the best and brightest in the western world.

Vista High School wasn't one of them. Most of my classmates were kids from struggling families. Their fathers were construction workers, avocado grove owners, gas station managers; some, like me, lived with their mothers after divorce had split their families. With my strange Australian accent, I got my fair share of the mockery high school kids everywhere dish out to those who are a bit different. If success in life depended on poring over textbooks, conscientiously doing homework and coming top of the class, I would have been a failure. With my buddies Dale Soderstrom, a golden-haired Scandinavian-American who laughed a lot, and Jerry Rudolph, a sharp storyteller built like a fullback, I did enough work to stay in school — but only just. We learnt a lot more on the football field and in our extracurricular exploits than we ever did in the classroom.

I took the academic course, which meant I could go on to college — university — when I graduated. I had no fixed intention of going to college, but in America every ambitious kid at high school sets his or her sights on college. I was mildly interested in English literature and history, and I did the basics in maths and science, but the courses were fairly easy and I didn't push myself. It was a bit of a farce: Dale and I enrolled in a course called 'chorus' — but neither of us could hold a note, so after a semester we drifted into drama and starred in the school play, largely because the drama teacher had a red-haired daughter called Madelene, a girl of great interest to us both. One year we decided to become audiovisual experts and got the job of showing educational films to the various classes. Jerry kept a wine bottle in his locker and we drank it between lessons; the three of us boasted that we didn't ever take a book home in four years of high school.

There were three main groups at the high school. There were goody-goodies from the established families who owned stores and big avocado groves. The goody-goodies drove new cars, got into their books, kept their noses clean and headed straight for college. This was a small group. The biggest group was the one I belonged to: the good-bad guys. We drove battered old cars, stole gas and avocados, raised hell and lived off our wits. The third group was the real bad guys, who hung out with low-lifes and seemed headed straight for reform school. My brother John was one of the real bad guys.

Sometimes there wasn't much to separate us good-bad guys from the really wild bastards. The boundaries weren't all that rigidly defined. Joe Walker, one of the two Vista sheriffs, came into the pool hall one day when we were illegally drinking beer — we were under 18 — and said 'I'm tired of kicking you guys out of here. Not only that — I know where you are now.' He took off his gunbelt, hung it on the rack and started to shoot pool with us. What the law forbade covered a much bigger area than what the sheriff would enforce.

Getting petrol for our cars was one of our biggest economic problems. Although I worked a variety of traditional jobs — I had a newspaper delivery route when I was eleven and I worked vacation jobs through high school — gasoline was often hard to come by. But one of the kids in my class, Max Jamison, worked part-time at the school washing the school buses, and he made the mistake of telling my buddy Dan Flemming where they hid the key to the gas pumps. Dan, later a labor organiser for the Carpenters Union, sneaked into the petrol docks once every couple of weeks and drew a discreet 10 or 15 gallons (50 or 70 litres) — nothing that you'd miss from a big tank.

But when he told me about it, the demand increased substantially. Pretty soon we had cars lined up there one night as if it were a regular gas station. We realised that that was it, that time they were going to miss the gas, so we decided to go for broke. I went home and returned with a 50-gallon drum; Dan found a couple of 5-gallon cans. Then we scrounged around the back of the building and found two 50-gallon drums of weed killer. We thought about that for a short time, then drained the drums and filled them with gas. Dan took the back seat out of his '35 Ford and loaded all the drums — the old car was right down on its axles — and took them to his parents' place. Dan had his bed in the garage, and he hid the drums there. He said 'If my dad had got on to it, it wouldn't have been too pleasant — but he didn't, or if he did he never said anything about it.' The next day, with 100 gallons of weed killer lying around the school yard, it was obvious something was up. A detective was summoned and interviewed Max Jamison and Dan and me. But we were never proven guilty and the school didn't do anything. Oh yes — we sold the drums of petrol and weed-killer to Jerry. He got a bargain. Unfortunately, there was a little too much weed killer in the mixture and it burnt out the engine in his 1940 Mercedes — Buyer Beware!

Dan tested his parents' tolerance, as I did Grace's. Once Dan hid a carload of stolen avocados in his room after we had picked them at night. When he came home from school his mother said: 'What're all those avocados doing in there?' Dan thought fast and said with a straight face: 'That's a very exotic kind of fruit, you know. It's the kind that can only be picked at night. They can't be picked during the day.' He doesn't think she bought it, but she didn't say anything.

I got the avocado caper down to a science. I went to a Vista salvage store selling army fatigues and left−over gear and bought miners' hats with lights on them, ideal for picking at night. Each time Dan dropped us off at the chosen grove, and Jerry and another guy, Frank Cox and I, did the picking and loaded up Dan's Ford. When Dan returned with the empty boxes we filled them up again. We made $50 or $100 a night with barely any effort.

Of course, there were risks. One night Dan, Jerry, Frank and I picked a grove clean of avocados. It took two trips in my mother's yellow 1932 Chevrolet, called 'The Rockcrusher' because it sounded like one. We carefully hid the first load behind the bamboo in my mother's back yard, then returned for the second load. At 3 a.m. we were on the way home when the local sheriff, Ed Speaks, apprehended us and carted Frank and me off to jail in

Oceanside, a town a few kilometres from Vista. Ed phoned my mother, who came to see us. I warned her about the avocados behind the bamboo. As the sun came up, Grace dug a huge hole and buried the fruit. Unknown to her, my buddy Dale was watching her frenzied digging and burying through binoculars, from his house 50 metres away. After Grace left for work, Dale wandered down in his vehicle, dug up the avocados and sold the lot while I was rotting in the Oceanside jail. Once again, my luck held. I was released after 12 hours.

Ed Speaks was a fairly understanding guy. He told Grace: 'All boys do things like that at some stage. I did it myself. But if they're not caught they can really get into trouble.' My mother was worried because we didn't have a man living with us; the detective gave her his number and told her to call him if she thought I needed a talking to. Then Grace discovered the freshly turned soil where Dale had removed the avocados, and she was furious: she called Speaks and he called me, told me to come over, and gave me a good dressing down. A week later I was put on probation in Grace's care.

Money was only a secondary motive — I think we really did it for the adventure, the excitement, the sense of outsmarting the authorities and developing a system which worked. But we ran it pretty close sometimes. I'll let Dale Soderstrom tell this story:

'We were in art class — our first creative class. Marshall Grenadis, who wasn't one of the guys we hung around with, was telling us about a rich guy who lived out in Gopher Canyon. His brother worked for him, Marshall said, and the guy had just gone on vacation. So Bob and I thought it was time to drop around and take a look.

'Sure enough, there was no-one there. Ol' Marshall was tellin' us the truth. We looked around and saw all these good things: there were four brand-new tyres on a horse trailer, and a huge box of tools in the toolshed. And no telling what was in the house.

'So we left. We were casing the place in daylight, because during the day you could have any number of innocent reasons for being there.

'That night we came back and parked about a quarter of a mile away and walked in. The last thing we could get would be the tyres, because if we pulled those off and somebody came by, it would be too obvious. So first we broke into the toolshed and got the tool box, as well-equipped as a mechanic's box, and set it down behind some bushes.

'Then we went over to the house and jemmied the window open. There was a whole bunch of rifles and pistols. It seemed like we were getting into the big-time. Bob said: "Let's take a pistol, or some of these..." I said: "Oh no, this is getting bad!"

'I guess he figured it was too. So we climbed back out the window. We didn't think of the silverware or anything like that — that was getting too big-time. But we took the four tyres off the horse trailer and threw them into the car with the tool box and took off.

'We drove to my house. It was still early evening, and we could see my mom there talking to a friend, and there we were unloading tyres and the tool box and hiding them under the house.

'Next day we went to school and Marshall told us right away that the damn place had been robbed. While Bob and I sat there with real innocent faces, Marshall continued: "Not only that, the sons of bitches stole all my brother's tools." He said, "My brother's going to report you guys to the cops."

'So Bob and I excused ourselves from the classroom and went out and debated what we should do. We ended up making a deal with Marshall — if he called his brother off, we'd give back the tools. But we could keep the tyres — they belonged to the guy who owned the place, and the brother didn't care about that.

'So we had four hot tyres, and we had to dump them fast, in case someone talked. So who did we sell them to? Ed Ward's dad. Ed Ward's dad was a retired New York City cop, as straight as a dye. He got a real bargain, $15 a tyre for brand new tyres. It's no wonder he didn't like me — he knew they were hot. But he also knew a good deal when he saw one.'

The guys who taught me most were my football coaches Charlie Bonebrake and Elmer Harritt. I wasn't a natural athlete like Jerry Rudolph, who burned off anything on the playing field, football, pole vault, shotput, track, but I was quite fast, I had been a quick sprinter over 75 metres at the Military Academy, I was in good shape, and most of all I was motivated: I was hungry to win. I played blocking back — Rudolph, the dynamite fullback, was enough of a bastard to say later I played 'left out' — and I was determined once I scored a place in the team to make sure I never missed a game, or even a minute of a game, through injury. I never took it for granted that I'd won a position on the side. I never accepted that I was an automatic pick. I always played as hard in practice as I did in the game. I broke my nose. I tore tendons. I pulled muscles. In one game I couldn't remember the second half of the game; it wasn't till I saw Charlie Bonebrake the following morning that I even knew it had ended in a draw. Charlie sent me straight to the doctor: it turned out I had concussion. But I was the only member of the Vista High School football team who never missed a minute through injury. Maybe that's obsessive — but I knew there were footballers that had a lot more talent than I did, and I felt it would be a real put down to be taken off the field because I hadn't pass-protected properly or I hadn't blocked properly. I've never missed a day's work through sickness either. Never. Poor Charlie Bonebrake — that really is his name — was a tall slender man with little authority as a teacher, something damaged about him. The big gift he gave me, one which has sustained me ever since, though I've been up against it many times, was confidence in myself. Thirty years later, when he was 68, he was sentenced to eight years' jail for molesting children — his first and only conviction. Elmer Harritt's gift was technique and refinement of skills; it's no good being confident if you're no good!

Jerry Rudolph was a year older than me — it was unusual to have friends outside your own year — and he delighted in scaring hell out of us in the initiation ceremonies for lettermen. (Players get their letters after a year on a high school sporting team). It went on for a week: the older guys grabbed a letterman, pinned his arms behind his back, stripped him naked, blindfolded him, told him they were going to burn his pubic hair off, held a flaming torch close — then jammed ice cubes around his genitals. Jerry reckoned 'you could hear the screams for ten miles'. He put me blindfolded in the back of his car with another buch of students, then went tearing off around a hill in the middle of winter. Rudolph was crazy: he drove like a racing driver. Everyone in the car was screaming, Rudolph turned into a sharp bend, screaming 'we're not gonna make it,' then opened and slammed the driver's door as if he'd jumped. I grabbed for the blindfold. I paid the penalty: Rudolph rubbed a red hot liniment on my crotch. 'Bob was standing there with tears running down his cheeks,' he remembers, 'he wasn't going to say a word.' Rudolph was completely crazy.

One day when I had cut school, he pulled up outside my house with a few other guys and shouted through a loud hailer: 'Your house is surrounded — this is the police.' I must have been a bit crazy myself; I came out in my pyjamas with a .22 rifle under my arm. Jerry says now 'If we did now what we did then, we'd all be in jail.' I believe him.

Actually, it wasn't until my last two high school years that I really started to raise hell. John lived with me and Grace for the first two years, and he considered me a goody-goody. We were opposites: I loved sport, he did his best to get out of it. I made friends with Dale Soderstrom and the football star Jerry Rudolph: he hung around with what he now calls 'a lot of deadbeats'. John says he likes the people on the edge, dropouts and other nonconformists, more than people like accountants and corporate lawyers — 'I find them more interesting than some of the other people you have to put up with.' He was embarrassed by his crooked teeth. Grace discovered it would cost $1000 to have them fixed, and she couldn't afford it. Besides, she was worried that he was getting out of control. She figured the following escapade spelt action. He nicked my car and drove across the Mexican border to Tijuana, got drunk, raised hell, and had his first sexual experience — with a Mexican hooker. He paid for her with a silver belt buckle he had stolen from the drugstore where he worked. Grace telephoned Reg and talked it over, and John went back to Melbourne, Mt Eliza and R.M. Ansett when he was 14.

Just before I entered my final year of high school, my mother took a job working for an aircraft manufacturer in San Diego 50 kilometres from Vista, too far to travel to school. I let it be known at school that this was the case, and in a friendly gesture Ed Ward invited me to stay with his family. This turned out to be all right with his parents; my mother, who was a friend of the Ward family, agreed, gratefully I feel sure, and I spent that year with them.

In my last year at school I started oganising a really good money-making operation: with Jerry and Dale, I ran illegal Mexican aliens from Vista to Fresno, about 160 kilometres north of San Diego, past the roadblocks set up from time to time by the Immigration Department. For that we charged $100 a head. For the longer run, to San Jose near San Francisco, we got $300 a head.

These Mexican aliens were generally, if somewhat contemptuously, known as 'wetbacks', because they swam the Rio Grande, the river that makes the border between Mexico and Texas, and the name stuck when they crossed the border on the west, into southern California. Most of the guys I smuggled within the U.S. were from the south of the long peninsula or sur called Baja California, a really isolated and dirt poor part of Mexico. They were young family men in the main, quite reasonable opportunists who figured that the six- or eight-week season of what the growers of California call 'stoop labor' in the market gardens and orchards equalled their annual income back home, and that the risks of a couple of nights in jail and deportation were worth it. Some had six or seven children. For the California growers they were cheap and quiet employees, who worked with a strength born of desperation on the back-breaking job of picking crops of lettuces, grapes and tomatoes. For U.S. citizens aiding and abetting border crossings or transporting aliens within the U.S. attracted tough penalties and the wrath of the authorities. But I never considered I'd get caught, and so gave this problem little thought.

This was the scheme: we used two cars, a lead car with only the driver, usually Dale, aboard, 10 minutes ahead of the payload car. We drove dead on 50 miles an hour. The idea was that if the lead car spotted an immigration roadblock, he should stop, get cleared, then turn around and hurtle back to warn the payload driver. The payload driver should let the Mexicans out, pass through the roadblock, then wait for them on the other side as they walked around the roadblock. It worked well half a dozen

CHILDHOOD AND YOUTH 33

times, and I was pretty confident.

I wasn't looking too far ahead: when we graduated from school we followed the custom of recording our ambitions in the yearbook. My classmates wrote down goals like joining the navy, going to college, or, if they were girls, getting married (this was 1951). I said my ambition was 'to retire to Australia'. I thought a lot about that possibility later, but in 1951 I think I said it because I couldn't think of anything else to say.

One night, not long after I graduated from high school — I was waiting for my draft papers for the U.S. Army, then fighting in Korea — I organised a run with Dale driving the lead car. Then Dale dropped out because he had a date with Carmen Trevino, a girl we had more to do with later in Alaska. Jerry Rudolph agreed to take his place, and we swapped cars, because I couldn't fit six Mexicans into my '34 Ford coupe. Jerry and his wife Margaret (they had been high school sweethearts, and married when Jerry was 17) drove off in the lead car; 10 minutes later I was on my way with a car full of illegal aliens. I drove along whistling cheerfully — and then, only a few miles out of Vista, I saw a roadblock. I couldn't believe my eyes! What the hell had happened to my warning system? Where the hell was Jerry? I slammed on the brakes, squealed over to the roadside and screamed '*Undulay — pronto!*' The Mexicans ran into the bush, but the immigration officer saw what had happened, sped up in his car and handcuffed me to my steering wheel. Then he raced into the bush, firing his pistol into the air, and six Mexican fugitives came out with their hands in the air.

The immigration officer took me to the nearest police station at Temecula. The questioning started. My story is 'it's my show, I'm driving them alone.' Then Jerry and Margaret came in and Jerry said casually 'Oh, there's Bob. Do you mind if I take my car back?' The cop stared at him and said 'What, he stole your car, did he?' I'm sure Jerry was tempted to have me charged with car-stealing, but he said, 'No, he just wanted to borrow it at a party, and I got a little concerned, so I followed him.' And of course I, being a true blue friend, didn't turn him in for his part in running the Mexicans. Jerry and Margaret left, and I was taken to jail in San Diego.

Next morning, after a night in a cell with the Mexicans,

I got lucky. One of the detectives at the San Diego jail had visited Australia, and he knew the name 'Reg Ansett'. When I registered for the draft, I used the name on my birth certificate, Ansett, not Campbell, which I normally used. (On one of his Vista visits, Dad was pretty upset that I was using the name Campbell.)

The detective asked 'Are you related to Reg Ansett?'

'Yeah, he's my old man,' I told him.

'Christ. What would he think about you being involved in this?'

'I guess he'd be pretty upset.' (What an understatement! In Melbourne, John had been picked up for riding a tram without a ticket, and when he was away on National Service, the old man received the summons. He wrote John a letter pointing out the embarrassment it would cause him if newspapers heard about it and ran the headline TYCOON'S SON WITHOUT A TICKET.)

The detective gave me a lecture about how greatly I was letting my father down, and when I told him I was waiting for my draft papers he said 'I guess two years in the army will fix you up.' So he let me go. It was a close call. Three things saved me: the luck that the cop had been to Australia, my name, and the fact that I was able to tell him a good story. I saw that the fact that my name was Ansett and that I was waiting for the draft were having an effect, and I talked them up for all I was worth. That was the last Mexican run.

My steady girlfriend at high school was Pat Whitfield — in the male pack I ran with she was called 'Flat Pat'. Her family had a construction business, and I worked as a builder's labourer for the family company at weekends and during school holidays. The last job I had with them was as security guard. They had built a school, and I had to guard it till they turned the keys over to the Education Department at the end of summer. I started at 5 in the afternoon and guarded the school till daylight the following morning, checking every sound, wondering about old noises around every corner. It was a great experience — but the job I had immediately after I finished high school taught me a lot more.

Like most high school kids in California, I had had some experience of the service station business, pumping gas, inflating tyres, not really very sophisticated. Then I landed a job at the Standard Oil service station in Oceanside, a small coastal town near Vista. Standard Oil had a training school which taught me everything I needed to know about the service industry.

On the forecourt in Oceanside, when a car drove in you would run out to it and ask if you could fill the tank. You'd check the oil, the fan belt, the battery water and the radiator, clean the windows, clean the floormats, check the tyres — it was simply incredible service, and you'd always try to sell something, a fan belt or a windscreen wiper or a tyre. Red Hostetter, the manager, was a guy built like a bull. No-one liked him, but for some reason he took a liking to me and made me his protégé and gave me extra responsibilities. I worked a lot of midnight shifts — I did a lot of midnight-to-dawn work in my early jobs — and Dale Soderstrom, who also worked for Standard Oil and who was often out boozing till 2 a.m. would drive over to sit and drink a few beers with me in the back of the station: it wasn't exactly rush hour at 2 a.m. Dale was talking about taking a trip to Alaska — Jerry Rudolph had gone up there and he had been writing me these letters about the well-paid jobs in Alaska. The idea of heading off to frontier territory, having some adventures and making money before we were drafted into the army appealed to me. When Hostetter heard I was keen to go, he thought I was reckless. One night when Dale was there drinking beer Hostetter said to me: 'Are you tellin' me you'd give up a career with Standard Oil to go to Alaska with that son-of-a-bitch?'

Dale was trying to pretend he was invisible. Hostetter was serious, and as an alternative offered me a job as assistant manager. I was tempted for two reasons: first, it would have put me one up on my buddy Dale — and we were very competitive guys; second, it would have meant I was the youngest assistant manager in the history of Standard Oil — throughout the U.S., not just in California. That appealed to my ego. But the pull of adventure was too strong: I said goodbye to Flat Pat and Dale and I headed up Highway 395 in his green '40 Chevvy — we called it 'The Green Hornet' — with VISTA-ALASKA OR BUST signs all over it in black and white, the high school colours. We had $150 between us, two rifles, two fishing rods, plenty of optimism, but no winter coats or reindeer boots or fur-lined gloves. All I had was a suede jacket to protect me against the Alaskan winter. I was 18.

2

Alaska, Japan and Australia

Dale and I were both gamblers. Even at 18 we knew cards and horses and the odds. But when we left Vista in mid-summer on 16 June 1951, if we had objectively set odds on our chances of getting to Anchorage, I reckon they would have to have been around 10 to 1 against.

It is a 4000-kilometre journey as the crow flies — about the distance from Sydney to North-West Cape, a good deal of it through rugged mountains on vile roads. First we cruised around Vista showing off our brightly painted VISTA-ALASKA OR BUST car signs; we wanted the whole town to know we were going. After all the goodbyes we got underway at 3.30 p.m. We made about 150 kilometres to Glendale, where a friend treated us to dinner. At Santa Barbara, another 200 kilometres up the track, I got sleepy (it was after midnight) and drifted on to the wrong side of the road, earning a citation from a traffic cop. On day two we applied ourselves more seriously and made it to San Francisco, copping a parking ticket in Salinas on the way up. Dale nearly lost his fingers showing some innocent bystanders in a small town we passed through the proper way to light a firecracker. I managed to collide with a road sign near Cloverdale, spinning the car around so it stopped facing the way we had come. Two mangled fenders didn't bother us; we checked into a motel and slept for 16 hours. After driving through magnificent redwood forests the next day we had supper at a roadside cafe and chatted through the meal with the old lady who cooked it. How much? we asked. 'One dollar,' she said. It seemed cheap. I gave her the dollar. As we walked out I noticed the disgusted look on her face — she meant a dollar each. 'Seeing that both of us are distinguished gentlemen, we hurried out to the car and left in a cloud of smoke,' I wrote in the logbook we kept.

Just before the Canadian border we spent $5 on sandwich meat, two loaves of bread, mustard and cigarettes for Dale. We had $97 left.

At the border there were two small problems: the Canadian immigration authorities required road travellers to Alaska to have $350 in cash or travellers' cheques. When we realised this, we figured, hell, we'd just write $300 in our chequebooks, cheques were as good as cash. The border authorities, naturally, said 'We can't accept a chequebook — you can write anything in a chequebook.' They turned us back. The second problem was our rifles: the Canadians required them to be plugged, and of course ours weren't, nor did we have any way of doing it. So on the drive to the next border crossing, about 300 kilometres away, we took off all the VISTA-ALASKA OR BUST signs. We told the border guards we were going to Vancouver for a few days and we would get the rifles plugged there. So we got through — on a pass that required us to have the rifles plugged in Vancouver, where we weren't even considering going, and which wasn't good for Alaska. Rubbing salt into the wound, the guards confiscated our $5 of food. 'I hope they choke,' Dale said.

We pressed on up the road — if you've ever ridden a bicycle down the Grand Canyon you'll have some idea of the conditions — and I made my first kill as a big-game hunter. I brought down a magnificent bird; Soderstrom described it as 'a cross between a chicken and a crow'. But it made a tasty meal. A few hours later we passed a lake with a few ducks on it. Dale grabbed a rifle and started banging away as if he were Rambo Stallone and 50 shots later bagged his first game of the trip. Every hour the muffler and exhaust became detached and bounced and rattled along the road, but with the inventiveness and confidence of youth we soon had it fixed — and considered ourselves master mechanics, working miracles with bailing wire.

The scenery was fantastic, wide, roaring rivers, huge

trees, wild, rugged mountains, but the road was narrow and very rough — in the places where it had been torn by the rain we had to drive for hours at no more than 15 or 25 kilometres an hour, any faster and we would have torn the car apart. We played games with ourselves to help pass the time while we were driving. Once I was asleep in the back seat while Dale was driving and I was woken by a rhythmical thumping. The car was labouring as if it had a flat tyre. I screamed at Dale: 'What the hell are you doing?' He'd worked himself into a sort of trance, measuring the miles on the speedo against the clock to make 30 miles in an hour and he was so obsessed with doing it that he hadn't noticed the flat. When we clambered out to inspect the damage the tyre was shredded and smoking; we were down to our last. We were doing some dumb things, but it never occurred to either of us that we wouldn't make it — when things went wrong we just figured out what to do and did it.

Travellers had been telling us all the way along that there was a bridge out on the other side of Prince George, a road junction town deep in the mountains of British Columbia. Sure enough, on 22 June about 1600 kilometres short of Alaska we found that the bridge was closed. There were ten cars waiting, though. A cutting about 50 metres long on the other side had to be filled in before we could cross — and the construction foreman warned that even then there was too much mud on the other side and he wouldn't let anyone cross. Everyone cursed him: they'd have been in Anchorage in a couple of days if he'd just get out of their way. Finally he said okay, he'd let this one caravan of cars through and then he'd close the road till 1 July. 'Look after each other — that's all the help you've got,' he said. We waited six tedious hours; I walked over the bridge to give my idea of supervision in road construction. Finally we were set to go. Each car-load was interviewed by the local newspaper and I saw from the opposite bank that Dale was thirteenth in line to cross. As the flashbulbs popped for the unlucky number, some wise guy yelled 'He's going to bust'. No sooner were the words out of his mouth than the muffler dropped off the Green Hornet with a crash. Dale whipped out, got under the car and fiddled with the bailing wire. While he worked I figured there was no way we'd cross the muddy section without the muffler coming off over and over again, I ran for a shovel to repair the road a little. It was no good: as soon as Dale hit the mud the muffler dropped off and the car surged up the hill wih a tremendous roar. We stopped and yanked the muffler off while the rest of the caravan passed by. A kilometre down the road, we got comprehensively bogged, and the only help we might have had was well on the way to Alaska. We were beginning to believe we were done for when along came a construction worker, a nice old guy who hobbled back to get his Caterpillar to pull us out.

Four punctures and 500 kilometres later we began to think we'd pushed our luck; the Alcan Highway's bad news. We composed a poem of the highway:
Winding in and winding out
Fills my mind with serious doubt
Whether the ass that build this route
Was going to hell or coming out.

In our eighth day on the road we decided to drive 24 hours a day and save on food as much as possible. About 1 a.m. on the ninth day we picked up a boy of about 15 who wanted a lift for 25 kilometres. During the drive he gave us a brief glimpse of life in the Far North: he said that each November he and a friend set off into the woods for six months, trapping for furs, and they set enormously long, wide lines of traps. He also told us he had made $10,000 in one good winter, and how to shoot and skin a grizzly bear. We were sorry to see him go.

We got to the Alaska-Canada border with $22 at 11 at night; there was a huge log across the road and a sign saying they would open at 6 in the morning. We had tried to doctor our pass to make it good for Alaska, but it was a rough job, an obvious forgery, and one of the guys waiting at the border said 'They're pretty strict on this, they won't let you across.' We thought we'd be done if we waited, and we managed to roll the log out of the way, crossed the border, and siphoned some petrol from a parked truck. Our money was tight, but we were across the border. We looked for a rabbit for breakfast, and after a few near misses with the rifle dead-eye Dale bagged one. We had found a nice little stream, made a fire and started to skin the rabbit when I saw a huge gathering cloud and ran for the car. Too hungry or too stupid, Dale stuck with the rabbit for another two minutes before he ran for the car, shaking like a madman, bumps all over his face. The cloud could have been locusts; it was mosquitoes. At the last gas station before Anchorage we pulled in at daybreak. No-one was up, and for some reason there was no lock on the pump, so we took 8 gallons, enough to get us to Anchorage, briefly debated whether we should leave the money but decided our need was greater than theirs, took off, and rolled into Anchorage with $US3.21, and 5 cents in Canadian money.

Jerry hadn't given me his address in Anchorage. I had written to him care of the Post Office, asking him to leave us instructions there. So we called in there just before it closed and asked the girl 'What have you got for Bob Ansett and Dale Soderstrom?' She looked at all the general delivery mail and said, 'Nothing.'

We didn't know what the hell to do, so we cruised up and down the main street, thinking maybe we might get lucky and run into Jerry. As we passed the bus depot, we got lucky; Dale spotted Carmen Trevino, Jerry's sister-in-law. I looked through the filthy window of the Chevvy and said 'No it's not Carmen — couldn't be.' Dale insisted: 'I tell you it's Carmen.' So I wound down the window, filthy, unshaven, looking like a bum after ten days on the road, and said to Carmen: 'Hi honey, want a ride?' Carmen spun on her heel and walked into the bus depot, and, feeling foolish, I said 'Goddamn you Dale, that wasn't Carmen.' But Dale knew Carmen well, he'd been dating her in Vista (in fact I often think she was the reason behind that mad trip) and we both knew that if it wasn't Carmen we were in for a cold hungry night for starters. Dale and I jumped out of the car and chased after her. Sure enough it was Carmen, stunned at seeing these two filthy red-eyed guys from Vista.

We drove two miles to Jerry's house; Carmen had been waiting for a bus home. Right on dinner time, we burst in on Jerry and Margaret and their two kids expecting we were going to make their day. Jerry, taken aback, just managed to conceal his displeasure at seeing us, but Margaret, a hospitable woman, immediately asked, 'Have you guys eaten yet?' Of course we were starving, and the answer was no. Jerry, who'd been working his arse off to feed his family, selling cars during the day and driving a cab at night, said loudly, 'Too bad!' Nevertheless, we sat down to eat with them and Margaret divided the quiche into extra portions. There was one slice left over: when Dale reached for it, Jerry jammed a fork into the table an inch from his hand. He made it clear while we were eating that he couldn't afford us.

We were exhausted from the trip, but with five adults and two children sleeping in one room and Jerry acting as if we were bad news, Dale and I went into Anchorage the next day. Target a job — any job. Jerry told us at breakfast that his letters about the town being full of jobs wouldn't exactly get an A for accuracy in a journalism course: it was actually tough to find work. That was obvious in the first hour of that first morning, but then we found the office of a Seattle construction company which was boring through a mountain to build a hydroelectric plant. There were jobs going begging — $200 a week for labourers, a fortune in 1952, about three times the pay in California, plus room and board. One thing puzzled us: we expected a queue a mile long, but there were only a handful of men applying. We were hired.

We moved to the base camp at the foot of the mountain about 100 kilometres from Anchorage and started work on the midnight to dawn shift in the 'Bullgang' that cleared the rubble from the tunnel rail tracks after each dynamite blast. They were working around the clock to get the tunnel finished before winter froze everything solid and made tunnelling impossible. We discovered that the reason no-one was applying for the jobs was that the company had a rotten safety record and the unions had black-banned it. We were there to circumvent the bans and let the company get on with the job, and that was fine with me.

The food was fine with me too: we ended our shift at 8 a.m. and then got into these magnificient American breakfasts, pancakes and maple syrup, steaks as thick as doorsteps, everything cooked to perfection by trained chefs. It was the best food I'd eaten then. The base camp was on the edge of a valley that grew the biggest vegetables I've ever seen — cabbages the size of basketballs, tomatoes as big as pumpkins. We were doing all right.

Within three weeks, the safety problems emerged. One

of the base camp buses taking the tunnel workers up the mountain had turned over and only just missed crashing down a cliff-face. Dale and I nearly fell off the side of the mountain. I had another close call when a railcar loaded with rubble hurtled past me as I worked at the side of the track — we'd struck underground water which was eroding the earth under the rails. I had to grab a metal stay and pull myself up and away: the car just brushed the back of my legs. If I'd stayed where I was my body would have been smashed into the side of the tunnel. A few days later another Bullgang man was crushed against the tunnel face by another runaway car, so I thought to hell with this! I've been to Alaska, I've done the trip and had the experience, I think I'll go see Pat Whitfield, who had moved to Oklahoma City with her family.

Dale, who got a job as a bus driver, thought I was crazy. 'How you gonna do that?' he demanded. 'I'll hitchhike,' I said. He drove me out to the crossroads about 35 kilometres from Anchorage and left me sitting on a little suitcase wishing my suede jacket was a fur-lined coat. I sat there for three or four hours, listening to what sounded like bears moving around in the darkness. The night was 20 hours long; most of the time I was hitch-hiking in pitch blackness. In my favour, I knew anyone who came by would give me a lift. Against me was the fact that nobody came by. Finally a truck picked me up — it was a 350-kilometre lift. But I spent a lot of cold, solitary hours on the damn Alcan Highway, and I was glad that the lonely hours guarding the school in the summer served to prepare me for it. In the end I made it to Oklahoma quicker than the drive up in Dale's battered Chevvy.

It was an uncertain time for all of us: the draft was universal, you couldn't get out of it except through physical disability or a deferment if you went to college, but you didn't know exactly when you'd be called up. When I left Vista, Pat and I hadn't made any firm plans, but it was assumed, without ever being said, that I would ultimately get a job and we would get engaged and married.

By the time I got to Oklahoma, I had really lost interest in getting married. Pat wasn't pressuring me in any way, but with the uncertainty of the draft and the uncertainty of my feelings, it just didn't happen. Pat went on to college and later became a very good teacher. I got a job pumping gas in Tulsa, Oklahoma then decided to go back to California.

I saw my old mentor Red Hostetter at the gas station in Oceanside, who told me Standard never re-employed anyone, that was Standard Oil policy, but there were exceptions to every rule. He referred me to Skeeter Quinlon, the guy Red had made assistant manager when I turned the job down. Quinlon was now manager of a smaller station at Carlsbad, a neighbouring town, and he employed me to pump gas for three months, then made me assistant manager — although by that time I wasn't the youngest-ever Standard assistant manager.

Meanwhile, Dale's letters told me of the fantastic time he was having, driving a cab and raking in money, I should come back up. Draft papers still hadn't arrived, I'd saved enough money to fly up, and Dale was my closest friend. This time I knew I was through with Standard Oil forever — they might make an exception, but they wouldn't allow me to make a mockery of company policy.

The flight from San Diego to Anchorage in a DC3, was cold, uncomfortable and prolonged. The DC3 barely cleared the mountains, and it had to put down for refuelling several times. On the last stop in northern Canada we had to wait 30 minutes while they refuelled; I was sitting with the wind knifing through my suede jacket — with the windchill factor I think the temperature was about 40 F below — and I didn't think I'd survive. The sub-Arctic cold has to be felt to be understood.

Dale met me at the airport and drove me straight to the Northway Cabs headquarters. He briefed me on how to impress the manager with my skills as a cabbie: he would leave me in his cab, then put out a test radio call. I had to respond with 'Roger, 51' — his cab number. Dale impressed on me that it was very important to lie about my age — I was only 19, and no-one could drive a cab till he was 21.

When the radio call crackled out, I grabbed the transmitter quickly (I wanted to be really fast and professional) and said 'Okay.' If I hadn't been sitting in a cab, I would have kicked myself. When I went into the office Dale was wearing a look that said, 'You asshole'. Nevertheless, the manager gave me an application form to fill out, and, exhausted and still not thinking, I put down my age as 19.

So then we had to square that away with the manager, but he was prepared to turn a blind eye. He knew Dale was a good driver bringing in plenty of revenue for the company, so he allowed me to change the age to 21 so there would be no problem when I went to the police for the licence.

Anchorage then was a raw, wide-open town. A lot of men looked half bear, half human — huge, bearded hairy men in lumberjack shirts — many of them on the run from the law or their wives or both. They were called 'sourdoughs' and they were the kind of people you didn't want to ask what their business was. Dale and I were just a couple of kids, wet behind the ears, and the other cabbies liked us because we were real goers. We became the pets of the organisation — and in the end we made more money than any of them.

We also became the pets of the girls who worked in the town whorehouses — and that made us a lot of money. For every john we delivered — they called them 'meatloads' — the brothels would pay us $6. I remember the first brothel I visited. Dale had told me where to go, and I took a meatload who had just come in from three months in the Klondike, the Canadian-Alaskan outback, knocked on the door, naive and 19, and said 'I'm from Northway Cabs and Dale sent me.' We sat down, and the girl asked the meatload: 'You wanna buy your cabbie a drink?' And the guy said, 'Sure, bring him a drink.' She brought the drink, and it was the worst-tasting concoction that's ever passed my lips. It was cold tea with a dash of whisky. So I sipped my cold tea while the meatload went inside a room for about a minute before he came out doing up his trousers. And then I found out that they charge the john $4 a drink, and I get the profit on my glass of tea. Four bucks in about a minute, plus the $6 delivery fee! What a terrific business this was! On the best nights we could make $200 with the cab fares, the meatloads, the tips and the whisky tea. We didn't actually solicit clients for the hookers, we just took them there if they asked, but Jerry, who was still working two jobs and falling asleep at stoplights, hustled. Whenever a few guys left the Last Chance Saloon or the Mint Bar or the Ten Forty Two Club, Rudolph was there asking 'You wanna go where the good times are boys?'

I hustled in other ways: cab drivers weren't allowed into the Anchorage train station to solicit fares — so I took off my Northway cap, put on my high school sweater, and got first bite at travellers who needed a cab.

Dale and I always drove the night, 7 p.m. to 7 a.m., because that was when business was best. When there wasn't much happening, we shot craps over a beer box set up in the back of one of the cabs. It wasn't penny-ante stuff: we would risk a week's earnings. One night we were going to continue the game in one of the cab driver's homes, and just as we were leaving a call came in: a guy called Diamond Jim Brady had a $40 job. So I took Brady to the back of beyond through the snow — the round-trip took about 8 hours — and when I got back the crap game was still going and Dale was crowing, he'd cleaned everybody out. I had the $40 in my pocket and I was ready to take him. But Dale was running hot and he cleaned me out in about 10 minutes flat. I was down to my last dollar when Dale threw the dice. It was a seven, a winner for him, but it was up against the wall — a cocked dice. Dale said 'cocked dice my ass,' and grabbed for the money. He was so cocky and I'd just done an 8-hour trip for nothing. He wanted my last buck from a crook throw. I saw red and hit him right between the eyes. After a brief break for Dale to attend to his fast-closing eye, he threw the dice again — and won.

We had to split our earnings 50-50 with Northway. After one crap game when it seemed the dice were loaded against us, Dale and I, sharing a room, shared a serious problem: the rent was overdue, we had to pay it quickly, and we didn't have the money. Solution: if I could keep all my earnings the next night, instead of turning half over to Northway, we could pay the rent.

So Dale became my 'passenger' and we pulled over at the end of a track near the Last Chance Saloon. The snow was a metre deep. I told Dale he had to belt me one — we were staging a robbery, and if there wasn't a mark on me, there was no way Northway would buy it. Dale, who was a beefy, powerful guy, was smacking his fist into his palm and saying 'how hard?' I told him again: 'It's got to be harder than that, we've got to make it look real.' So Dale hit me, and it was a pretty good one, knocking me down, but there was no blood. I got to my feet, a bit stunned, and told him 'You've got to do better than that.' So he hauled off and really let me have it over the right eye. I flew through the air with my eye split open and blood pouring on to the snow. Dale started running for the Last Chance; I make a radio call: 'Northway 45, mayday, mayday.' The cabbies are pretty good at looking after each other, and in less than a minute there was a cab driver bending over me and asking 'Christ, what happened?' I told him 'some guy with a knife nailed me.' He could see Dale's fresh foot-prints in the snow, and charged off after him. When he got to the Last Chance he saw Dale there, his trousers wet to the thighs from the snow, feeding money into a poker machine as if he'd been doing it for hours, and panting like a dog in midsummer. The cabbie cried out, 'They got your buddy!' And Dale, putting everything he learned in high school drama classes into it, looked amazed and panted out, 'What do you mean?'

I described my attacker in some detail at the Police Station — a man pretty much like Dale, six foot, 190 pounds, around 20 years old. The cop looked at me as if a lightbulb in his head had just been switched on, and said, 'I know the guy — I've got his mugshot here. He got out of a jail a couple of weeks ago.' He pull out the mugshot — a real mean looking son-of-a-bitch — and I looked at it thoughtfully and told the cop: 'No, that's not him. I'm sure that's not him.' The last thing I could afford would be to have somebody arrested. The next day the story made page one of the *Anchorage Times*: ROBBER SLUGS LOCAL CAB DRIVER, GETS $20. And we paid the rent. I'm glad I haven't had to earn every $20 I've made like that.

Because of the well-paid unskilled jobs, there was a big black community in Anchorage. This was still the age of rigid racial segregation in the southern states, and blacks were the poorest paid, worst educated and most desperate for work of all the racial groups in the U.S. Eastchester Flats, 8 kilometres from Anchorage, was the Harlem of Anchorage: black, poor, dirty and dangerous. Even the police stayed out. One night Dale got a fare to Eastchester Flats from a guy of Eskimo descent called Buck. Not many of the cabbies would go into Eastchester — a white guy was just looking for trouble down there. Dale pushed his luck:

'Buck came in from Nome. He was a huge guy — looked like a gorilla. He wanted a cab on charter for three days while he "looked for nigger gals". The Northway owner was a friend of his, he said Buck was good for credit, and Buck needed a cab with him all the time for three days. He found a woman called Ruthie with a debilitating stutter. I took them to a hidden gambling parlour with a bar out front and made a deal with the proprietor for a commission on Buck's drinks and gambling. Okay. After three days with Buck at $6 an hour, he owed me a bundle, but when I put him on the plane for Nome the bastard refused to pay. So I went back down to Eastchester figuring at least I'd get my money from the gambling parlour. When I walked in, I saw 50 pairs of black eyes turn to me and I could almost hear them thinking "What the hell's this white guy doin' here?" I walked up to the proprietor — a dumb nineteen year old — and demanded my money. The barman says "I don't know what you're talking about." So I started to explain he owed me $150, he's not cheating me, this is an illegal joint and if I don't get my money I'll call the cops and have the place closed. In front of all his friends at the bar, he pulled out a roll of greenbacks big enough to choke a horse — he had a goldmine there — peeled off two twenties and dropped them on the floor. I just looked down at them — I wasn't going to pick them up. Then the guy suggested we go out back. And I was dumb enough to do that — I was too young to be scared, I was just ignorant. But when we go out the back he peeled off $150 and gave it to me — I guess he just didn't want everyone to see him do it. When I walked out the two $20's were still on the floor. I didn't pick them up. I got a three-day education out of it anyway.'

Anchorage in the early 1950s was the sort of town where weird things like that happened all the time; it sure opened the mind up to possibilities! I often feel oddly grateful for those two trips there at that time. Perhaps Reg felt the same about the Territory in the 1930s...

I was pretty flush after six months; then in April 1952 our draft papers arrived; we had the option of doing our basic training in California or Alaska. We organised to do it in Alaska so we could keep driving cabs at night, and Northway were thrilled with that because we were major income earners for them, our staged robbery notwithstanding. They gave us a month off to go back to California before we were drafted. We took separate aircraft down to Seattle because of the fear that if the plane crashed we would both be lost to the world! We also took out insurance policies for $10,000 on each other's life. I went first, and sat by the radio in Seattle waiting for the news that Dale's plane had crashed and I'd got my ten grand, while Dale had his ear glued to the radio in Anchorage. We took our savings to Vista and Las Vegas for a last fling. We had devised what we believed was a foolproof system for the roulette wheels in Las Vegas — and we blew our money of course. I fell in love with a magnificent girl, Sally Gunning, Sal-Gal, and spent the rest of my money on her. The only trouble was we had no money to go back to Anchorage — so we had to settle for basic training at Fort Ord in San Francisco.

On the Army bus from Vista to Fort Ord, we stopped overnight in Los Angeles. Dale and I slipped out of the hotel via the fire escape, rented a car, drove the 150 kilometres back to Vista for one more night on the town, then got back the next morning and slept all the way on the bus to Fort Ord. Until I joined Budget in 1965, that was my only rent-a-car experience — and I don't remember the name of the company!

In our first week at Fort Ord, I got together with Dan Flemming, my old Vista High School buddy, who had nearly finished his basic training, and did some serious beer drinking — a can of beer was ten cents in those days — but I was nailed for it: newcomers weren't supposed to drink. I spent the next three weeks marching around the barracks all night on guard duty; still working nights.

My mother remarried while I was at Fort Ord. I slipped away, absent without leave, for four days, to be with her in Las Vegas — and while I was away they had the tests for the most critical part of basic training, rifle shooting. We were graded as an expert, a marksman, a rifleman, or we failed. I had a guy standing in for me and I was graded an expert — top score, and I was 700 kilometres away at the time.

I loved basic training. I didn't want to go overseas — the Korean war was on at the time — and I was still infatuated with Sally Gunning. I decided to go into the paratroopers, which meant that after six months' basic training I had to re-enlist for another two years. It meant more pay. It also meant I had a three-week break between basic training and re-enlistment, when I was to do jump training at Fort Benning, Georgia. The army paid my expenses to get to Vista, and I spent time with Sally, then visited Pat in Oklahoma on the way through to Georgia.

It was clear my mustering out pay wasn't going to go far. I got in touch with Ron Hewitt, who looked after my father's company interests in the U.S. and asked if he could lend me some of Reg's money to buy a car. He said he couldn't. This brought a letter from Reg on 15 October 1953. I still have a copy — I showed it to my own son Ron recently when he asked for my help — and I think it shows something of our relationship.

My father wrote:

Dear Robert,
I am sorry to hear from Mr Hewitt in San Francisco that you have been communicating with him regarding the purchase of an automobile which I understand you told him you have now bought and cannot pay for, and if this is the case you are most certainly a very foolish young man. Mr Hewitt sent me a copy of his letter to you, dated September 22, where he advised you that he could not assist you to obtain an automobile, and quite definitely that is the position.

Mr Hewitt is a friend of mine whom I called on once before to assist you to return from Alaska — a position you should never have got into had you been a responsible type of person. (Actually, I spoke to Hewitt about going back to Australia when I was in Alaska, but nothing came of it.) At the time you communicated with me from Alaska I was in Tahiti, a country where communications are very difficult, and the only way in which I could assist you was by calling on my friend Mr Hewitt whom I have since repaid for the monies which he paid out on your behalf.

Mr Hewitt has no funds of mine in the United States nor, for that matter, has anybody else, and I am more than concerned with your communications to him and your requests for financial assistance. I now regret very much coming to your aid on the previous occasion as you have proved quite irresponsible and completely ungrateful.

Would you please remember this in future, that I have no funds in the United States of America. It is impossible to obtain dollars in this country without Government approval and Government approval can only be obtained for very special cases. I certainly could not, even if I wanted to, get dollars to buy you an automobile — I cannot even get dollars to buy myself one.

Kindly do not communicate with Mr Hewitt and remember he was doing me a personal favour when you previously needed assistance. He is not my lawyer in the United States and has no method of helping you. I have now told Mr Hewitt to completely disregard any request you may make to him.

Now Robert, you are over 20 years old. You are in the Army and you are being well paid. If you are being transferred from one side of America to the other, the Army will pay for your transfer costs, and under no circumstances will I assist you when you are being well paid and should very easily be able to stand on you own feet. You are now a fully grown man and you must make your own future in life, and the sooner you realise there are no short cuts and no easy ways to success, the better for you.

Ninety five per cent of all the young men in the United States, or, for that matter, anywhere else in the world, are forced to make their own way in life and their success, or otherwise, is entirely in their own hands. If they want automobiles, they must earn sufficient money to buy them. The same goes for all the other amenities in life. The quicker you realise this and knuckle down to making a way for yourself, the quicker you will have your foot on the first rung towards success. I suggest to you that you work hard in the Army and endeavour, in due course, to qualify for a Commission. This may not be easy to achieve but it is possible. I would certainly be much more impressed if I felt you were making progress under your own steam. Even if it were possible for me to assist you financially which it is not, it would be of no real use to you. In fact it would only postpone the time when you ultimately realised you must make your own way.

Well now, Robert, you are completely on your own feet and your future is in your own hands. Stop trying to get things for nothing and wake up to the fact that the good things in life must be earned.

The salutation at the end was simply 'Yours' and he forgot to sign it. The matter-of-fact tone was typical of my father's letters: he was that sort of person. It had no great impact on me: I was still young enough to try things on to see what I could get away with.

After three months of jump training I was the fittest I'd ever been — and even if I had cut corners and gone AWOL in basic training I shaped up as a paratrooper. There were 90 in my group — only 45 actually graduated. Of the remaining 45, five were offered positions as jump instructors, and I was one of them. But that would have meant I stayed at Fort Benning, and I wanted to go to Europe. All the sages at Fort Benning reckoned the army would always send you where you didn't want to go, so rat-cunning Bob Ansett, given the choice of Korea or Europe, put down Korea — and then I was marked for Korea! I was assigned to join the 187th airborne division.

I didn't get there, though Dale did, as a military policeman — I think he spent more rest and recreation leave time in Japan than anyone before or since. When I got to Japan, en route to Korea, General Maxwell Taylor, later a key military leader in the Vietnam war, was trying to build the best-ever U.S. Army football team, and with my football background I was recruited during the refuelling stop in Tokyo the minute I stepped off the plane. North of Seoul, the 187th made a jump behind enemy lines to cut the retreat of North Korean troops, in an action planned by General MacArthur. A great many drowned in the bay, a few died from enemy fire. These terrible wasteful and sad casualties were typical of the paratroopers' lot in those days. Maybe my obsession with football saved my life. Statistics suggest it is likely.

I played army football the same way I played it in high school — I was determined never to miss a minute of a game through injury, or because the coach ordered me off. And I made it. I wasn't a superstar, but I always logged up the most playing time of any guy on the team. The closest I came to breaking my record of 60 minutes play in every game was in the second last game of the second year in Japan. I was a blocking back, an opponent fumbled the ball and I went to pull it out and a guy fell on my right elbow with all his weight and turned it back. I thought the arm was broken — it was the worst pain I have ever experienced. But there were only 10 minutes left in the game and I wasn't going to go off. I found it difficult to straighten the arm for the next two months — I played the last game with the elbow taped up in a plastic support, and developed a technique of using my shoulder in tackles. I knew I just had to suffer through that one game and I would have the whole summer for the thing to heal. (As it turned out, I was selected in the Army All-Star team to play against best of the Navy, Air Force and Marines. We played the Air Force at the Rice Bowl on New Year's Day and though we lost it was a great game: both teams got a trip to Hong Kong.)

My summer job was as manager of the Sugami Hara swimming pool. I had 25 Japanese lifeguards working for me. It wasn't the most taxing job I've ever had, and pretty soon it struck me that I could easily disappear from the army. I took my name off my bed at the army base, took my name off my wall locker, took all my clothes and disappeared to a little flat in Tokyo. When Dale came down on leave, I planned to devote the whole week to rest and recreation, not that there was much rest.

I had formed a relationship with a girl who worked as a hostess in the Blue Gardenia, the bar where I hung out. Bar hostesses weren't prostitutes and they usually were very attractive girls. I had been all but living with my hostess for a couple of months, when I discovered she had a boyfriend in the merchant marine.

Late one night I was sitting at a table with a buddy drinking Jack Daniels mixed with beer, drunk as a lord, when a guy came at me with a broken beer bottle. A big Japanese beer bottle. Though I could barely see straight, I moved quickly when I saw that jagged bottle coming at me, and I ended up on top of the guy on the floor, pounding him in the head. I was mad and drunk. The next time I went back to the Blue Gardenia, my hostess told me her boyfriend had a broken nose, broken cheekbone and a depressed forehead, and he had put out a contract with a hit man to kill me. 'Whatever you do, get back to the base, don't come into town, and don't come anywhere near the Blue Gardenia,' she said.

I took her advice.

Dale and I found another nightclub, the Macombo, and I found a new girlfriend. On Dale's second R&R, we walked into the Macombo, and the saxophonist who played there, Takami — one of the best jazz saxophonists in Japan — told Dale he wanted him to meet 'Newface', a hostess who had just started there. Dale crossed the bar and sat at a table with Newface. Before long, he was into his pitch — she was a really beautiful girl — but after a few minutes the doorman approached him and said, 'There's somebody outside who wants to meet you.' Dale cursed, excused himself, and went downstairs, where he found his girlfriend from the previous night — it wasn't his night; she was also Takami's girlfriend. While he was trying to straighten things out with Judy, I saw an opportunity across a crowded room, and I introduced myself to Newface. It turned out her name was Kazuko, and not only was she very attractive, with a wonderful figure, but she was also intelligent and well educated, from a successful family. I fell in love with her, not right there in the nightclub, but after a few dates I knew she was for me. After six months of persuasion she moved in with me; we took a flat halfway between the base and the city and she gave up hostessing.

Kazuko — she anglicised her name to Karen when we married — was my reason for trying to get the hot-dog franchise for U.S. sport in Japan: baseball was starting to boom, and American football was being played at the army, navy and airforce camps. The crowds were huge, there were no hot-dog stands and the opportunity to make good money was so obvious it screamed for attention. Dale dreamed up the idea and we went as far as costing it, researching what we would need for equipment — it wasn't much, the hot-dog business isn't capital-intensive — and finding out the potential market. The one thing we didn't have was money. So I wrote to my father explaining the idea and asking for a loan. I knew the idea was right, but Reg didn't think much of it. The Japanese ate rice cakes, he said, there was no Oriental appetite for hot-dogs. We didn't have the sophistication then to know how to put an idea like that to a bank or finance company so we dropped the idea.

But Reg was wrong. A few years later, Dale was drinking beer in Phoenix, Arizona, watching a telecast of a Japanese baseball game. During a break there was a quick interview with the guy who had the hot-dog franchise, and the announcer said, 'And now he's a millionaire.' Dale dropped his beer.

Dale hadn't been doing much after his discharge — he got out seven months before me and he was living with his sister in Los Angeles, getting by on his winings at the track — he was always a good punter. When I got back he drove up to San Francisco and moved into the Fort Ord barracks with me, living off the U.S. Army as if he were waiting for his discharge like the rest of us. It was two weeks before he was discovered.

On the day of my discharage we got two quarts of Ten High whisky, the cheapest bourbon, which was all we could afford, and drove the 750 kilometres back to Vista, reminiscing about the good times in Japan and hitting the Ten High. Dale couldn't hold his liquor as I could; at Long Beach just south of L.A. he sideswiped half a dozen parked cars in a row — wham! wham! wham! wham! wham! wham! — and there was a motorcycle cop right behind us. He took Dale straight to jail. I asked the cop: 'Look, I only got out of the Army today — can you give me the car keys and I'll make sure he gets it back.' Eventually the cop turned over the keys and I drove down to San Diego in Dale's car. He spent three days in jail.

When I left Japan I told Karen I'd be back and we would get married. I guess thousands of Japanese girls heard that from Americans during the Korean war at the end of rest and recreation leave, but I was in love with her and I meant it. If I could have returned as a hot-dog millionaire, so much the better. When I got back to California my mother was against my marrying — she thought I was a lovestruck kid infatuated with a beautiful girl (she was right to some extent) and that I should wait a year and then if I still wanted to get married, she wouldn't oppose it. Reg was opposed — he thought I was too young — but he was a bit dismissive. He told Grace: 'Robert would never do a thing like that.'

I decided to take up a football scholarship I had with the University of Utah. Utah was an eye-opener for me: it was Mormon-dominated, and a dry state. It was a strange place, difficult to understand. I lived in a dormitory for football players; we used to go to these quasi-nightclubs where people drank 'set-ups' — that is, you brought in your own bottle of whisky and they would sell you seven-up and mix the drinks.

The pre-school training went okay; we had a coach, Cactus Jack Curtice, who later became one of the top American college football coaches. I loved the football and I was getting a G.I. benefit of about $80 a month, plus the scholarship payment of about $15 a week. The scholarship also paid for board, books and tuition, so I was doing pretty well. But when the academic year started I had great difficulties. I had been out of school for more than five years, I'd lost the habit of studying, I hadn't used my brain academically since high school, and although there were some pretty undemanding courses for us 'jockstraps', as they called the athletic scholarship holders, I just couldn't hack the classwork — I was only half committed to it. After the football season I decided this wasn't for me.

I went to see Dale in Los Angeles. I was going to go to San Diego to look for work, but Dale asked, 'Why not look here?' Of course Dale gave me a lot of confidence — he'd been looking for work for about a year and was still unemployed, living as a punter. But he insisted, picked up a newspaper and started looking through the employment ads. I noticed that a milk company wanted drivers for home delivery — and though I wasn't interested in a home milk run, the ad sparked the thought that Carnation

Milk might need people for the wholesale runs, which appealed to me much more. Dale and I took ourselves down to Carnation and they had a couple of jobs going; they hired us both.

I got an apartment three blocks from Sunset and Vine when everything was happening in West Hollywood. I could drop in to a little nightclub seating 50 people and hear Stan Getz playing tenor saxophone or Stan Kenton and his big band. For the price of a few drinks I listened to those legendary musicians for hours. I had to start the milk run at 6 a.m., so staying up late was rough, but some nights it didn't make any difference. On one of those nights, Errol Garner was playing piano and around 10.30 Dale and I were ready to quit when Frank Sinatra walked in with Lauren Bacall — it was just after Humphrey Bogart died. I'd been a fan of Frank's since high school, I have every record he's ever made, so Dale and I refuelled our Jack Daniels and sat back. Around midnight, Frank sauntered over to the piano where Garner, an incomparable black musician, was playing — he sat on two telephone books because the stools were too low — and for the next two hours Garner played and Frank sang. It was just magic. We left around 2.30; with only a couple of hours before we started work, Dale and I stayed up over coffee until we picked up our milk trucks. I drove down the Santa Ana Freeway, still loaded with Jack Daniels, on my way to Disneyland. I nodded off, but jerked my head up just in time to see a concrete bridge embankment coming at me. I swerved the top-heavy truck; it flipped on its side. I had to climb out the passenger door as if I was exiting from a submarine. I stuck my head out and there was this amazing sight: the whole freeway was covered with milk, glistening white, like snow. I climbed out, figuring I had a problem — what I'd just done was a sackable offence — but I could cope with it. A car behind me stopped and I said to the driver: 'Did you see what happened?' He said 'Yes.' I said: 'Did you see the guy who cut me off and made me swerve?' He said 'No.' So I told him: 'You'd better keep going.' That was my story. I stuck to it, and I got away with it — though I wasn't too popular at Carnation for a few days. When Dale got back from his run and found I wasn't there, he affected not to be surprised. 'I figure I've whipped his ass again,' he told a driver, meaning he'd finished his round quicker than me.

I bid for, and won, the route through Watts, the black Los Angeles ghetto which burned in the 1965 race riot. In 1966 Robert F. Kennedy said the Watts blacks were 'an army of the resentful and desperate,' but 13 years earlier, for me they were my customers.

Although any white in Watts felt conspicuous, I wasn't uncomfortable. Where I went to high school, there was literally no significant racial consciousness among the Mexicans, Chinese, Japanese and whites. There were no blacks, but I had had contact with many black Americans in the Army and my relations with them were no different to my relations with the whites. In Watts in the late 1950s racial feeling hadn't polarised as it was to later. Anyhow, I was young, fit and fearless; I was friendly and sipped wine and coffee with them; and I pretty soon got to be seen and known around the place. The people who ran the corner stores and supermarkets and liquor stores were fine people. The liquor stores all had a metal grate over the service window, and they kept a gun under the counter. Drugs weren't a problem then — it was alcohol and poverty which was causing the crime, the grates and the guns. One morning I called at a corner store to make my delivery and the place was sealed off. The police told me my customer, a black lady called Maria, had been shot in the head for the money in her till. Three months later Maria was back, a big scar on the side of her head, and looking a bit lopsided, but back on the job. Another morning, approaching the tram-track intersection with Sixth Aenue, I saw the head of a white man in the middle of the tracks, eyes open, staring at me. Apparently the tram had cut off the head and dragged the body on — there was no sign of the body. That head reappeared in my nightmares for years afterwards. But I personally had only one incident on my run — a black guy pulled a case of butter from my truck. I had no trouble catching him. He turned out to be a guy with two convictions, a loser.

While I was with Carnation I returned to Japan briefly and married Karen. We had magical times in those early years, but the Los Angeles smog was giving me trouble: my eyes would burn at the wheel of the milk truck, and the photochemical smog clogged my lungs and gave me the dry heaves by late morning. Visits to my mother in San Diego with that clear sweet air left me thinking that it was crazy living in poisonous air, particularly with a young child. My eldest son Ron was born in 1958 — and I decided to move to San Diego.

I bought a house in Clairemont, an outer suburb of San Diego and got a job with a bread manufacturer, Oroweat, of which more later,and became friends with a guy who lived two doors away, Pete Kemmsies, a construction site clean-up man, a footballer, water skier and beer drinker, a guy after my own heart. We were both a bit wild, bringing up kids and working for wages. We laughed at the same thins; we would do anything to bring each other down. We went water skiing on the Colorado River at weekends. Kemmsies, Pete's buddy, Bill Mitchell, a painting contractor and I, often headed off in the morning with 24 cans of beer each, skied all day under the Colorado Desert sun and drank the 24 cans. Once, jumping the wake behind Pete's boat, the ski dug into deep water; I flipped over the top and the ski whipped back. The metal skag on the end opened my right leg — I've still got the scar — but because it was so close to the bone it wasn't bleeding much. I taped it over with two bandaids and went right on skiing.

They were wild, yahooing weekends. Once Bill Mitchell, a big guy who couldn't take much sun, wanted to leave a day early, and Pete voted with him — they forced me to drive them back in my Buick. I had 24 cans of beer under my belt and I was mad as hell. I planted my foot and stayed on 120 m.p.h. I thought Bill and Pete were asleep in the back — actually Pete tells me 'we were sure it was all over, we were gonna be killed, but naturally we weren't gonna say anything' — and I dozed off and drifted into the centre lane. Suddenly I saw a huge truck coming at me head on — it couldn't have been more than 75 feet away. I just turned the wheel enough, I had the sense not to turn it sharply, and the tractor just grazed the Buick. It's the only time I've known I was an eyelash away from instant death.

I've always been obsessed with flying and Pete Kemmsies had a pilot's licence. One day, after five hours' beer drinking, and playing liar's poker in the Fallout Shelter, a bar by the Montgomery Airfield, Pete and I got into a serious discussion with an aeroplane mechanic called Digger and another guy we'd never seen before. The question was: if you turned off the engine in mid-air, could you stop the propeller revolving, or would the windmill effect keep it turning no matter what you did? One thing led to another and finally we had to settle it. Pete, Digger, the stranger and I went to the airfield and climbed into Pete's Cessna Skylane 182, just before midnight. Here's Pete's account of what happened next, at 5000 feet:

'We fly around, and we're havin' a hell of a job to get the prop to stop windmillin'. Eventually we work it out so the prop stops turning and we just glide along silently. Then I figure, belly full of beer, I've never done a landing with the engine off, a dead-stick landing, and here's my chance to try it.

'I figure that with the engine off I'd better come in a little high — I don't want to drop it short — but on the final approach I see I'm way too high. No problem. I'll just start the engine, go around and try again.

'I turn it on — and nothin' happens. The engine won't start. Now I've really got a problem: I'm about 100 feet up, half the runway's gone, I'm gonna overshoot, and just beyond the end of the runway is freeway 395, eight lanes of high — speed traffic: I can see the headlights.

'I have two choices — land in the parking lot by the airfield or try to get it down on the runway. I thought if I landed in the parking lot I'd have a hell of a time explaining that away. I slipped the Cessna violently sideways and just got it down in the last third of the runway. We stopped just touching the airfield fence. Ol' Ansett kept saying "Why wouldn't it start? Why wouldn't it start?"'

We went and had a beer as if nothing had happened — but the stranger, who had never flown before, asked Pete, 'Are all landings like that?' and walked into the night — he didn't even want a lift back to the Fallout Shelter.

Pete was a larrikin of the air, and I encouraged him. We would have a few beers at the Fallout Shelter, then take off and head for San Diego Aiport and we'd touch down — and take off immediately, while above us huge jetliners were circling waiting for us stupid bastards to touch and go while they're burning fuel at $1000 a minute. Often we headed off for a private airfield with a bar, have a few beers, then take off for the next one — an aerial pub crawl.

I was particularly proud of the lawn at my house — I kept it watered and fertilized, trimmed like a golf green — and of course I needled Bill Mitchell and Pete Kemmsies, who didn't give a damn about their grass. Their yards looked more like cow paddocks. My needling got to them. One afternoon they were drinking in Rosalie's Bar and got to chatting about that bastard Ansett and his lawn. So Mitchell, who's about 250 pounds, drove his Ford Ranchero down to my house and onto my precious lawn — and then he burnt rubber across the lawn, tearing great shreds out of it. I charged out of the house, and there were Mitchell and Kemmsies holding their sides laughing. I knew I couldn't take them both, so I had to laugh — but I was seething with fury.

Pete and I were good mates. The intense competition between us was, I suppose, part of the ritual of young men proving themselves — to themselves and each other. I think, despite all the yahooing, that I was a pretty level-headed guy, and the cheque I brought home each week from Oroweat proved I knew something about the commonsense principles of running a business. Pete never believed that — he thought that though I was conscientious and hard-working I was sometimes a bit of a mug. Pete:

'One day Bob arrived my house and he's got this big grin on his face. He had four eggs. He put them on the table and said "I bet you can't tell which two of these are hard-boiled." I looked at the eggs, felt them and said: "These two right here." Bob's face fell. He spun the eggs — hardboiled eggs spin longer — and sure enough, I'd got it right. He never could figure out how I could pick them without spinning them. How did I? The hardboiled ones were still warm! He can be a dummy — but I guess people like it that a big-time entrepreneur can be a dummy. It shows he's vulnerable, he's not the perfect hotshot who knows all the answers.' Most of the staff at Oroweat were political liberals who voted for John F. Kennedy in the 1960 presidential election, fell under the spell of Camelot and grieved after his assassination as if they had lost the last best hope for America. I thought the liberals were mostly bleeding hearts with soft heads, and I wasn't too shy to say so. A liberal Democrat lived in the next house in Donald Avenue. It was an election year, 1964, and one Sunday morning we got into an argument about Barry Goldwater who was the Republican presidential nominee against President Lyndon B. Johnson. The 'liberal' hit me with a coffee cup and broke my jaw — it was wired shut for six weeks.

The fights with the bleeding hearts at Oroweat weren't that bad, but it seemed to me and Pete that America was turning left politically, there was increasing government intervention and regulation of business, initiative was being stifled, public debate was dominated by characters of social vision but no experience of business realities. Politically, Australia under Robert Menzies was looking much more attractive to me than America under the Democrats. Besides, I had been thinking on and off for years about whether I'd go back to Australia, I had passed the milestone of my thirtieth birthday the previous year, and although I was making good money with Oroweat I figured it was time to start a substantial career. To be quite candid, I thought that if my father hired me as an Ansett Transport Industries manager, it would be a good deal for both of us.

It all crystallised one night in Peter Kemmsies' kitchen — we were talking about our kids' education. Pete had three young kids, Danny, Jeanne and Tommy, and I had Sherrie, Ron and Tim. We didn't think much of the educational trends in California. Discipline was a dirty word. Neither of us wanted our kids growing up in a country where people depended on welfare and government handouts, and it seemed to us that America was heading towards socialism if Barry Goldwater lost the election to President Johnson. In April I made a bet with my Oroweat boss, Frank Dell, a bleeding-heart liberal. If Goldwater won, Frank would push a golfball with his nose one mile down the Kearny Mesa Road — I had lovely visions of my boss crawling down the street. But of course Goldwater was the long-shot underdog, and in the weeks before the election I started to measure the mile on my breadtruck speedo. On 4 November I set a new North American record for pushing a golfball with the nose, wearing a sign:

I WAS FOR BARRY — AND STILL AM

Pete Kemmsies took turns with me and Frank walked

alongside us, crowing. The event was covered by television cameras, and the *San Diego Evening Tribune* ran the story under the headline:
NOSE PRESSED INTO SERVICE:
ELECTION BET LOSER TEES OFF IN MILE-LONG GOLF BALL DRIVE

I wrote to my father telling him I was coming home and suggesting he might like to send over aeroplane tickets to take me to Melbourne — but the old man didn't think much of that idea. He wrote back saying he felt I was coming to Australia for the wrong reasons. I suppose refusing to buy tickets was his way of underlining the fact that there was no easy ride for me in Australia because I was a rich man's son. I sold my house; Pete sold his business. Pete and Muriel and their three kids, and Karen and I and our three, boarded the steamship *Iberia* in Los Angeles on 5 February. Kemmsies, a fiercely independent guy, told an Associated Press reporter as we left: 'If our children want to grow up to do things and think for themselves without government interference, they'll have to get out of the United States. Opportunity here just isn't what it used to be.' (He said in 1985: 'I was mistaken. Australia is more socialist than the United States — but going to Australia was the best thing I ever did. I can't say a bad thing about Australia or Australians'.) The angle for the story of our departure was that we were going because Goldwater had lost. That wasn't actually the finest, palest shade of truth, because we had booked our fares to Australia before the election, but Goldwater's loss certainly sealed the voyage for Pete and me — and Karen was strongly in favour of immigrating.

On the voyage out I deliberately spent the profit on the sale of my house: I wanted to start running the minute I hit Melbourne and I knew if I had a cushion, enough money to last the family for a few months, it might make me lazy or complacent. I wanted to get some runs on the board and I knew a financial spur would be the best motivator. I suppose that's one of the answers to a question people ask me a lot: What motivates a motivator? Survival's part of it.

Because of the publicity about my return to Australia, Neil Smith, then an Ansett Transport Industries executive, later chairman of TAA, met the *Iberia* when it docked in Sydney and arranged to have us hidden in the Captain's cabin to avoid reporters. He smuggled us off the boat and flew the Ansett family to Melbourne. The Kemmsies stayed on the boat; we met them a few days later in Melbourne. When I hit Melbourne with my family, every reporter in town was looking for this son of Reg Ansett's who'd returned home because Goldwater lost. But it was a while before I spoke to the press. Ross Alexander, my father's public relations man, had a few beers with me in Lou Richards' pub, The Phoenix, crowded with reporters from the Herald and Weekly Times building just across Exhibition Street, but no-one spotted me. The Kemmsies and Ansett families, four adults and six children, moved into a one-room flat above a chemist's shop opposite the Botanic Gardens. After 20 years I was home again. Now what? I never sat around long asking myself questions like that. I went to see my father.

3
An Ex-greasemonkey's Luggage

Now I have achieved some success as a businessman, people are curious about how I did it, what were the keys or even *the* key to Budget's and my success, what special qualities and experience led to the philosophy behind the company, even looking for tricks or hidden sources of assistance or expertise or finance. (It is deeply ironic and amusing to me to hear that my father is still, after I've served 20 years as a Budget executive, suspected of having slipped me a few quid, that our public feuding was 'a publicity stunt'!) Sometimes my answers don't seem to be 'enough', they are 'too general'. Often, because these questions are asked and answered during question time at public speaking engagements, there is not time to go into my experience in detail and make the connections between the actions at all levels of the company today and the things I knew when I took my luggage off the *Iberia*.

A lot of the answer has to do with odinary things. We are still reaping the benefits of good, smart people's hard work traipsing around travel agents wearing out shoe leather without complaining about it; people who greeted car renters with a smile and friendly attention while they were worried about things at home, people who ran the vacuum cleaner nozzle around the top of the trim on the floor of our cars to remove those bits of trapped fluff they didn't pick up on 'the old once-over'; people who saw and approached travellers in unfamiliar airports when they looked lost and showed them where to find the toilet.

Some of this work went on in the 1960s; some of it happened yesterday; some of it will go on tomorrow. It adds up to thoughtfulness, courtesy, hard work, persistence, initiative, self-motivation, determination, self-organisation — all the things we routinely see wanted in the situations vacant ads. These are essential ingredients and there is no secret about them, though often I wonder how many of the advertisers get what they want and what the managers placing the ads do to encourage and foster the qualities they seek.

I welcome the opportunity to explain at length where I took on the mental equipment that fitted me to take on Budget. To do that I have to go back in the story of my life and look more closely at the three key jobs I held when I was in my teens and twenties. Everything I've done since has been the application of fundamentals learnt selling bread and milk and, particularly, selling petrol and garage services on the forecourt for Red Hostetter and Standard Oil in Oceanside, California.

I was 17 when I went to San Diego for the Standard's week-long training course — I had to pay my own way there — and it was a real eye-opener. Everything — *everything* — was devoted to customer service. First lesson: when a car pulls in to the petrol pumps, whatever you're doing, you drop it and *run* to the car. Second lesson: Don't just say, 'Yessir, can I help you?' or 'Good morning ma'am.' Be positive: you know they're there because they want petrol, and you're there to sell it. Say, 'May I fill the tank for you, sir?' The guy might have in mind buying $10 of gas, but if you suggest a full tank the chances are he'll think 'why not?' And you've got extra volume right there. You put the pump on automatic, then you release the bonnet and check the oil. It's a bit dirty, so you say to the driver 'The oil's a bit dirty'. You check his service sticker and point out, 'You've done 1200 miles since your last oil change — it'll only take me two or three minutes to get that oil out and replace it.' (Standard used fast oil-sucking pumps that did the job in a couple of minutes.) You check the radiator water, and if it's a bit dirty you suggest he could use some radiator cleaner. You check the fanbelt — you often find cracks in fanbelts — and ask the driver 'Have you seen that?' You have to be careful not to overdo it — but drivers often appreciate it because there's nothing worse than a broken fanbelt and a seized engine when you're out in the middle of nowhere.

Then you wash the windscreen, inside and out, checking the wiper blades — there's nearly always some deterioration in the rubber. You check the tyre pressure, and while you're at it, check the quality of the tyre. Then you get a whisk broom and sweep out the mats.

If you do all this cheerfully, with enthusiasm, we were told, a driver might pull up planning to buy $10 of petrol, end up spending $20 or more, and pull away pleased and happy and more secure because of the service and the experience.

Red Hostetter was a big tough guy with a piercing whistle and a voice like a foghorn. He was an absolute disciplinarian, physically intimidating, and he ran as tight a ship as I've ever seen. Nobody was ever five minutes late when they worked for Hostetter. I couldn't have faced him. It was just out of the question.

His garage was as immaculate as an operating theatre. If you dropped a spot of grease you would immediately get a scraper out and put some kerosene on it. I had to clean the lavatories — to meet Hostetter's standards of spotlessness I did it two or three times every eight-hour shift (I worked mostly midnight to 8 a.m.). We wore white overalls that were always as clean as dinner suits. This was all part of the image: Hostetter taught me that a spotless garage tells the customer straight away that the place is well-run by people who care about service and know what they're doing. Even if the service is flawless, if a customer gets a subconscious impression of sloppiness because there's grease on a uniform, he won't be back.

Whenever a car pulled up at the pumps and I was working at something else, Hostetter would give his whistle, so loud it hurt my eardrums. It became a bit of a game: if I was lubricating a car 20 metres away from the pumps when a driver pulled in, I'd drop everything and sprint to stop his whistle.

We were always busy; there were no coffee breaks. If there were no cars at the petrol block and the phone wasn't ringing you'd be doing a lube or an inventory or washing the yard. There was a points incentive system on sales: if you sold tyres, wiper rubbers, radiator cleaner and floor mats worth $1,000 during a week you'd get a bonus of around $25. For me it wasn't the money, it was the challenge that I relished: I just had to get the most points each week. I found attitude was everything. You might run, wash, suggest and clean totally correctly — but if your manner wasn't cheerful and enthusiastic you would not make the sale, the points or the commission. The tips were another, fairly minor, incentive: at nights when people had had a few drinks and were feeling more generous you might get tips.

There was no really idle time — although when it was 3 a.m. and Dale came around with a six-pack of Budweiser and there were no cars and Hostetter was sound asleep I admit I sometimes relaxed. Hostetter was a strong character. I never got to know him intimately — he wasn't a manager who would have a beer with the boys — but he commanded my respect. In the army I met a number of guys like him, sergeants who were as tough as hell, but you knew that below that exterior there was an inner man — who was also as tough as hell. You could rely on them when the going got tough; they didn't have the kind of toughness that looked like concrete on the parade ground but you knew would be eggshell under pressure. Hostetter wasn't like that: he wasn't a phoney. His character was too strong for him to do the dirty on you, and I knew he would back me if I was right and it was important. He was highly respected in the Standard Oil organisation, he had the biggest service station in California south of Los Angeles and he broke all the records in sales and performance. Like me, he hadn't gone beyond high school. Like me, he wouldn't tolerate anything but excellence. I learnt another fundamental from Hostetter: I enjoyed working in a service station that did things well and presented a good image. A pleased customer pleased me. Working well pleased me. Getting more bonus points than the other greasemonkeys pleased me.

If you've got the wrong attitude to the customer, all the product knowledge, all the MBAs, all the formal skills don't mean a thing. Attitude counts more than any other thing — and attitude is perhaps the most difficult thing to get right in business. In the early years in Budget, when I coined the slogan 'Can Do' our people earned less than they would have earned in comparable jobs elsewhere, worked longer hours and the amenities and offices were often pretty dreary. But Budget people had the same attitude — 'Can Do.'

People respond to strong leadership, as I responded to Red Hostetter. And the leader must reinforce the attitude that the most important person in the business is the customer. The moment the senior Budget management are not prepared to give up their cars if a customer wants it, then the state managers would stop giving up their cars, and the branch managers and so on. That would mean the customer is no longer the most important person and the managers have priority.

When executives join Budget it's tough to adapt to the company culture: no matter what your track record, you have to prove yourself within the company — the past doesn't count. If you have a company car and they're out of cars in the rental office, the manager is the first to give his up. That's what people expect.

On Saturday mornings every manager in the company is in the office, in part because they know I am. A few years ago our first human resource manager joined Budget, and he refused to come in on Saturday mornings because he had family commitments and so forth. That was the major problem he had in being accepted into the company: he couldn't, wouldn't, be accepted because he violated our culture by staying away on Saturdays. In itself that's trivial. It's also a small matter whether a manager gives up his car when a customer wants it. But collectively these small things are crucial: you can't have a commitment to customers if you have a lot of fat cats on the payroll who don't have that commitment. Lip service is easy — everyone does it. Acting it out is harder: we do that.

Skeeter Quinlon was one of Hostetter's assistant managers, very sharp, a nice guy who used to win all the sales contests, one of the boys. He was better at selling than Hostetter, but he wasn't as strong a leader and manager of people. When I came back from my first trip to Alaska, Quinlon was the Standard service station manager at Carlsbad, just down the coast from Oceanside, and Hostetter used his influence to breach the Standard policy and get me rehired as Quinlon's assistant manager. Then that damn Dale Soderstrom got on the phone and told me about all the money he was making in Anchorage and I quit. It wasn't with too much regret: I didn't think that after two years in the U.S. Army I'd really want to make my mark in a Standard Oil service station. I guess I learned in Carlsbad that being a brilliant salesman wasn't enough; Quinlon was brilliant at selling, but he wasn't complete.

Hostetter's example as a leader built on my experiences in the army. I discovered in the barracks environment in the U.S. and Japan that there are followers and there are leaders and, without seeking to do so, I became a leader. I would set the tone of the group of friends I acquired. I think the army disciplined me.

One night at Fort Ord we went on a full night forced march; it was my turn as platoon leader. We were heavily loaded. The sixteen men took turns of ten or fifteen minutes carrying a heavy submachine gun, and after about six hours of this a black private jacked up and refused to carry it. I took a stand and told him 'You're going to carry it.' He pulled out his bayonet and threatened me with it — it was only a threat, he wasn't going to use it — and I let go with a stream of abuse, a really forceful flow, unusual for me. That stunned the guy. I said: 'This machinegun is going to sit where it is, it's not going to move unless you carry it — and when we're asked where it is, you're responsible.' In the end he picked it up and carried it. I think that was an important moment for me. I just reacted instinctively, without thinking about it at all, in front of sixteen guys, with the bayonet sharpening the drama, and it worked. A person can react in all sorts of ways in a situation like that, by showing fear, or backing down, but I reacted instinctively and asserted leadership. In the Army I became a specialist first class quicker than anyone else and it sharpened my talents and discipline and gave me more confidence: I came to feel that whatever I wanted to do, I could do pretty well.

Carnation Milk had no training school. I took over a route covering Burbank and Monrovia in East Los Angeles. On two mornings I'd go to Disneyland, and I had some aircraft factories where I'd leave huge metal cannisters for the factory canteens, and several liquor stores which took small deliveries. I got the hang of the business, and apart from turning over my truck one morning and washing the freeway with milk, it was fairly uneventful.

After six months the driver for the Watts area left; this left the route open to bids from other drivers. The most experienced of the bidders got the route. Since I'd only been with Carnation six months I wasn't confident about scoring Watts, a high-volume route with a couple of big supermarkets and substantial demand for milk, chocolate milk, orange juice, cottage cheese, butter and eggnog. But I got it.

I developed a good rapport with the black, Chinese and Hispanic shopowners. That was the key to my job, because the only way you could increase volume would be by getting better displays in the shops — there wasn't much chance for expansion by getting new customers.

When I left the plant at 6 a.m. I had to double check the inventory and sign for it — from that point on the milk, eggnog and butter were my responsibility. If I left with $300 worth, I'd have to come back with cash or credit to that amount.

We were paid a fixed income of $75 a week plus a commission on volume; I usually made an extra $25 or so on volume and I think I sold more eggnog than anyone else in the company; I would drive about 65 kilometres a day and make 25 or 30 calls. I developed a friendship with a driver for a rival company, Foremost, and used that to measure how I was doing competitively — and of course I was always competing with Dale Soderstrom. If I couldn't sell more eggnog quicker than Soderstrom I reckoned I should give the game away. This was consolidating what I'd learned at Standard Oil: make sure you know what the customer wants, then give it to him, plus a bit more. The liquor stores and corner shops and supermarkets all wanted to sell produce quickly: I tried to show them by my enthusiasm and my reliability — my image — that I could help them do it.

Chance plays a big part in everyone's life. You have to be open to the opportunities chance creates. When the Los Angeles smog had troubled me for more than two years, I noticed a housing development on one of my visits to Grace in San Diego. I went to the government to see if I was eligible for a G.I. housing loan — and I was. The interest rate was 3.25 per cent. I put down a deposit on one of the houses — without having a job in San Diego. At the end of the street was an Oroweat factory, the only business close to the house. I went to the manager and explained I would be moving from Los Angeles in six months, and what were the chances of getting a job? He said 'There's nothing now, but who's to know in six months?' So I gave him my number and kept in touch and a month before the house was finished a job came up, I went down for the interview and was hired — it worked out beautifully.

Oroweat was the first company to bake a big variety of breads, to really expand the range outside the staple of white sandwich bread, and when I started the Americans were just getting interested in rye, wholewheat, pumpernickel, potato bread, raisin bread and the like: Oroweat had 25 different varieties. I had to fight the other bread companies for shelf space in the supermarkets. The supermarket managers monitored shelf space very tightly: if you weren't getting turnover they would take space away from you, which meant your turnover would go down — it was very competitive. Once again I started work at 6 a.m. and worked till 2 in the afternoon. The trick was to order from Oroweat exactly what I needed — if I ordered too much the left-over loaves would sit in the truck overnight and lose their freshness. If I ordered too little I'd have to waste selling time returning to base for a refill. I started out with a high-volume route — I guess I just was lucky to have a huge supermarket, Unimart, which took a big proportion of the thousand loaves I loaded into my truck each morning.

When the other bread manufacturers saw the volume Oroweat was generating with breads outside the standard high-volume white bread, they started to add some rye, pumpernickel and oatmeal bread. The two keys to getting good displays were a good product and I had that, and good relations with the store managers. I worked very hard at the latter.

To get more display space I would get a special line, selling two oatmeal loaves for the price of one, displayed in a big bin — and to get that I had to sell the idea first to the Oroweat managers and then to the supermarket managers: it was selling at both ends, and I ran the route as if it was my own business. I thought of myself as a self-employed small businessman buying product from Oroweat and selling to the stores. It was basically the same operation as my Carnation job, but there was a higher dollar return on commission at Oroweat, and therefore more incentive. I built up my sales and in the year Barry Goldwater lost the Presidential election to Lyndon Johnson and Pete Kemmsies and I decided to go to Australia, I was the highest paid breadseller among my Oroweat rivals in San Diego County.

When I arrived back in my hometown I carried my most important luggage in my head — the lessons I learnt at Standard Oil, Carnation and Oroweat, in the U.S. Army and on the football fields in California, Japan and Utah. All that I've done at Budget in the last 21 years has been to apply those fundamentals. I don't mean that they've been useful company slogans. I don't mean that they're a shorthand summary which make an interesting after-dinner speech. I mean I've applied them *obsessively* every day for the last 21 years.

My starting point is that you're in business to create a customer. If you think you're in business to make a profit, you've got your priorities wrong: the first objective is to create the customer. Profit follows.

As part of the process of creating the customer, you find out what the customer wants. You must not give the customer what you think he or she wants — you damn well find out what he wants and then you give it to him. That's an absolutely fundamental premise for a successful business, but you'd be surprised how few really adhere to it. There's a lot of lip-service, but lip-service can send you broke when it makes your employees think they're doing it right when they're way off course. What you want is obsessive application of the principle, throughout the company.

In the service industry, as I found out while I notched up bonus points at Standard Oil, customers respond to cheerful and enthusiastic people. That's a commonplace, of course — everybody knows it — but you have to find creative ways to have your company staffed throughout by enthusiastic, cheerful and responsive people. In the first place, of course, you hire enthusiasm — that's the first quality Budget managers look for in job interviews — and you create mechanisms to encourage and reward enthusiasm. Each business finds its own mechanisms.

In the car rental business I've found that the key is *competition*. Australians might not be famous for their pursuit of excellence, but they respond very well to competition. Beating the competition by doing the ordinary things well — making the cars cleaner, answering the telephone quicker, makes people feel good about what they are doing, it creates a daily element of excitement and drama. There is a huge difference between trying to do things well and trying to do them better. If the cars are well turned out and the telephones answered quickly, people tend to relax and ultimately get bored: we're doing pretty well, so where's the panic? But if the goal is to beat the competition you can never relax or get bored: the game's still going on.

The basics include treating a customer the way you would a close friend or relative. You welcome them into the office the way you'd welcome a friend into your home. You're pleased to see them — you should be, they're your living — and you want to please them. Image is vital, as Red Hostetter taught me in his hospital-clean service station. If people in a rental office look harrassed and the place is untidy, this creates an immediate psychological impact on the customers. They're on edge. They're not confident the car will be what they want. Things could go wrong — an untidy office creates the impression that things *are* going wrong. If paperwork is required for a booking or booked pick up, and the person at the desk says, 'Now where did I put it?', however innocently, the customer fears it has been lost, and it's going to take damn quick retrieval to alter the impression of sloppiness created.

Over the years, I've learnt about areas of business I knew nothing of when I was 31. In the year of the publication of this book I'm deeply involved in finance, for example, and I don't pretend that 20 years ago I had more than the foggiest notions about the intricacies of high gearing ratios, what is a reasonable research-and-development spending percentage of annual turnover and what is dangerously high or dangerously low and so on. Even so, every day I'm struck how often the final decision, the one that leads to action, in the end stems from ramifications of the central customer-orientation and competitive philosophy that was the only business skill I had in my luggage in 1965.

4

Uphill and Roadblocks

R.M. Ansett, known throughout the administrative layers of Ansett Transport Industries as 'R.M.' (never, but never, 'Reg'), wasn't disposed to kill the fatted calf for this prodigal son. I got to know some of the Ansett executives during my first months in Melbourne. I liked them and I think they would have welcomed me to the team, but R.M. was an old-fashioned man who believed in keeping his private life and his corporate life entirely separate. In one sense I can see his point.

Perhaps my father sensed even in 1965 that Bob Ansett would not be contained in a corporate structure created by someone else, that his corporate child could not contain his son, but at the time his rejection hurt. I asked if I could borrow a car to look for work. He said: 'How about trying Avis?'

My return created some family apprehensions for Reg — I think I was an embarrassment to his second wife, Joan, and their adopted daughters, because most people knew nothing about his first marriage. Suddenly I had materialised out of nowhere, with newspaper headlines about Reg Ansett's forgotten son. His entry in *Who's Who in Australia 1965*:

> ANSETT, Reginald Myles, Aviator, Chairman and Managing Director Ansett-A.N.A., Ansett Transport Industries Ltd. and Subsidiaries; Dir. Pacific Air Maintenance & Supplies Ltd. (Hong Kong), Cathay Pacific Airways Ltd. (Hong Kong), Cathay Holdings Ltd. (Hong Kong), Woolcord Fabrics Ltd., Petroleum Investments Ltd., Universal Telecasters

(Qld.) Ltd., Chairman Mornington R.C.: son of C. J. Ansett, Mt. Eliza, Vic.; *b.* Feb. 13, 1909, Inglewood, Vic.; *ed.* St. Sch. and Swinburne Tech. Coll.; *m.* June 17, 1944, Joan McA., d. R. Adams; *recreations,* flying, horse racing and game shooting; *clubs,* V.R.C., V.A.T.C., M.V.R.C., Roy. Caledonian Vic., Vic. Amateur Sports; *address,* 489 Swanston St., Melb., and Gunyong Valley, Mt. Eliza, Vic.

No mention of my mother or John or me!

I had come home to a fair bit of publicity, but no money, and both Pete Kemmsies and I were getting dangerously low on funds. Pete had sold his plane and construction business in California. Four adults and six small children lived in a one-bedroom flat over a chemist's shop. One night I borrowed $500 from my brother John, came home with an armful of meat and groceries and invited John and his wife Cynthia over for dinner. For Pete that was too much. He said in 1985: 'We had been sharing everything, and you had run out of money. Then I ran out — and we were literally finding it hard to buy food for our families. Now I'd spend my last dime for all of us — you should have shared that meal with us too. I've never forgotten it.' In retrospect, I'm ashamed of my thoughtlessness. I just didn't think. Pete died shortly after he said those things, shot in his San Diego house by his girlfriend's jealous ex-boyfriend.

My father knew Eric McIlree well. McIlree is an important figure in this story and he had a host of seemingly contradictory character traits that puzzled a lot of people who knew him. He was vigorous and had a quick, sharp intelligence. He was a genuine entrepreneur. He flew planes and was a skin diver. Late in his tragically short life, he learned to play the organ and would inveigle his guests, in the most charming manner, to join him in singalongs at his parties, which were often lavish. It could not be said he was a handsome man, but his bravado and panache made him very attractive to women, and he had dozens of girlfriends, quite trying the patience of his wives, of whom his widow was the third. His employees were seldom caught on the hop by Eric — a cloud of cigar smoke was the unmistakeable early warning signal that he was about to descend. Men loved his company too. As well as being a raconteur, he could be a very shrewd adviser and a thoughtful man to talk to about issues. He was a confidant of Harold Holt and Henry Ford, both of whom were visitors to Dunk Island, which he owned. Harold Holt had a retreat at Bingal Bay just across the channel from Dunk Island which attracted a great deal of gossip about 'goings on' there. It is said that Henry and Christina Ford's marriage nearly joined others that had foundered there.

Yet he was capable of great affection for the women in his life, and his children. A great labrador dog was a nearly constant companion. He was a warm friend of Arthur Rylah, onetime Attorney—General of Victoria, who figured in a minor scandal when trying to help Eric get Avis into New Zealand.

He could also be as tight-fisted as hell: he would want a site, it would be perfect for his purposes, the buyer would be willing to sell and, to everybody except Eric, the price would be right. Negotiations would drag on interminably, the deal would be jeopardised by price haggling more than once — and more than once the site was lost. He simply had to screw the other party down, and the need was psychological, not good economic sense. When I told him he was penny-wise and pound-foolish, he didn't bother to make a case. That aside, he was a tough, shrewd, good operator, easily the most interesting man in the rent-a-car business, and I respected him.

No-one who met him forgot him, and McIlree stories abound. Of my own memories, one incident surprised me and I've never quite managed to put it into place since. We had both been summoned to see my old man at his office and while we were waiting for him, Eric was un-characteristically nervous, patting down the sparse oiled hair of his mainly bald pate. Then he turned to me and volunteered this part of his private self: 'I spend the week-end with the Prime Minister of Australia or the Premier of Victoria. But I'm always scared shitless when meeting Reg Ansett.'

When my father rejected me, I figured that first, I

wanted to be in transport — my interest in the industry could be genetic — and second, I wanted a part of the industry in which my father was not involved. That left two choices: rental cars or taxis. Since I'd already exhausted my interest in cabs in Anchorage, there it was.

I applied for a job at Hertz, then a tiny company sharing 15 per cent of the rent-a-car market with 49 other operators (Avis dominated the industry with 85 per cent of the market). Hertz offered me the position of Queensland manager; when I mentioned this to my father he called Eric McIlree and told him of my interest in rent-a-cars. In May 1965 McIlree offered me the job of chief executive of Budget Rent-a-Car. Starting salary: £25 a week. I accepted immediately — and for every day of the next 20 years did my best to beat the hell out of Avis.

It was a job — but it wasn't a job which would have attracted a long queue of aggressive and experienced executives in those days of full employment. The first Budget office at 253 La Trobe Street, Melbourne, was an old garage, with a fleet of six cars, run by an old Avis employee who was marking time till his retirement. It was owned by Eric's family company, Shellbank Holdings, and it was designed by Eric purely as a weapon to protect Avis from attack at the bottom end of the market — the people who would walk in and drive out, who weren't interstate executives on expense accounts, but who wanted a cheap car for a few days, and who paid cash.

I was lucky I started relatively late — I think if I'd tried to start my own business when I was in my twenties I would have made a Godawful mess of it. One night after I'd been drinking with friends at Essendon Airport I was driving back to Melbourne in a Ford Galaxy with my cousin Stan Nicol when a guy tried to run me off the road. I chased him, pulled him out of his car and belted him. As I drove off with the guy lying beside his car Stan said: 'I know you didn't think twice in America about doing things like that, it was second nature to you, but here you're heading a business, you've got your father's reputation to consider, you could endanger everything.' It was strange advice coming from Stan, a guy who drank more than anyone I've known, who was a legend at the Torquay lifesaving club and who had more friends than anyone I've ever met. He wanted to live fast, die young and have a good-looking corpse. And he did. He died in 1974 after a debilitating knock on the head with a surfboard in Queensland, and had the biggest funeral I've ever attended. Stan was a great influence on my adjustment to Australia, even though he did everything wrong, and he was my closest friend in Australia; his sister married my friend John Stevens, Budget's Queensland manager. I never forgot his advice.

When I became the Budget chief executive, all I knew about the company was what the name implied: that it offered cut-rate car rental. I hadn't heard of Budget Rent-a-Car in the U.S. I had no management experience. And my sole encounter with the car-rental industry was the night Dale and I slipped away from the U.S. Army in Los Angeles to see our girlfriends in Vista.

But I was competitive to my toenails. I knew from my years playing gridiron that persistence and determination would beat talent, even brilliance, and since I had no management experience, I wasn't inhibited by preconceived ideas of what would work and what wouldn't; I thought everything out from first principles. When I went to Avis for a period of 'training' — it wasn't really training, it was just exposure to the Avis organisation — I discovered that what I had to beat wasn't brilliance. But it was formidable — Avis had nearly nine-tenths of the market, a government-guaranteed monopoly of the airports which generated most of the car rental business, and a virtual monopoly of the hotel and motel business. Much later, the media were to make use of the David taking on Goliath theme — and it really seemed a bit like that at the time.

I had read a book I liked, Robert Townsend's *Up the Organisation, How to stop the corporation from stifling people and strangling profits*, outlining his views on a host of business and management concerns. He was the man who coined the famous slogan for his company, Avis, in the U.S.: *When You're No. 2 You Try Harder*. (This referred to Avis U.S.'s position behind Hertz, the U.S. market leader.) I loved its customer-service orientation and its brilliant use of an unpalatable fact to go on the attack. The book contained a ton of interesting and useful thoughts and advice, but the cover type struck the note I thought I should strike in my new job:

> If you're not in business
> for fun or profit,
> what
> are
> you
> doing
> here?

Since the chances of making a profit in my first year at Budget were two — Buckley's and none — I figured I'd try to have as much fun as possible.

My first day at Budget was really exciting. At the pokey, dilapidated office, the nice old-timer was sitting not renting the perfectly roadworthy six cars — the fleet, in fact — in the dingy garage. But it was my first chance to show what I could do, and my excitement was real. I looked across the street to Kay's Rent-a-Car, a rival cut-rater and saw this sign in their window:

> 10/- A DAY
> AND
> 1/- A MILE

So I hand-lettered my own sign, for starters, and put it in the window:

> NOTHING A DAY
> AND
> 1/- A MILE

That sign was my first shot in a small war that has absorbed my energies and the energies of hundreds of other troops in the car rental business.

It was intuition, not cost analysis, that led to that decision. But it was a good one; it was mileage charges that brought the money in anyway, and we had lost very little potential revenue to gain a dramatic competitive edge.

My competitors thought I would ruin what there was of the company without a daily minimum: they were so blinkered by the status quo they didn't even calculate how little the day rate brought in or contemplate matching the pip-squeak in La Trobe Street. My first day opened up tremendous possibilities, even though we failed to rent a car!

Although Australian workers are said to be less motivated than Americans, less willing to give everything to the job, less interested in going the extra yard just for the satisfaction of a job well done, I knew that they were ferociously competitive in one arena and did very well in it. That was the arena I enjoyed most and from which I had learned most in America: sport. I figured that if I set Budget's goals, not as abstractions like 'the pursuit of excellence' or even 'the best service at the best price', but as *competitive* goals — to beat the opposition, and do it every day — Australians would respond to that.

We also needed to create what psychologists call a 'positive mind-set'. At the end of my first month at Budget all our cars were out, and I was walking into the office congratulating myself when I heard my secretary, Helen Smith, talking on the telephone to a potential customer. (Helen took the calls and I washed the cars in those days; we were the total Budget workforce.) 'I'm sorry,' she said, 'but all the cars are out.' That was perfectly true, but what struck me was the pleasure in her voice as she said 'no'. There's a certain human pleasure in turning down somebody who wants something from you. A few years ago I waited in a long line for tickets to see the movie of David Williamson's play, *The Club*. Just as I got to the window, the ticket lady looked up with a magic smile — and pushed out the SOLD OUT sign. It was her moment of superiority — and if you want to see someone else who has enjoyed those moments, look in a mirror.

After thinking about this problem for a few minutes, I coined a slogan — the first Budget slogan — of two words: Can Do. There's always a solution to problems in business — if you don't believe that, you shouldn't be in business. Next time all the cars were out and a customer called in, Helen said 'Yessir, can do'. I had about 10 minutes to procure a car for rent. I *ran* around the corner to the Avis office in Elizabeth Street, rented an Avis car, drove it back to La Trobe Street and rented it to our customer. Some people would think that was lunacy, because Avis's rates were higher than ours, and we *lost money* on the deal. But I looked at it like this: we had created one more satisfied Budget customer, instead of creating an impression that we weren't a serious business. We were investing in the future — even though, to my chagrin, we were doing it by creating more business for Avis: between 1965 and 1970, Budget became the largest single user of Avis cars in Australia. Naturally, we didn't go on losing money on it, but negotiated a discount deal with Avis to narrow the gap between their rate of hire and ours. I always argued that my discount was not enough for such a good customer!

I've never felt doubt about a major initiative — I'll come back to that later — but sometimes minor problems look like they're going to beat you.

In 1965 I wanted a site for Budget in Adelaide, on the corner of Frome Street and North Terrace, right across the street from our rival, Kays, but the estate agent said: 'It's being used as a car park, the owner's happy with the income and we wouldn't be interested in leasing it to you'. I had a search of the property records done and located the owner, a lady who lived close to the city and the next time I visited Adelaide I went to see her. She was a dear old lady of 84. I told her over a cup of tea how much I wanted that block of land. Her main concern was that she wanted guaranteed parking spots for herself and her son; that's why she didn't want to lease it. I told her if she leased to me there would be a parking spot for her as long as she lived. I got the site.

Four years later, the old lady sold me the site, on condition that she would still have her parking spot. I agreed, thinking she probably won't need it much longer. She was 88 then. But she kept driving for another six years, pulling up right in front of where the customers parked, creating havoc. But it was still worth it.

In 1965 only 3 per cent of the Australian population had rented cars — the entire industry generated only around $10 million of revenue and Avis had $8.5 million of that. The market was corporate executives, company directors, people who drank Chivas Regal and flew first-class: I was interested in the economy-class passengers who wanted to rent a car for a weekend in Surfers Paradise, then drop it off in Brisbane. Beer drinkers who wouldn't think renting a car was the equivalent of hiring a car without the chauffeur, a luxury for the well-off. They would think of it as a time and cost-saving equivalent to a taxi, and for me they had one great virtue: there were a hell of a lot more of them than there were company directors in silk shirts. (Male company directors: in those days a woman renting a car was a novelty.) And the same well-off men who rented cars when they flew to sales conferences or to board meetings would rent them when they flew from Melbourne to the Gold Coast on holidays. The whole industry was confined to Australians who were very comfortable.

Curiously, although Eric McIlree started Avis in the early 1950s — he entered an agreement with Avis U.S. in September 1955 to use the name 'Avis' exclusively in Australia, in return for licence fee payments including $2 a year per car — Budget U.S. had not registered their company name in Australia. Morris Belzberg, the President of Budget U.S., says, 'My understanding is that we hired a lawyer to register the name, but he saw fit to go to Eric McIlree, who of course registered it.' Registering business names is so easy and commonsense you'd think only a dummy would overlook it, but Budget U.S. did, and as I'll explain later, so did I. Never assume your competitors have got the basics covered: sometimes even in the best-run companies, they haven't.

Just before Eric McIlree hired me, he had changed the name of his down-marked company from AAA Drive Yourself Pty Ltd to Budget Rent-a-Car Systems Pty Ltd. That was a marketing step forward — 'Drive Yourself' tells potential customers nothing about the company that they don't know already: what else could a rent-a-car company be but drive yourself? The advantages of the first alphabetical listing in the Yellow Pages ('AAA') are dubious at best. Budget implied cost-consciousness, giving us a symbolic advantage over Avis and Hertz even in the company names: what the hell does 'Avis' imply to a first-time car renter in Ulladulla who wants to meander down the New South Wales coast, spend a day at Wilsons Promontory and drop the car off in Melbourne? If he knows *avis* is the Latin word for bird, does he care? If he's a radio buff, he might think of the German physicist Heinrich R. Hertz, who died in the 1890s and gave his name to the unit of frequency which measures electromagnetic waves, but when he's renting a car, would he give a damn? Of course many people had heard of Avis and Hertz because of the overseas companies with those names, but as names, on a scale of one to 10 they were one.

Although McIlree held a controlling interest in Budget and he was formally in a position to control me through the company, he didn't exercise this control. If he had required me to run the company on his guidelines, I would have quit. But I had to struggle for my autonomy: at the start, all our accounting was done by Avis, our cars were bought and disposed of by Avis, our payroll was handled by Avis. Even our premises were inherited from Avis. Eric had a benign view of Budget, because my efforts to expand Budget worked directly in favour of his family, who owned the company, but the guys who managed Avis never shared this view. I can understand that: to them Budget was competition.

So we couldn't compete with Avis in the corporate market — we weren't permitted to have credit accounts or credit cards. (Diners Club was the only consumer credit card then, but we did use TAA, Avis, Hertz and Ansett customer cards as evidence of credit-worthiness.) Budget customers paid cash for a service peculiarly unsuited to cash transactions. We weren't permitted to pay commissions to travel agents, which shut us out of the tourist slice of the industry cake.

It didn't make sense. I told Eric: 'If you really want an operation that sits outside a competitor offering cars at a cheaper price, sure, they might walk across the street because of the price — but if they can't get a car delivered, if they can't pay for it on credit, if they can't book it through a travel agent, then it's not going to become an ongoing business.' We could have a short, sharp shock effect on the rental business, and we did. But we couldn't grow. At that time the market was too small, there weren't enough people who wanted to rent a car without the full booking and credit services — and there were dozens of corner-garage rent-a-car businesses going broke to prove that. If Budget continued solely as a walk-in, drive-out company, it was headed for oblivion. I think that was Eric McIlree's intention, and he saw Budget as a temporary weapon to wound the cost-cutting competitors.

What he didn't take into account was that I wouldn't accept it. I wasn't going to devote my energy and whatever talents I had to a company that would be phased out.

I didn't see my career as being a temporary defensive weapon for Eric McIlree and then dropping out when it suited him. I was committed to the job.

Once I listened to Rafer Johnson (the Olympic decathlon champion who was with Bobby Kennedy when he was shot in Los Angeles in 1968) explaining commitment: 'A pig and a chicken are walking down the highway and they see this sign: "Ham and Eggs 95 cents". The chicken says he reckons that's good value. The pig doesn't think so: "From you, it's a contribution," he says, "but to me it's a total commitment".'

At the start, the Avis master insurance policy was broadened to include Budget cars — all six of them. By October 1967 Avis set up as a self-insurer, and the subsidiary insurance company, Auto Accident Consultants Pty Ltd, administered insurance for Avis and Budget — but as separate entities. Not long after, we negotiated our own agreement with General Motors Holden. Each step was a cut in the umbilical cord with Avis — or to put it another way, we were like a colony fighting for its independence, except that there was no war. We took over functions one by one, even though the Avis managers quite rightly saw us as competitors. McIlree, even when we were taking customers from Avis, continued to smile benignly. Within three years, I had won my debates with McIlree and the Avis managers and Budget was a fully-fledged car rental company which delivered cars, accepted credit and paid commissions to travel agents.

But we were still a tiny company with an insignificant share of the market: there was good business growth, and airline growth, which meant people were travelling more often and renting cars more often.

We needed more visibility, particularly in the hotel and travel industries, which generate most business outside airports. We had an introductory offer to guests at various high-turnover hotels, offering a $3 discount; we distributed Budget shoe-shine kits to hotels and put litter bags in all Budget cars. The litter bags told our hirers that Budget cares about the environment, its clients' convenience and its own cars and staff, this is a company with a social conscience which believes in good housekeeping. We also distributed sewing kits and kids fun items like Budget balloons. We negotiated an arrangement with

Mobil Oil to hang 'Agent for Budget Rent-a-Car' on most Mobil service stations around Australia — all aimed at creating greater visibility at little cost to Budget.

The California connection was still strong — and it still is today. I made my closest friends in California, and we've stayed close for twenty years. I know people tend to drift away from one another when they live on different continents, their interests change, they become different people, they can't keep up that day-to-day sharing of experience which is the basis of many friendships, but Dale and Dan and Jerry and Ed Ward are still among my closest friends — partly because of what we shared in our formative years and partly because we haven't changed all that much. Pete Kemmsies, who went to Adelaide selling Cessnas for Ross Aviation for a while before he went back to California, said: 'I don't think I've ever really grown up — and to tell you the truth, I don't regret it either.' I don't feel like that — but I still felt connected to, and comfortable with, the larrikin kid who was robber Robert. I was quite shocked when Pete told me he was going back to the States, and I tried to talk him out of it. But he was broke, his wife was unhappy, and he felt he could always come back to Australia. He did, but only for visits.

Dan Flemming visited on a brief working holiday in 1967, and returned totally broke to California — he hitchhiked across the States because he was out of money. He had worked a year as a carpenter in the Oceanside Fire Department before I talked him into coming back. I gave him a job as counter-clerk in the La Trobe Street office. By then I was working very long hours to create a national Budget network and I was on the road more often than I was at home.

In the first year we opened offices in Sydney, Surfers Paradise, Launceston, Hobart, Adelaide, Brisbane, Rockhampton, Cairns and Townsville. In 1966 we opened in Perth, Mackay and Devonport. But in Melbourne, I was growing apart from Karen. We seemed to have less and less in common.

Dan came with me to Sydney and I offered him the job of Sydney manager. Money was tight then, and I suggested he should stay at the YMCA till he got a place to live — but he baulked at that. 'You can forget it,' he told me. A few weeks later we flew to Perth and rented a building by the Blood Bank. Dan thought it was funny to start Budget Rent-a-Car in Perth at a time when we didn't have a single car for rent and he didn't have one to drive. But he should tell the story:

'I hired a carpenter to build some cabinets, I painted the walls and I went around town passing out the Budget pamphlets at the travel agencies and hotels, and got posters up around the place, A client would walk in, no cars visible, and I'd call Avis and they would bring the car around. Of course the customer would do a double-take: "What the hell's goin' on here?"

'Then we got a big Ford Falcon and painted it up with he Budget sign and colours. I'd park the car on a parking metre in front of the Kays Rent-a-Car yard — that used to piss them off something fierce.

'I spent three months there, but it was fairly lonely — Perth is famous for its nice friendly people, but I didn't find them open and friendly, for some reason. But I did have some fun. I met Paul Rigby, then the *Daily News* cartoonist, now working on the *New York Post*. Rigby was mad. I got involved with some crazy limp-fallers, a bunch of guys who go out drinking in the Palace Hotel or the Esplanade and suddenly fall en masse to the floor. The limp-fallers were all members of the Lager Lovers' League, one of those bizarre west-coast groups that was famous in Perth for a while and was good for a few laughs — for me it did a lot to make up for the isolation of Perth and the loneliness that I felt in all that sunshine with all those people famed for their friendliness.'

Hiring friends is an added risk in business, because if things go wrong you can lose not only an employee but also a mate. That didn't happen with Dan — but there were frictions. Once I saw him slouched over the counter filling in an application form and told him to stand up straight, and he resented it. Dan, now a labour organiser for the Carpenters Union in Vista, had something of the union attitude mindset even then, and he wasn't interested in giving the extra effort to make Budget a winner — he called it 'donating overtime to the company'. We've stayed friends though — if you choose your friends by their ideology you have a narrow range of interests — and friends.

Although Dan didn't take to Perth so easily, I had always enjoyed it, and I made some good friends on my visits — John White, a local playboy, who was a mate of Paul Rigby's, Des Legget from Qantas, Nev Taylor from Avis — at the time my closest friends in Australia were in Perth.

In 1968 Dale Soderstrom came for a visit, and I wanted to give him a good time, so I arranged a round-Australia trip: I could use each stop either to look at establishing a Budget office, or to visit an existing one. I talked Frank Pascoe, the Ansett general manager, into giving me two round-Australia tickets. I don't think my father ever knew of it.

We flew to Perth, had a few days off, then set off on MacRobertson Miller Airlines (MMA) through the north-west.

The flight from Port Hedland to Darwin changed my life.

As the hostess finished her speech about safety, exits, oxygen masks and life jackets under the seat in front, I nudged Dale and said: 'Hey Dale, that's a good looking hostie, why don't you throw some of your wonderful charm at her?' Like a lot of American men, Dale had heard some wonderful things about Aussie girls, and he'd set his heart on getting one. The hostess came back up the aisle and speaking to us both, delivered the usual VIP invitation. 'The Captain sends you his compliments, and if you'd like to go up on the flight deck you're most welcome.' We thanked her kindly and chatted briefly.

At Derby we stopped, and while we were stretching our legs under the boab tree, the hostess, whose name was Josie Chadwick, told the other hostess: 'One of them's Bob Ansett and one of them's Dale Soderstrom, but I don't know which is which, and it's driving me crazy. I'm going to rifle a briefcase and see if I can find a name.' So she went through my briefcase, found a business card, and then knowing who was who, came back and said to me: 'Mr Ansett, if you would like to go up and see the Captain you're most welcome.' A few minutes later Dale sauntered up to Josie while she was making coffee and started chatting her up. He didn't make much progress; we left the flight at Kununurra and Josie flew on to Darwin.

Josie was relieved that that flight was over. I found out later that she'd been to a party the night the flight left Perth at midnight — hostesses are not supposed to drink for 12 hours before a flight — and when she saw the VIP list with the name 'R. Ansett' (she thought it was my father) she told the other hostess, Barbara Livie: 'I feel sick, I don't think I can handle this at 3 o'clock in the morning.'

A couple of days later Dale and I caught another MMA flight from Wyndham to Darwin and damned if Josie wasn't on the plane again. Dale did a smooth-talking line for her again and set up a date in Darwin.

We all went to the Koala Hotel, then Darwin's top hotel, and Josie was talking to the pilots and crew, smiling and flirting, and Dale was getting really upset: he felt he'd been stood up. I said: 'Oh Christ, get out there and talk to her and see how you go.' He said: 'No, stuff it. I'm finished.' It was probably a misunderstanding, part of the difference between Americans and Australians: the Americans are much more formal and get confused by free-floating Aussie ways where you make the rules up as you go along.

I went into Darwin to see about setting up a Budget office. When I got back I saw Josie having dinner at the hotel with a pilot and, joining them, I told her that Dale was feeling hurt. We had four adjoining rooms in the hotel, and half a dozen of us ended up in my room drinking and talking — I got more and more interested in Josie, and Dale was getting more and more drunk, and as mad as hell. He wanted to drive Josie's boyfriend's MG sports. So a deal was struck. The pilot would take him for a drive in the MG if Dale would model the new bathing suit he'd just bought in Las Vegas. We were all under the weather, and Dale posing in a ridiculous little bathing costume was hilarious.

Next day Josie, Dale, another MMA hostess and I drove to a beautiful waterhole near Darwin, Berry Springs, where you could swing on a rope like Tarzan. Josie swung off this rope with a wild scream of pleasure and plunged into the waterhole, and I started to get interested: I'd never seen a woman behave like that before.

That night Josie had dinner with a friend; Dale and I joined up with the aircrew. When I went to bed, I saw the key in Josie's room next door and I thought it was an invitation. (Actually, all the MMA crew left their keys in their hotel doors in those days, it was a code within the airline, family feeling within the company — a locked door meant the person behind it wouldn't be regarded as one of the team.) I thought — I'm a sophisticated man of the world, I know how to play these games; I'll stand her up! Josie and her friend decided that Dale and I would have these terrible hangovers next morning — so they organised to have these greasy breakfasts of bacon and eggs delivered to us at 7 a.m. I guess that was about our level of interest then, good fun times, but we saw quite a bit of each other in the next three days — never exchanging a word about the key in the door. Before she went back to Perth I told her Dale and I would be in Hayman Island in three days, and asked her would she try to get there? But it wasn't possible.

On my next trip to Perth — the cyclist Nick Brown was riding across the Nullarbor with a Budget back-up car — I sent her a telegram saying COMING TO PERTH, KEEP WEDNESDAY NIGHT FREE. She thought that was 'quite flash'. Josie:

'I thought it was terrific having dinner — but when he said he had to stay over another day, and "what about tomorrow night?" I said "I'm sorry, but I'm doing something." He complained: "Jesus Josie, I come all this way and you've just got Wednesday." I said: "Well you only said Wednesday."' About six months later Josie resigned from MMA and, with a girlfriend, took her first trip to Europe.

I'd almost forgotten her by then. But in Rome she had a sudden impulse to send me a postcard, thinking, 'That's funny — why do I want to do that?' She was having the sort of fun you do when you're young, travelling with no money, seeing what turns up in chance encounters, living for the moment.

'Rosemary and I caught the train for Florence in Rome — we had to stand up the whole way, and we had an orange each as our meal for the day,' Josie says. 'We got talking to some Lebanese architectural students, and they said "Where are you staying in Florence?" And of course we said "We don't know", which was true. These wonderful chivalrous students abandoned their beds to us, took us around Florence and gave us a great couple of days. We went to London, Paris and New York. Then we had this standby ticket from New York to Perth and we stopped off in San Francisco where the Qantas crew showed us around. When we got back to Perth we both decided the old home town was too boring, so we thought we'd go somewhere in the magical Eastern States. Rosemary had relatives in Sydney: I didn't care where I went, so Sydney it was.'

Josie was beginning to feel hooked on the travel industry — she liked the travel, the stopovers in the best hotels, the generous food allowances — but she was also beginning to feel trapped. In the life of flight and cabin crew, because of the odd hours and travel she found she only saw her kind of people and she was becoming insular. Some of the pilots, especially, she found egotistical and boring. Josie was getting locked into her own little aircrew world, so she thought she'd try for a ground job with an airline.

She and Rosemary went to Qantas and BOAC and the others airlines asking eagerly 'Have you got any jobs available?' The women behind the counters would say, looking them up and down: 'What qualifications do you have?' They quickly found out that flying for MMA didn't qualify them for anything — except another job as hostesses.

So Josie applied to become a Qantas hostess — and had an amazing job interview. There was a table of interviewers, six men and a woman, and the first question was: 'Do you shave your legs?'

Josie swallowed.

'Oh yes.'

'Tops and bottoms?'

Josie never forgot that: 'It must have been a bit of shock treatment to see how you would react to impertinent male passengers — but there's no way they'd get away with those questions now.'

After a few weeks of unsuccessful job-hunting Josie was getting desperate. She wrote to me saying: 'Guess what? I'm in Sydney looking for work, and I'm not having much success — I think I'll have to hang out the red light.' I called and offered her a job as the first Budget Sydney sales rep, then on my next visit signed her up — which was just as well.

The day she signed, Qantas called to say she'd been accepted for the air hostess job. At that stage she would much rather have flown for Qantas than hawked Budget literature around Sydney travel agents, but I persuaded her that the application form she'd signed was actually a two-year contract and she couldn't back out. She accepted that, thinking 'Well, better make the most of it,' but I often wonder how things would have turned out if I hadn't applied that extra bit of strategic pressure.

When I hired her, Josie was about as qualified for the job as I had been for the job Eric McIlree offered me. She had a bubbly personality and that was about it. She had no sales experience, she knew nothing about Sydney from one end to the other. On the other hand, Budget in those days was not in a position to entice the best sales people in Sydney.

Josie's experience was much like other early Budget newcomers: they had to make it up as they went along. The goals were set; method was the individual operative's business.

'When I started I looked up the travel agents in the yellow pages, then went through with a biro marking all the numbers in George Street — I'd write the numbers on my arm, catch a double-decker bus, and march into the travel agent saying: "I'm from Budget and we've got economic rates." I never said *"cheap rates"*. I had to convince people we weren't a fly-by-night organisation — there were agents, lots of them, who had never heard of Budget.

'Quite often I discovered the Avis rep hadn't called for six months — they could afford not to in those days because there was no competition — and I'd make sure I called every month with an up-to-date rate card, tried to establish a rapport and showed them I was genuinely interested, and that Budget was an efficient company that provided service that kept customers happy. If our customers were happy, so was the agent. Actually, many of our Sydney customers in 1969 were prostitutes who would come in off the street — Kings Cross is five minutes walk from the Budget office — with fishnet stockings, lurid makeup and glazed expressions; they did more miles than the businessmen. I worked like a drover's dog — Robert got me into competition with Pat Collett, the Melbourne sales rep. It was Sydney versus Melbourne, me versus Pat. After a few months I beat her sometimes — she started in front because there was no sales rep in Sydney before me, so her figures set the standard. But he pushed us: I burst into tears once when he said 'I see you dropped a few this month' because I wasn't used to competition. I thought I was just doing a job: at first I took it as a personal affront. I saw around 25 travel agents a day. The figures went to Melbourne and Robert told Pat: 'Well Josie saw 120 this week: who have you seen?'

I was becoming more and more distant from Karen, dating Josie on my visits to Sydney. It was a stressful time for the three of us, with the added complication that I was Josie's employer. She didn't tell anyone in the Sydney office about our relationship, and our work relationship was brisk and professional — I didn't let my feelings about her interfere with encouraging her to compete with Pat, but you can't really keep these things secret in a small office: once I sent her some red roses and signed the card 'Graham' — my middle name — and Josie was mystified about the identity of her secret admirer. But she was probably the last person in the office to guess.

We went for our first weekend away in the winter of 1969 — to Thredbo. Josie wasn't the best on skis and she ended up black and blue. When she got back to her flat in Elizabeth Bay she called on a Kings Cross doctor, a nice fatherly man who saw she needed more than creams for the bruises, encouraged her to talk, and told her gently: 'Josie, married men do not leave their wives.' When she told me that I said: 'You don't think you're breaking up a marriage, do you? Because you're not.'

The end of a marriage, breaking the ties of 13 years, is never easy, and although by that time there was really nothing left of my marriage to Karen, I needed time. Josie gave me time, although sometimes she wondered what she had let herself in for. 'Robert would call for breakfast at 7 a.m., and that was the most wonderful time I could expect to have for the rest of the day,' Josie says. 'I started thinking "Is this what it's all about?" It was too good to stop — but I didn't sit down and look at the facts realistically and work out what was going to happen in the end. I wouldn't recommend it to anyone. Your life's really not your own.'

What did Josie see in me?

'Robert talked about things that the ordinary guy on a date wouldn't or couldn't. Politics, national events. He didn't have to come on strong or play at being something that he wasn't. At dinner one night I looked at him and thought "I could still enjoy talking to him when I'm 70." That was important to me. And I did have a history of going for older men, which I think was — I can say it now — looking for a father figure.' Josie's father, Mr Reginald Chadwick, died suddenly ten years before when she was a teenager.

I had had enough of this STD relationship after 12 months. On my next visit to Sydney I told her how it was wonderful to come up and have dinner but it wasn't enough; she had to come to Melbourne. She decided to bite the bullet, packed her things in a station wagon, drove non-stop Sydney to Melbourne and moved into a flat in South Yarra. She continued to work for Budget. Pat Collett had become pregnant and Josie replaced her in sales. I moved in with her 9 or 10 months later. Karen remained in Melbourne, working in sales and public relations for a firm selling Japanese jade.

Back in the office, things were going well, but problems were looming. In 1968 we showed a profit for the first time — a very modest profit, but it was a milestone passed, psychologically good for the team and useful in arguments that had to be made to get round the problems I saw for the future. The no-frills market just wasn't big enough to keep Budget growing. But in going after the mass market, we were competing directly with Avis, and our restricted advertising with the Scot in the green kilt (now winking at cents, not shillings) was seen by the Avis management as an attack on them. That was fine with Eric McIlree, because his family still took the Budget profits. He could say 'Well, if Budget's going to produce $200,000 of profit a year why not let them have a go, even if it does take some business away from Avis.' I regularly produced a business plan, had it approved by the directors, and that was the start and finish of McIlree's involvement. If we didn't meet the business plan forecasts, of course, the directors wanted to know my response. Since McIlree's family company, Shellbank, appointed the Budget directors and could sack them, theoretically he could have kept a tight rein on me — especially since Avis was also in the 'no-frills' market by then and offered cut rates in their downtown offices. But he acknowledged the realities, which were that to survive, Budget would have to compete against Avis as strongly as it did against Kays, Hertz and the other companies and that this would require management autonomy for Budget. Anyway, he knew I would not accept dictation from him for long.

Although Budget did very little poaching of our competitors' management then or now, the rent-a-car industry in Australia has a curiously incestuous history. Eric McIlree, the dominant industry personality, hired me in 1965. Another strong personality, Alex Katransky, came from Dominion Rent-a-Car in New Zealand and started Kays in Melbourne. Bill Maher succeeded McIlree at Avis and now works for me as a special consultant, and resident director, in New South Wales. Doug Wooten, another McIlree man, joined a Katransky man, John Murphy, took over Kays and later merged with Hertz. Another Kays man, Bern Bruning, started Thrifty in Melbourne and moved to Sydney. I ultimately took over Katransky's old New Zealand company, Dominion, in 1983 and Thrifty as well in 1984.

From my first days with Budget to the early 1970s, we had the benefit of solid general business growth together with aviation growth, which meant there were more executives flying interstate more often, and therefore renting cars more often. But the user base — those Australians who were rental car customers — hadn't grown all that much: by 1970, for example, 5 per cent of Australians had rented cars — not a spectacular growth from the 3 per cent who rented cars in 1965.

Apart from a few spot ads in travel magazines, we didn't advertise until 1968. We had no money for expensive advertising campaigns in those days. My instruction was that, as company policy, we had to work to get free media exposure — free ink, the Americans call it — every single day of the working week. That's still company policy — and although it's true that we have a $4 million paid advertising budget today and that there has not been a story about Budget published in a newspaper or magazine or telecast or broadcast every working day for the past 20 years, it's also true that we have achieved more effective media exposure than any company I can think of. Today it's rare if a day goes by without some exposure of either Budget or me in newspapers, magazines, television or radio somewhere in the country.

We tried some stunts at first. In 1968 Norm Curran, the Budget manager in Melbourne, saw a newspaper picture of a guy walking down Little Collins Street without any trousers, a shot of him with his arse hanging out, and he said, 'Hell, it's remarkable how people can get into the newspapers — let's see if we can come up with something creative for Budget.'

The two of us put together the idea of a parade through Melbourne to liven things up. We built it around the advertising slogan we were using then:

THERE IS A WAY TO BEAT BUDGET RATES!
RIDE A BICYCLE
RIDE A HORSE
RIDE A POGO STICK

We got Paul Jarman, a top jockey, on a horse. We got Vic Brown, who had just ridden a bicycle across the Nullabor, sponsored by Budget, on a bicycle. We got Des Tuddenham, the captain of Collingwood, on a pogo stick. We got a bunch of go-go dancers on the back of a truck, and a group of Budget girls on a stagecoach. We had a whole range of horses and about twenty-two different display groups. We started the parade on the corner of Elizabeth and La Trobe streets, outside the Budget office. The idea was to cover the square of the central business district, go down Elizabeth Street to Collins Street, turn up Collins Street, then up Russell Street to La Trobe and back to the office. We overlooked one detail: Russell Street is the Victorian Police headquarters. People were staring out windows, listening to the band playing, stunned by this unannounced parade, Moomba out of season. Someone from Russell Street called the Budget office and asked what the hell was going in. I was the only one there: when the cop asked for the name of the person who would accept the charges for breaking every regulation in the

City of Melbourne — animals in the street, no police permit, blocking traffic, health regulation violations — I gave the name of a Kiwi car washer whom I knew was going back to New Zealand the next weekend. We never heard any more about it. It was a very successful parade.

My first five years at Budget, 1965 to 1970, were really my apprenticeship in setting up and operating a national organisation. At the end of 1970 we had Budget offices covering the continent and Tasmania from Brisbane to Bunbury, from Darwin to Devonport.

In Sydney we operated, along with all the other car rental companies, on William Street, the would-be boulevard running from Kings Cross to Hyde Park. Early in the 1970s we got notice to quite from our landlord, the Westfield Corporation. They were going to demolish the building.

We spoke to our lawyers, who said, 'Don't worry about it. Under the Landlord and Tenant Act in New South Wales it'll take them six months to get you out.' But it was a problem: we simply had to have an office on William Street, and there was nothing available. One Saturday when I was skiing at Mount Buller, the Westfield people moved in with armed guards and took possession. Our Sydney manager, John Nettlebeck, refused to leave the building. He called the police. The police removed the guards and there was a stand-off: the Westfield guards ringed the office from outside and told John: 'People can leave the building — but no-one's going in.' No employees, and no customers.

When I got there late on Saturday night I'd hurt my knee skiing and I could hardly walk, but I talked to John on the telephone and passed notes under the door. We managed to wedge a cot through a barred lane window for John to sleep on; he used a fishing line a customer had left in a car to hook up hamburgers pies and beer — the window was about 10 metres above the lane.

Next morning we set up a mini-bus as a temporary rental office. An American customer said to me, 'This is the strangest car-rental arrangement I've seen in my life. Where do I return the car?' I told him, 'Right here.' He couldn't believe it.

On Monday I went to see Frank Lowy, the Westfield managing director, and explained my plight to him. In the end he said: 'I'll tell you what I'll do. I'll give you 30 days to get out. But to get the 30 days you must lodge with me a bond of $50,000 and if you aren't out by midnight on the thirtieth day, you forfeit the bond.' I didn't like it — Budget couldn't afford to lose $50,000 — but I had no choice. Lowy removed the guards and I went back to the Budget office.

As I was explaining the situation to John and the other Budget people I looked across the street and noticed the Playboy Club, which I knew had had some financial difficulties. We went across the road and looked at the building and discovered there were two entrances: maybe the Playboy Club could use one and we could use the other? I talked to the owner, Theo Morris, who later bought the Chevron Hotel in Surfer's Paradise. Morris was a tough bargainer. He forced me to pay much more than the space was worth — the negotiations took five days — but the next weekend John Nettlebeck, who had worked in the building industry, (we made him our head contractor after this, and he went on to build our Peel Street headquarters) went in with jackhammers and had all the carwashers working all weekend, ripping out huge plaster of Paris figures that made the place look like a grotto. Then we hired some builders who worked flat out for three weeks. The thirty days were up on a Sunday; on the Friday there was still no carpet laid, no telephones installed and no office furniture in place. The floor was rough concrete and the carpetlayers said you couldn't lay carpet on it. We went back to our old office and ripped up planks of masonite and cut them as floor covering. We finished laying the masonite at 7 on Sunday night. While the carpetlayers beavered away — on Sunday night! — PMG workers, nourished by a few cases of beer, shifted the telephones from across the street. At 11.55 p.m., in front of independent witnesses, we locked the doors on our old office, minus the floorboards. We arrived at the new office at 6 a.m. and washed the windows. The desks arrived at 6.30. We opened for business an hour later.

Despite the growth, the fun, the challenges and the successes, I was getting frustrated: I wanted my own business, and I couldn't see any clear way of buying Budget. When I asked Eric McIlree if he would sell me equity in the company, he said he had a firm policy that either he or Shellbank owned 100 per cent of the enterprises he was involved with. Roadblocked there, I got together with a few good people — John Ansett, lawyer and interested party; Norm Curran, a senior manager and our ad man, Charles Anzaratt — and designed a concept for a company to be called 'Ansett Rent-a-Car'. We developed a good prospectus and booklet, a presentation strategy for developing it based on my experiences with Budget, and even went as far as having the uniforms designed.

All I lacked was the capital — about $250,000. I spoke to Mobil Oil, who provided all the fuel for the Budget fleet. Mobil were interested, but they were having problems in Australia at the time, so they didn't want to bankroll me. I approached our bankers, the ANZ, who said the funds would be provided — so long as I could get a guarantee from my father.

When I approached him, he said the Ansett organisation might be interested in getting into the rent-a-car business, but he wasn't very enthusiastic about my scheme and I wasn't interested in ending up as a subsidiary of Ansett Transport Industries. What I wanted was some form of personal backing, either a loan or a guarantee. My father said, 'Look, if there's one piece of business advice I can give you, it's this: *never* give a personal guarantee. That's a strict policy I've had all my life. If somebody needs help, you're far better off to lend the money yourself.'

Naturally, I asked him if he would lend me the money.

He gave my document setting out the concept of Ansett Rent-a-Car to Ralph Cooper, the ATI finance brain. Ralph had the document for about two months; I was getting pretty impatient and I finally called and said: 'Dad, I just want an answer — yes or no?'

It was no.

Soon after, I discovered two things: first, Eric McIlree somehow found out about my plan for my own company — which would of course threaten both his companies, Avis and Budget. Second, Ansett Transport Industries had surreptitiously registered the name 'Ansett Rent-a-Car.' So I was roadblocked again: I could not get the funding, the name was lost to me, and McIlree was likely to fire me. He was white-hot: he accused me of trying to double-cross him. That was not true — I'd made it crystal clear when I asked him about selling equity in Budget that I wanted my own company.

Eric didn't fire me. Perhaps he thought that Reg might take retribution if he did: McIlree was dependant on the Ansett organisation to produce a lot of business for Avis. But that might not be fair to him — perhaps he felt I had made one mistake and everyone's entitled to one. He ended up offering me a percentage of Budget's profits, which gave me an incentive to maximise company profitability. I accepted, but I wasn't hooked by the incentive because we were still in the developmental stage, and trying to maximise profit would have hindered Budget's growth.

I've never forgotten that incident. I accepted the old man's decision not to lend me the money or guarantee a bank loan without any recriminations. But I was very disappointed in the way the name was registered. It was sneaky. If he or Ralph Cooper had rung me and said 'Look, we have to protect the Ansett name, we can't let you have it for a rent-a-car business, so we've registered it,' that would have been proper — indeed, given Ansett's proprietorial interest, it might have been difficult for me to register the name. But that wasn't done. Nobody from Ansett Transport Industries had a conversation with me about it.

(I'd like to say the incident taught me a lesson I've never forgotten — make sure all the I's are dotted and the T's crossed before you put a project at risk. I'd like to say I've done it ever since, but it isn't true. Years later, when I was making one of my speeches to a community group, a guy in the audience, Terence Trourig, asked about my ambitions in air travel, and I said 'One day we will have an airline called Budget Airlines — a walk-on, no-ticket, low-cost arrangement.' I forgot about it for three weeks, then asked our solicitor to register the name. He discovered that 'Budget Airlines' had been registered a week previously by Trourig. We had the name registered in every state except home state, Victoria — and we had to pay Trourig $20,000 to get the name back. Naturally, I didn't like it, but I do admire his opportunistic spirit. (No individual, and no company, is perfect, and none ever will be.)

I had suffered a setback, but it didn't affect my determination to have my own company at all. I bided my time, and continued the Budget expansion.

5

Driver's Seat

Eric's decision to keep me on meant that being fired is a business experience I've never had. I don't like firing people — and I hardly ever do it. (Once in the early years I had to fire a man and I took a bottle of whisky to his hotel room in Sydney. We both got drunk and at the end of the evening he reckoned I was doing him a favour by letting him go.)

When it becomes obvious that a Budget manager isn't going to make it in the company, I try to create a situation where they will resign of their own accord.

The Peter principle applies in Budget as in other corporations: having done well in a lower level some people are promoted and reach their level of incompetence. If that happens I've got to redirect them tactfully back to the things they did well previously. It's a real skill: you've got to be able to polish the image of the job they've left six months before. Of course it hurts — it damages people's images and their egos, but the good ones accept it. Borderline ones don't; they move on.

In a dynamic company growing rapidly, as Budget was in the early 1970s, you take punts with people, knowing that they have limitations, but hoping they'll rise to the occasion. Sometimes you're wrong, but this is the risk in companies that promote from within as much as we do.

Getting people to fire themselves is a very Australian strategy. It's not applicable, for example, in America. It takes patience, but in a small country where a company has a high profile like Budget, it's better to do it that way than create vindictiveness and hate.

The pattern tends to start with people losing productivity, getting a little lazy, setting themselves up in attractive offices and isolating themselves from the hard cold realities of the business. These are pretty human traits. But if an executive running a division of Budget has been meeting with me, for example, every two months for a half-hour talk on how the division is going, and then he is required to meet once a month and the reporting procedures are tightened, he realises he's under scrutiny. If he accepts it and lifts his game, the problem's resolved. If he says, 'I've got where I am by doing it my way and I'm not going to accept your interference,' the problem's resolved by our parting company.

A senior executive failed in a job I'd appointed him to and resigned. I talked him out of it and appointed him to another job. But he wasn't doing well in that either. One day he came in and said: 'I've just had it — I think it was unfair when you took me out of my previous job.' He offered his resignation again. I accepted it. A friend of his who still works in the company told me he was really disappointed I hadn't talked him out of his second resignation. 'Never complain, never explain and never resign,' is good advice I believe.

Eric McIlree was a man of generous appetites, a partygoer, a man who liked the company of pretty women: in some ways he was an old-fashioned playboy, although without the softness and lack of purpose that that label implies. He liked to have people around him, to be the centre of attention, and to tell stories. Late in 1973 he went to a celebration of his fifty-eighth birthday. During the party someone in a crowd asked Eric when he was going to turn Avis into a public company and take a holiday. Eric said, with his storyteller's timing: 'I'm going to take a very long holiday: I've got the big C.'

McIlree had cancer of the bowel; his body was riddled with it. There was no 'woe is me' about him: he knew the cancer would kill him. ABC television made a documentary about his preparation for death; he was pictured in the papers with his infant daughter saying that his greatest regret was that she would not remember him. In the last months of his life he made decisions as he had always done. I talked with him for two hours in the new Budget office in Peel Street and asked him how he saw Budget's future. Eric said he had set up a trust, headed by John Reid, later to become a controversial chairman of the Australian Bicentennial Authority, and two others, a lawyer and an accountant. His estate would be run by the three trustees. Things would go on as they had.

I pressed ahead: 'Well, given that Avis will lose your entrepreneurial drive, wouldn't it be time to reconsider whether you might sell some equity in Budget to an employee?' I meant, of course, me.

Eric replied simply: 'I think it's inappropriate for us to discuss that. My instructions to the executors of my estate will be that it's inappropriate for the McIlree family to share in the ownership of an enterprise.'

I thought the word *share* implied that while they would not sell me part of Budget, they'd consider selling me the whole company. But it wasn't the time to press him on it: he was going back to Sydney to die.

I drove Eric to the airport that afternoon. I never saw him again; he died three months later.

I initiated negotiations with John Reid to buy Budget from the McIlree estate, and this dragged on till late 1974. Then I discovered that Eric had given a direction to his trustees not to sell the company to me. I resented this. I thought I had a good working relationship with him. I'd built Budget into a profitable company, it was a valuable asset, it had cost him nothing, and I thought I was entitled to some recognition for what I'd done. I guess he gave that directive because he thought that without his flair and drive, Avis would be vulnerable to an attack from Budget. Avis management were adamantly opposed to Budget being sold to me. Finally, I put a proposition: if I couldn't buy Budget I'd cut loose and go my own way. My stand put pressure on the trustees: if they didn't sell Budget to me, could they get as good a price from anyone else? They made me an offer: they would lend me the money to buy Budget, and retain control till I paid back the loan. They wanted a buffer zone, a few years' breathing space before I made a full frontal assault on Avis.

Already the gloves were off between Avis and Budget: for years Budget had shared the use of the Mobil service station at Melbourne's Tullamarine Airport with Avis, but after Eric died the Avis management raised hell and said Budget should not be at the airport at all. They booted us off.

In early 1974, however, I had an interesting conversation with Stan Hamley, an executive of the Australian Guarantee Corporation, the finance company owned by the Bank of New South Wales, now Westpac. This was a lucky break: Stan had an assistant with a friend whose son worked for Budget, and he heard through this connection that I was looking around for funds. Hamley, a man who speaks with the measured detachment of an intellectual, as if nothing in the world is capable of moving him to anger, was in charge of the AGC's business investments. He had noticed, he said, that the rent-a-car industry was a great user of funds. The AGC was a great supplier of funds. Since I had approached Mobil, Shell, the National Bank, the Bank of New South Wales, the ANZ, and the AMP without finding anyone prepared to risk money on a company which had grown from nothing to a turnover of $1.5 million generated by, in 1974, 150 highly motivated and skilful people working 25 outlets where in 1965 the corresponding figures were 2 and 1, Hamley interested me. (The financial institutions were interested in bricks and mortar, not in cash flow.)

Although temperamentally we are opposites — Stan says 'by disposition I prefer to be an unknown' — he had always enjoyed working with entrepreneurs, relates to enthusiasm and drive, and brings a hard intelligence to the formulation of long-term corporate policy. When we began negotiations I had one fundamental difficulty — I had very little money of my own to put into the purchase. It's the most constant challenge for entrepreneurs, and one of the questions I'm most often asked: 'How do you get the money to build a business?' My answer is, 'You've got to be prepared to risk whatever assets you have. If you've got a house, you've got to be prepared to mortgage it; if you're prepared to risk your own money, to back your idea yourself, you're much more likely to get a financial institution to back you.' In my case, the AGC backed me as an individual rather than Budget as a company, which meant I had to have my own capital in it if Stan was to persuade the AGC board not only to buy equity in the company, but also to finance my shareholding.

In the beginning we tried to work a deal whereby I could own 51 per cent of Budget — but I just couldn't get enough personal funds. In the end — it happened quite quickly, in about three months, I borrowed $40,000 from Mobil Oil as a personal loan, AGC financed the rest of my shareholding, AGC acquired 55 per cent and I had 45 per cent. Stan became Budget chairman. He was the buffer between me and the AGC board, a role he played particularly well. I had no contact with other AGC executives.

Now he's left the AGC, Hamley has a rather acid view of the corporation. 'The AGC's role in life is to do tacky things,' he says. 'A large bank like Westpac [the Bank of New South Wales's new name after merger] has to have an AGC to do scungy things that the nicer bankers don't want to do — deals with used car dealers, scungy personal loans and things of that kind.

'The directors were a group of bankers and accountants who in terms of disposition had an average age of about 123. When I left AGC eight years later, none of the directors had met Bob Ansett, and the thought of coping with such a wildly optimistic entrepreneur was just too daunting. Even though that wild optimism translated into growth and profit, it didn't matter too much. Boards of directors really are not so much motivated by the bottom line, the profit, but by their own comfort or lack of comfort. One would like to think that people take decisions upon logical grounds, but they almost never do. The thought of having to cope with an Ansett without a handy tool [himself] was just too terrifying. None of the board had ever been a businessman, and that was a problem.'

Hamley based his decision to get AGC into Budget, apart from its growth, profitability and market position, on one main factor: me. 'Budget is Ansett — no more, no less,' he said. 'Bob's a person of incredible determination. He's a very good motivator of people. He's a surprisingly good selector of people. And he's a very hard worker. He's capitalised on his assets — his family name, the weakness of competitors and so on, but I don't think those are the primary reasons for his success. If he didn't have those primary attributes he wouldn't have been able to capitalise on the opportunities.

'Bob spouts forth at great length with really quite trite sayings, such as "Can Do" — but he not only fervently believes in them, he makes sure they are reinforced within Budget. He's got between 20 and 50 such maxims, his encapsulations of management principles which he reiterates at every opportunity. Most managers say these things, but they don't mean it, and they don't make sure that it happens. Bob's got a bit of magic about him that he can make it happen.

'It's not an entirely novel approach. It's not a breakthrough in the theory of management. His management style can be criticised as easily as it can be praised.

'Budget is a personality-driven organisation. In the Budget management structure there are at least 20, and perhaps closer to 30, people all reporting directly to him. No management book you can read will say that the number should exceed seven, or perhaps five. In an institutional sense, it is impossible for him to manage it. Under logical heirarchical management it just couldn't happen.

'But it does happen because he has made all the appointments, he knows all the people, all the problems, all the nuts and bolts.

'If he got knocked over by a tram tomorrow,' Hamley says in his undertaker's voice, 'it would have a dramatic effect on the Budget image, because to the public he *is* Budget — the television presenter who is also the owner and chief executive. But it would have an even more dramatic effect on the management structure — there would have to be a quite dramatic departure from the management structure that presently exists. The presenter bit would be fixable. The management thing would be fixable too — but nowhere near as easily. Not without a lot of anguish.'

The AGC directors sold AGC's share in Budget in 1982 to me and Stan Hamley — but I'm getting way ahead of myself. On 20 December 1974 I bought Budget under the arrangement with AGC — realising a goal I'd kept steadily in my sights for nine years.

Josie and I were in Sydney when the transfer took place on the day the deal was signed. Naturally, we celebrated. It was an impromptu party at the Sydney office with Budget employees, John Ansett, who was my lawyer on this occasion and a couple of business friends who blew in for a few grogs. Josie and I woozily caught the last plane to Melbourne that night. My first major business decision as co-owner was to order champagne in-flight.

6

The Airport Concession War

I'd been meeting my father on Fridays quite regularly. There was no invitation — I just went to his office late in the afternoon and had a few drinks with other Ansett executives. I was drinking more information than beer, blotting up the things that were said, trying to understand how a big organisation like Ansett Transport Industries (ATI) operated.

My main impression of my father at work was his power, the confidence he projected that anything he wanted to happen would happen. He had the aura that for him *anything* was achievable. He wasn't overbearing, though, and the senior Ansett people certainly weren't deferential towards him. It was fascinating to see him in that environment, with his own people, in his own building and in the pub. I was in awe of him.

Our relationship changed to a more equal one after I bought Budget. He was interested in what I had to say; before the purchase he wasn't interested. Late in the 1960s, and in the early 1970s, he had tacitly acknowledged that I was moving in the right direction, what *he* thought of as the right direction. But it wasn't till I bought the company that we became more equal. I think it surprised him. He never thought it was on the cards that a major financial institution like AGC would put its faith in me.

The Friday talks over drinks weren't long sessions. Reg flew home to Mt Eliza by helicopter and he had to be there by last light. In the winter months he had to leave by 5 p.m. Four days after our champagne celebration of the Budget purchase Josie and I were married in Perth, the ceremony at her mother's house followed by a roistering Swan River cruise. Cyclone Tracy brought us abruptly back to earth, destroying our Darwin office along with much of the rest of the city on Christmas Eve 1974. Half our cars were too badly damaged to drive. Bob Atkins, our Darwin manager, made the rest available to people streaming out of the ruined city to Mount Isa, Alice Springs, Adelaide and Perth. Dave Addison, our Melbourne truck manager, drove an eight-tonne Ford truck with a portable fibro office on the back, from Melbourne to Darwin in 10 days, and we were back in business in a couple of weeks.

I was beginning the most important phase of my career. For the next four years I would devote myself wholly to the campaign to break the Avis airport monopoly, a fight on behalf of my most fundamental personal and business value, my belief in free competition, and against entrenched complacency in Avis, the Department of Transport and the Federal Government — and finally against the corporate power and lobbying strength of my father.

We had done a survey of airport car renters a year earlier and discovered most of them believed Avis was the only company on the airports because they were the only company that could *afford* airport offices: they didn't know Avis was the beneficiary of a Government-granted monopoly. The 10-year Avis agreement with the Department of Transport was due to expire in 1979. To give competition a go in the airport car rental market, we would have to change the political climate — that is, *let people know* about the monopoly — and try to educate the politicians and bureaucrats.

Before we hit stride with this campaign, Josie and I flew to America to negotiate an agreement with Morris Belzberg, the President of Budget U.S. I'd previously been visited by a U.S. franchisee who visited Australia and suggested we made contact. He told of Morris's charm and of a change of mood in Budget U.S. At that time our connection with Budget International was nil and the previous management was no friend to Budget Australia. We explored the possibilities of working with each other, but this was a period of galloping inflation internationally and Whitlam's Australia was catching its fair share, so talk of 2 or 3 per cent of turnover going to his organisation could have wound up being very expensive indeed; profit-to-turnover ratios in rental car operations are low worldwide in the best times, and this added an extra dimension of danger for us. Still, the connection had real value for us — it created new customers in foreign cities who could book a car to travel in Australia, served Australians overseas and it equalised combat conditions with our competitors. As seed money I offered A$1 a car per year royalty base. No deal.

After telephone negotiations back in Australia, we struck a deal of $1 a car a month. This gave us affiliation with 2000 Budget offices and the big central reservation centre in Texas. We could now book hire cars for Australians from Lismore, New South Wales in Lima, Peru or Little Rock, Arkansas, or London, England, the big Australian jump-off point for Europe. And vice versa for the foreign traveller here. Their market and operations programs were a mine of trend-spotting information and their expertise in franchising particularly interested me.

Morris would have preferred us to pay a royalty rate based on turnover to Budget U.S. but he recognised his weakness in Australia: I had the Budget name and I'd built a thriving business. We arranged for Morris to visit Australia to see how things were going and talk the agreement over. If either of us was dissatisfied, we would pull out. Morris says 'Bob impressed me then as an aggressive, energetic individual — and he just kept innovating, with his showmanship and flair,' which was typically nice of him.

On my return to Australia I went to the Trade Practices Commission in Canberra and argued that the Avis monopoly breached the Trade Practices Act: it was a monopoly in restraint of trade. The Commission looked at it and said the Avis agreement, if made between two private companies, would be a clear breach of the Act. There was only one catch, and that was catch 22 — the Act explicitly excluded Government departments. As it was the Department of Transport which had the agreement with Avis, the Act did not look like being much help to us. Later we made submissions to the Trade Practices Review Committee, and won assurances that government instrumentalities would from then on adhere to the spirit of the Act (the Avis agreement was made before the Act came into operation).

So far so good. On 27 August 1975 this full-page advertisement, signed by me, appeared in the *Australian Financial Review*:

> If you want to rent a car at any airport in Australia and you haven't made arrangements in advance — then you rent an Avis car. That's that! You are forbidden by law to sign a contract with any other company within the boundaries of our fifty domestic airports. That's the freedom of choice you have. You are barred from shopping around for a better deal. It's not fair to you. It's not fair to my company, my employees. I would like to see it changed — for all our sakes.

Beneath was a petition to the Labor Transport Minister calling on him to honour the Whitlam Government's pledge to 'remove barriers to free trade caused by monopolies'.

The same month I took off in the *Budget Bird*, a chartered propeller-driven Aero Commander sporting the Budget logo. With me was Reg Hodgson, our marketing manager, Kate Cooksey, our fleet coordinator, Josie, and my daughter Sherrie — Josie's and Sherrie's smiling faces appeared beneath headlines showing the impact of our first campaign flights in Queensland: 'Challenge to Car Hire Rights' said *The Cairns Post*; 'Wants Airport Monopoly Broken' reported the *Rockhampton Morning Bulletin*. 'Bob and his Budget Bird try to break rent-a-car monopoly — Protest flight to Coolangatta,' said the wordy *Gold Coast Bulletin*, while in Brisbane *The Telegraph* headline enthused 'Pretty Good Start to "War"'. If we had just been arguing for a fair go for Budget and nothing more, I doubt that the news organisations would have been interested — thousands of companies want free ink and free air time and try all sorts of stunts to get it. But we were on a fundamentally political campaign, arguing for freedom of choice for consumers and the benefits competition would bring: better service, wider choice of vehicles, lower prices. We weren't arguing for Budget to replace Avis as the airport monopolist: if we had, the journalists would have stayed away in droves. We were arguing on behalf of the customer and, in the end, of the car rental industry itself: even Avis might lift its game in a competitive environment, although I confess I didn't waste any time thinking about that. I wasn't altruistic: I was operating from self-interest, but a self-interest which would benefit the customer. That's the way corporate competition is supposed to work.

Late in 1975 Peter Cullen, a Canberra lobbyist who had been Prime Minister Gough Whitlam's private secretary, read a newspaper article about the Avis airport monopoly. Cullen, who says the hardest thing about being a lobbyist is drumming up new business because good lobbyists are always working themselves out of jobs, wrote to me, Hertz and Kays, suggesting the three locked-out national firms should get together to lobby so we could all get a share. He came to see me shortly afterwards. I told him if he wanted to include Hertz and Kays he could forget me, because I wouldn't team up with a competitor. He went back to Canberra and thought about it for a while, then said 'Okay, how about me working for you?' We agreed on a price — actually, I think Peter undersold himself. His work was of great value for Budget. We needed his contacts, his understanding of the public service mentality, his knowledge of the subtle political dynamics of Canberra.

Peter believed there was no chance of the Government cancelling the 10-year Avis contract before it expired in 1979, so our strategy had to be to use all the influence we could to make sure the new contract provided, as far as possible, an 'open go' for everyone. In these preliminary meetings I told him that philosophically I believed there should be no restrictions on car renting at airports — or anywhere else, of course. It should be open to anyone — as it was at many airports. At Shannon Airport in Ireland, I told him, there were 13 car rental companies.

Although in principle all airports should be open to all car rental companies, including the 160-odd local companies dotted around the country, in practice there's not much sense in having local companies on airports, because if a guy in Double Bay, Sydney, is flying to Melbourne and wants a car when he gets there, he's not

THE AIRPORT CONCESSION WAR 115

going to telephone Melbourne to order it. He'll book the car in the Sydney office of a national operator. So for practical reasons the airport fight was between the four national operators — Budget, Avis, Hertz and Kays. Except, of course, that it wasn't, because Avis had it all. My argument was simple: throw open all airports to all national operators, because that would mean more rental business, and therefore more revenue for the airport authority, cheaper rates and better service for customers and improved industry efficiency. The argument against us, Cullen and I thought, could basically be summed up: what was good for Avis was good for Australia.

I started writing letters to every member of the Federal Parliament, to create an awareness that something was wrong. Some MPs, both conservative and Labor, wrote back expressing sympathy. A week or so later, I'd release the letter to newspapers and reporters would call me for comment, then call the MHRs and Senators and maybe the Minister for their comments. This simple strategy achieved four objectives. First, it let the politicians know what was going on. Second, it generated public indignation about the monopoly: no-one likes a monopoly, especially not when they're paying for it, as they always are. Third, it publicised Budget's lower rates. Fourth, it tapped the Australian sympathy for the underdog: Bob Ansett and Budget were seen as little guys taking on the giant Avis and the Australian Government.

We presented a first petition with 10,000 signatures to Charlie Jones, the Minister for Transport in the Whitlam Government. He just ignored it. He had no interest in changing the status quo. Charles Halton, who was brought out from Canada as the transport Czar, the Transport Department Secretary, was also a waste of time for us. I got nowhere with him: he wasn't interested in competition at airports. He liked the status quo within the airline industry and the car rental industry. He seemed deaf to reason: there was no physical space for Budget at airports, he said, it was all too much trouble for him. Peter Morris, who replaced Jones as the Labor shadow Minister for Transport, was sympathetic and said the Opposition would support opening the airports to competition, but it didn't believe the Fraser Government should break the Avis contract and in any case the decision was up to the Fraser Government and we would have to convince them.

My first breakthrough was when Peter Cullen and I saw Phillip Lynch, the Treasurer in the Fraser Government. He had political problems at the time over his Surfers Paradise property deals, but he was the first senior Government person I met whom I felt genuinely wanted to do something about it. He was empathetic. I thought I was making headway. Then I met Peter Nixon, the National Party Transport Minister and although I respect and admire Nixon, I think he was a captive of his Department, he left things to Halton and the Department of Transport public servants, and the Department was pushing the cosy family line: we know Avis, we've dealt with them for 10 years, don't rock the boat.

Morris Belzberg visited Australia in 1976 to get acquainted with his newest affiliate. Morris, a gentlemanly executive with the old-fashioned manners common in corporate America, admired our standards of service — but he was horrified that we didn't feature price in our advertising. Although 'Budget Drives Your Dollar Further' had become one of the best-known slogans in Australia, we didn't mention dollars and cents in our advertising. Morris thought this shocking. He would fire his advertising agency if it ever produced an advertisement that didn't feature price, he said. Budget worldwide advertised itself as the biggest discounter in the industry.

My experience was different. For two years, from 1965 to 1967, we had established outlets close to our competitors on the basis that people would choose Budget since our charges were so much lower. But we had found that the car rental customer wasn't prepared to abandon a known standard of service and a familiar brand name to save a few dollars, and that the customer attracted by lower prices was a high-risk driver — more accidents, more bad debts, more cars not returned. In 1967 when we evaluated what Budget meant to people we found to our disappointment they tended to equate cut-rates with cheap service: Budget, they thought, had cheap rates, second-hand cars, dicey insurance and rotten service. Price is important — no-one wants to give away money for nothing — but it's also part of the customer's perception. 'If you charge nothing you're worth nothing' is still part of consumer psychology. A year later, Morris saw the need to change Budget U.S.'s image from a discounter to a company that provided a high level of service — a change which flattered me, because I saw the part I'd played in changing the philosophy that governs the Budget worldwide system which now has more than 120,000 cars in more than 100 countries.

Early in 1977 I heard rumours that Avis was on the market, that a couple of companies were interested in buying it, and that one of them was Ansett Transport Industries.

At one of our Friday talks I asked my father about it. He said his company had looked at Avis, but they weren't interested in buying it. He showed me some information ATI had gathered about Avis, its market share and profitability. That interested me, because his figures confirmed what I knew about Avis, that it wasn't trading all that profitably — and they were concerned that they had only two years before the airport monopoly might have all the substance of a pricked balloon. My father thought the current year, 1977, was the peak of Avis's value, because from then on they'd be sliding towards the end of the airport monopoly. When I asked him more directly about his interest in Avis, he said, 'Oh, we're really not that interested.'

I said: 'If you're serious about buying into rent-a-car, it may be that there's some way you could buy into Budget.' In the two years I'd owned it, Budget had doubled its size. We were showing a lot of progress. But my father shrugged his shoulders and said: 'We look at all these things that come along, but we're really not that interested in the rent-a-car thing.' After that I raised the issue of Avis with him every Friday, but he would laugh and say 'Don't believe everything you hear or read.'

But he was, for the first time in our conversations, really interested in the rent-a-car industry all of a sudden. I told him I didn't care who owned it, it was a tired company, it was a dog, the management had lost direction, they had no flair, there was only one way it could go and that was down — and I was going to help it along. In my naivety I gave him information about the real state of the industry, the relative market shares and Budget's growth rate. This was much more accurate than Avis's information — they had always underestimated me and Budget's growth rate. He was building an accurate profile of the industry: I was being used. (My observations about the Avis management being tired actually helped persuade Sir Reginald Ansett to buy the company: he figured that with Ansett owning the company and appointing entrepreneurial managers, things could only improve.)

On Friday 14 December he called me at 4 p.m. and said, 'Look, we've made an announcement to the sharemarket, embargoed till 5 this afternoon, that we've just bought Avis.'

I was stunned, I was silent for a minute. Then I said: 'You realise this is going to put us on a path of confrontation. I'm going to be fighting for my survival. If you own Avis you're putting my livelihood at risk. Now Avis is not a company being run by ineffective trustees — it's part of a massive, dynamic organisation that produces a lot of business for car-rental companies. We're going to have one hell of a battle over this.'

'I don't understand what you mean,' my father said.

'To you it's just a subsidiary. To me it's my whole life and I'm going to be fighting like hell — I see your buying Avis as a great threat.'

'You're over-reacting. Avis is a subsidiary. We've always provided business to them through in-flight reservations and nothing's really going to change.'

'You've got a major contract coming up in two years and with your political clout you're going to make it extremely difficult for me to break the airport monopoly.' My tone was cold and concise, but underneath I was furious. And I was hurt. I felt betrayed.

'You're over-reacting.'

That was the end of the conversation. He was genuinely surprised by my reaction: I think he had underestimated me ever since my return to Australia. He didn't think I would fight the way I did.

Josie remembers me saying when I got home that night: 'Now I know what it means to be stabbed in the back — and by your own father.'

I responded aggressively, drew attention to the Trade

Practices Act and said this was a perfect example of what the Act was designed to avoid. I coined the slogan 'Number one in '81' and Budget staff wore the button with the new slogan from then on. At the time, widely accepted market share figures showed Budget ranking third behind Avis, the big boy, and Hertz, which had merged with Kays in 1976, so the slogan reflected my confidence that I would win the fight to bust the airport monopoly, and having done that, outbid Avis and Hertz to get on the airports, and having done that, to beat hell out of them in open competition. I went to Canberra to talk to the Trade Practices Commissioner and two weeks later the Commission decided to take action against Ansett.

I spent six weeks at the Trade Practices Commission case against Ansett in the Federal Court — one of the most important things I've done in my career. I thought I knew the car rental industry very well, but after the hearings I knew it in minute detail, the fleet sizes, the successful States, the unsuccessful States, the activity at every branch, every airport, in Australia. The Avis and Hertz people came in and gave evidence — and then they disappeared. No-one else involved could be bothered to sit through it. But I did. I knew the amount of business each city was doing, and by extrapolation the amount each airport was doing. I read the transcripts, of course — Avis and Hertz had access to the transcripts, though whether they bothered to read them I don't know — but many times the hearing went in camera and you couldn't get the drift of what was going on behind closed doors unless you were in court. And I was.

I was in effect the whole case for the prosecution. When I started my evidence the Avis counsel, Andrew Rogers, asked, 'Would you like a seat?' Rogers had a very indirect style of cross-examination: he was Mister Nice Guy, and I could never tell where he was heading — unlike Jim Gobbo, the QC for ATI, now a judge, whose nickname in the profession was 'the barracuda'. I liked the barracuda because I could tell where he was heading. But I told Mister Nice Guy I preferred to stand up. And I did, for three days. It was partly a psychological manoeuvre: you present an attacking image if you're standing up, and partly because I think you're more alert when you're on your feet. You can get a bit lazy if you're sitting down:

your mind can drift. I didn't want to drift: I thought afterwards that anyone who can survive that sort of cross-examination could survive the Vietnam torture chambers. It was that intense. Josie said afterwards: 'It made me feel sorry for murderers, seeing what they were doing to Robert.'

The basic question for Justice Northrop was whether ATI's buying Avis meant Sir Reginald Ansett's company was in a position to 'control or dominate' the car rental market. Given that Avis was by far the biggest company and had, according to their evidence, 46 per cent of the market (Budget had 16 per cent), and that 65 per cent of Avis business was written at airports I thought we had a pretty persuasive argument. My concern wasn't just with Ansett and Avis: I was certain TAA would acquire Hertz.

The two airlines shadowed each other's moves: if Ansett bought Hayman Island, TAA would acquire Dunk Island. The me-too reflex ruled. We would then have to fight two competitors owned by airlines, and if it was Avis and Hertz on the airports under the new contracts, the battle would make David versus Goliath look like an equal fight.

My success in the marketplace — Mr Justice Northrop said 'In all seriousness Mr Robert Ansett claims that Budget will be number one in 1981' and found that Budget was expanding faster than Avis — actually told against me. Justice Northrop reasoned that there was 'strong and effective competition in the car rental market in Australia... It cannot be said that Avis dominates that market in the sense of having a commanding influence...'

The judge found that when the Avis contract ended, it was 'likely that the Minister for Transport will grant airport authorities to at least two and possibly more rental car operators... I find that after 30 June 1979 the market share of the rental car market now held by Avis is likely to be reduced substantially...'

When he heard this, Peter Cullen said: 'He seems to know more about it than the Department, or the Government.' Naturally I hoped the judge was right, but his judicial 'finding' was not binding on the Government, and his expectations were not law in the Department of Transport.

As a result of Justice Northrop's decision, everything was at risk for me. The strength of the Ansett organisation and all its subsidiaries would make it very difficult for us. My father had all the financial resources, all the advertising avenues, all the political clout. I came back with my brother John, the Budget lawyer then, to the Peel Street office and had a meeting with my executives. The ABC asked if they could film my reaction to the decision in the board room. We celebrated, drank champagne, and said in effect 'We have not yet begun to fight.' I made a 'V for victory' sign for the cameras. At times like that it's a leader's job to keep everyone's spirits up, to look forward to the next fight, to stay cheerful and optimistic. What I really felt was that I had suffered my worst defeat: I thought Budget had been set back five years. In a letter to all Budget employees and licensees on 15 June I said 'The court decision was a personal loss, but not necessarily a sustained, damaging loss for Budget... Ansett will institutionalise Avis, escalate rental charges and accept a rundown in their market share. Airport entry is the real issue. You as members of the Budget team can be justly proud of the company's performance in tackling the Ansett giant octopus and be confident that ultimate victory, Number 1 in '81, will be even sweeter after last Tuesday's knockback.' I immediately set up a meeting with TAA executives to explore the opportunities presented by TAA's loosening its ties with Avis.

It might have been a knockback, but it didn't slow our momentum. When Ian Reinecke of the *Australian Financial Review* reported Budget's move into on-line computerisation in June, he noted that 'the smallest of the big three rental car companies, Budget, is at least six months ahead of its two major competitors in implementing such a system'. Our $150,000 worth of hardware and $80,000 of software would have excess capacity for some time: it could handle our planned doubling of fleet and turnover by 1981.

Three months later the Department of Transport announced the terms of the new airport car rental contract. There would be one national operator represented at all 58 Commonwealth airports. There would be a second position at each airport, tendered for airport-by-airport. To me it was another disaster. In all my conversations with the Department I might as well have been talking to a brick wall. If Bill Maher, the Avis managing director, had written it himself he couldn't have done better. It was a farce. Now my adrenalin was really pumping: I flew to Canberra and went with Peter Cullen to see Charles Halton, the Department of Transport secretary and explained the problem. Since Avis had three times our turnover, if Avis offered the Department 5 per cent of turnover, we would have to offer 15 per cent to match it. The whole thing was loaded Avis's way; the Department was looking after its old mate. It was just like the 'open public tender' called in 1969, when no car rental company could match Avis's size, turnover and network: when you have in effect only one company able to make a competitive tender, it's a farce. Peter Cullen said it was like calling for tenders to supply food around Australia when the only contenders were the McDonald's hamburger chain and Harry's Cafe de Wheels. In a memo to all Budget managers and licencees on 1 September 1978 I said the terms were 'nothing but a charade designed to confirm Avis' long-term airport monopoly'. I pointed out that if Avis won the national position and several companies shared the airport-by-airport position, Avis would still have a monopoly because the competition would be impotent: it would not have a national reservations system, or credit-card system or be able to offer one-way rentals.

A week later I wrote to Prime Minister Malcolm Fraser saying 'we believe the tender will become a matter of considerable public controversy' and argued that the terms were against the spirit, and probably the letter, of the Trade Practices Act — we had a leading Queen's Counsel's opinion to this effect. I said Avis had 70 per cent of airport business and paid about $700,000 to the Commonwealth. Any competitor would have to offer more than this. If Budget offered $700,000 or more, its losses, with only 15 per cent of the airport market, would be 'enormous until it could build its share to around 70 per cent, which would take years. So while on the surface it may appear to be a competitive tender, it is just not so; only the present franchise holder can secure the national tender. May I respectfully suggest that you can quickly satisfy yourself on this matter by asking officers in the Department of Transport if they consider it is even remotely likely that Avis will not be the national operator.' I

THE AIRPORT CONCESSION WAR 123

asked to meet the Prime Minister to put my pitch to him personally. In November TAA announced it had acquired Hertz.

Cullen really saved the day for me. He explained that Malcolm Fraser had established a Prime Minister's Department unique in the Westminster system. The Department had a range of experts to deal with each ministerial portfolio so the Ministers, or their departments, couldn't put anything over the Prime Minister. Cullen arranged for me to see Jim Hickey who was responsible for transport within the PM's department. Hickey, who Peter would talk to over a beer once in a while, was brilliant. Now retired, he was the clearest thinking public servant I'd ever come across. He immediately saw the point of my argument about stacked tendering and said, 'That's wrong, that's absolutely wrong — I'll go to bat for you with the Prime Minister'. We also talked to Peter Nixon. On 23 September the Prime Minister replied that he had a Department report on the matter, he knew of my meetings with Nixon and the Department officers and 'I wish to advise you that the question of the form of the tenders is soon to be examined by the Cabinet. In the circumstances there would be little advantage in arranging a meeting at this stage.' It was the best knock-back I could have had.

At the Cabinet meeting the first item on the agenda — of all things! — was the airport car rental agreement. Fraser persuaded Peter Nixon that there had to be more than two operators, so it went back to the Department. The Department came up with a proposal that still disadvantaged us: two national operators, a third position open to airport-by-airport tenders. They assumed Avis and Hertz would get the two national positions because of Ansett and TAA, and of the third position, Budget, Thrifty, Letz and anyone else who was around would divide them up. *The Age* said the decision was a victory not only for Bob Ansett, but 'for common sense as well... the decision recognises that there is room for genuine competition in the car rental field and that in a free enterprise society a monopoly, or even a duopoly of the cosy kind proposed by Avis and Hertz, is a contradiction in terms. We welcome the Government's endorsement of the free enterprise principle.' The Avis managing director,

Bill Maher, whinged that one of the three companies would 'go to the wall'. Avis and Hertz would be forced to serve all the airports and 'a pirate' would be allowed in to 'take off the cream'. Doug Wotton, the Hertz managing director, said 'Having competition is fine by us, but having too much competition is going to rebound on the public....' I could hear losers talking.

The deck was still stacked against us, but I thought I'd reached the limit of public support and a campaign against it would look like whingeing. Our business had grown by 35 per cent during 1978 because the public identified with our 'Freedom of Choice' campaign. I felt they thought, 'Okay, this guy has stood up and challenged the system, let's give him a try.' Now I felt they thought 'You've got your chance — let's see what you can do with it.' I accepted the challenge.

For the next two months I sat down with John Kleinig, our general manager, and Duncan Lietch, our operations manager, and worked out what to bid at the best 46 of the 58 Commonwealth airports. We assumed Avis and Hertz would get the two national positions: because they were backed by Ansett and TAA they could bid whatever they needed to win, whereas Budget couldn't afford it. But I was quite confident Budget could get a national network out of the airport-by-airport bids. Because of my six weeks in the Trade Practices Commission case against Ansett, I knew the industry in comprehensive detail. I think that decision to spend six weeks at the court hearing was perhaps the most important of my business career. We lost the battle, but using the opportunity it presented, we won the war. We worked out how much business we could expect at each airport if we spent $X in advertising, how much we could afford to pay the airport authority, how much to offer as a minimum guarantee and how big a percentage of turnover and so on. All our energy went on the airport-by-airport bids; on the big ones we sometimes spent days on our calculations. I was extremely confident: if we lost one of the 46 airports I would have been very disappointed. We would pay the Department a total of $2.4 million for the 46 airports — and we threw in some insurance: we would pay another $200,000 if we were accepted on all 46 airports. So if Thrifty, Letz, or another competitor overbid at one airport, we had a $200,000 buffer.

When we finished these calculations we put them together to make a bid for one of the national positions — just for the hell of it, as it were. The bid was $3.1 million. We thought the odds against us were 100 to one. On 31 March, the day the tenders closed — they had to be delivered to the Department by 2 p.m. — the documents were being frantically typed and copied; we didn't have word processors then — and I said, 'Throw another $50,000 on the national bid — just for the hell of it.' Actually, we guessed Avis and Hertz would bid around $4 million. It was then 1.20 p.m.; we finished the documents in a mad scramble, then gave copies to two people in separate cars — in case one had a smash or something — and they made the delivery with five minutes to spare.

On 1 May we got the results. They could not have been better. Hertz won the first national position with a bid of $8.1 million. Budget won the second with $3.15 million. Avis placed third with $3.1 million. The bids mirrored the industry strengths and weaknesses.

Before we analyse the business effects, it seems fitting that Australia's superb newspaper cartoonists' comments on the war be recalled:

126 BOB ANSETT

'NEIL' AND THE HERALD & WEEKLY TIMES LTD

THE AIRPORT CONCESSION WAR   127

I understand *The Australian's* sub-editors in 1979 were unhappy with Pickering's first comment on the issue, and he re-drew it (*below*):

LARRY PICKERING
& NEWS LTD

LARRY PICKERING & NEWS LTD

LEAHY

THE AIRPORT CONCESSION WAR   129

THE YEAR OF THE CHILD.

D INGRAM

THE AIRPORT CONCESSION WAR 131

Said Sir Reginald Ansett:
I had all my plans set
On maintaining my rent-a-car monopoly
How *could* my son topple me?

HORNER AND THE AGE

Hertz was paranoid about Avis and Ansett so their bid was nearly $5 million more than it needed to be, offering nearly three times what we did, consequently crippling their marketing and advertising efforts over the five years of the contract. It was the greatest overkill for a tender that anyone had heard of, and the sort of thing you would expect from a government-owned enterprise not subject to the financial discipline which governed us. They got the national position, but no joy — in fact they lost $20 million during the life of that contract. Any other company would have gone into liquidation.

Avis was killed by over-confidence. They were so sure they would win a national position after so many years as the Government favourite that they didn't put the effort into the airport-by-airport bids as we bid. As a result, though they won Melbourne, Sydney and Brisbane airports, they lost Adelaide, Perth, Hobart, Canberra, Coolangatta and ended with only 11 airports. Their network was fractured. And at the airports, if you haven't got a whole network, you haven't got a chance. Within a year the Avis market share was smashed: in the first six months of the new airport arrangement its share of airport business fell from 55 per cent to 35 per cent, while Budget's mushroomed to 35 per cent. In one of his greatest misjudgments since he turned down me and Dale Soderstrom for help with the Japanese hot-dog franchise, Sir Reginald Ansett said the day the contracts were announced that Avis's 'viability as a business will not be impaired'.

But it was not as if winning the national airport tender meant we would automatically cruise to 'Number one in '81.' On the contrary: the real fight, to beat hell out of the competition, was just beginning. Despite its grotesque overbidding, Hertz believed it could get the lion's share of the 5-year $100-million airport market, because of the help it would get from TAA and its lower establishment costs, particularly at TAA-owned terminals. In *The Age*, business writer Nigel Wilson said '[Bob] Ansett is in a quandary. His company is third in the car rental stakes. To acquire more market share — even just to approach his goal of No. One in '81 — Budget's rates will have to be just that much more attractive than the competition, at a time when the company's operating costs are rising. This means Budget has to hang on to its "downtown" market — the sector it picked up from Avis and Hertz — and capture at least half the airport traffic. The task won't be easy.'

During the lead-up to airport entry we had been expanding rapidly, largely through franchising, which began on 1 June 1977. The franchise gives the buyer use of the Budget name, a hookup into our network and the benefit of our national advertising campaigns and the publicity Bob Ansett and Budget generate as sources of news. The franchisee is self-employed, not on the Budget payroll, takes his own risks and acts autonomously. By late 1977 we had sold franchises covering the north-west of Western Australia, Gippsland Victoria, Toowoomba and Ipswich in Queensland, Newcastle and Cessnock in New South Wales. On Norfolk Island, Cec's Car Rentals became our franchisee and in New Zealand Dominion Car Rentals joined up with a fleet of 700 cars. We had also been gnawing away at the airport market, introducing mini-buses with two-way radio in 1976 to take passengers to and from our off-airport offices. Now we had from 1 May to 1 July to open at 58 airports — as long as it had taken us to put the airport bid together. We acquired 350 cars, hired 50 more people and spent $0.5 million on airport rental desks.

Ansett-Avis was tardy and grudging in adjusting to the reality of the new arrangement. With 10 days to the start-up date of 1 July I pointed out Ansett's failure to grant Budget desk facilities at the airline terminals it owned — Sydney, Brisbane Cairns and Wynyard — whereas TAA had already done so at its four terminals. I said 'With Ansett Airlines it's business as usual, with the air traveller be damned...How long has the community got to tolerate the arrogance of this company?' I argued that this arrogance naturally followed while the airlines were protected by law from competition and suggested it was time 'the Minister gave both airlines appropriate notice of termination. Under the Act, this means five years' notice. So what are we waiting for?' (In the end, Ansett refused Budget access to their terminals, so we set up mini-terminals in offices rented just outside the Ansett terminals. I also made sure Ansett's behaviour was widely publicised. This enhanced Budget's 'underdog' image — and many Avis customers switched to Budget out of sympathy for us. When Sir Peter Abeles and Rupert Murdoch took over 18 months later, we were allowed into the terminals.)

We also commissioned a marketing survey which showed that Budget's 'brand awareness' was on a par with Avis' and Hertz', that most people had sympathy with us because they identified us as the underdog in the airport fight. But now we had won that fight, people felt the time had come for us to deliver. They thought Budget should do something for the consumer, now the consumer had done something for Budget in helping to smash the monopoly.

That was fair, it seemed to me, and not only fair — it was a marketing opportunity. I introduced 'Flat Rate', based on the premise that renting cars at so much a kilometre troubles drivers a bit because they don't know how much they'll be up for. They could guess, they could estimate, they could calculate, but they couldn't know. People didn't like that: it contradicted their normal experience. When you check into a hotel you know what the dollar number's going to be on the bill. When you buy a watch or a Scotch or any old hotch-potch, you know the price. People didn't like driving with one eye on the odometer checking off the kilometres, and they didn't like the surprise at the end of the run when they multiplied the kilometres by the rate and added on the daily charge. In Flat Rate we offered not only certainty but a low rate as well: for example, the old Budget unlimited kilometre rate was $34.50; under Flat Rate it was $20 a day.

I borrowed $350,000 to advertise the flat rate and bought spots in every Sunday night movie in every capital city in Australia. The ad featured me with a huge pair of scissors cutting the 'red tape' surrounding Tullamarine Airport, explaining Flat Rate and saying we would accept Avis credit cards. Three-quarters of the entire population of Australia saw that ad in six weeks. Avis responded with an ad headlined:

WE PUT THE FLAT RATE TO THE TEST. AND IT FAILED.

The theme was basically that Budget was trying an old Avis idea, though they didn't mention Budget. I couldn't believe my eyes — or my luck. It's one thing to spend money to advertise the innovation of a competitor half your size — but to publicly proclaim that you're a failure! It opened the door to a tactic which suited me down to the ground — response advertising. The next morning, the same newspapers carried a full-page Budget ad headlined:

AVIS, THAT'S ANOTHER TEST YOU FAILED — BOB ANSETT

The body copy suggested that Avis's airport bid was 'a classic of business miscalculation,' promised Avis credit card holders that we would process them 'at least as quickly as Avis' and asked Avis: 'If you thought flat rate was such a rip-off, how come you currently offer it at your city offices? And how come you offer it to major business accounts? Let's face it Avis, Budget Flat Rate has caught you flat-footed!' Hertz weighed in with star footballer-motivator Ron Barassi shaking his fist at readers and asking 'Why rent a Budget car when it isn't any cheaper?' Hertz's new pricing policy, the ad said, was parity: whatever Budget did, Hertz would match. I was willing — and dropped to $7 a day at William Street Sydney before Hertz hollered uncle. My ad the next day was headlined:

BUDGET HURTS HERTZ EVEN MORE

I suppose I went too far when I ran an ad featuring a Hertz photograph of Barassi with the headline

DID YUH HEAR WHAT YUH SAID YESTERDAY BARASSI?

The Hertz lawyers told me I'd 'broken every copyright law in Australia'. (Hertz hired Barassi to offset my impact as a presenter — but the ploy failed and Barassi soon disappeared as Hertz spokesman.)

I promised I wouldn't do it again — and took out Australian citizenship. I'd lost Australian citizenship through the grant of American citizenship because of my service in the U.S. Army. It seemed a good time to formally become an Aussie again — particularly since the Hertz managing director was then an American.

If they wanted response advertising I was more than happy: I had the track record, the visibility and the enjoyment of combat which meant I was fighting on home ground. When I presented an ad headlined:

THE BUDGET CUSTOMER HAS THE LAST WORD

presenting research showing 92 per cent thought Budget's rates were lower and 72 per cent thought our service better, I finished saying: 'If anyone would like a copy of the research, just drop me a note and I'll send it to you.'

I had two requests. One from Avis. One from Hertz.

We took $17 million of Avis' business in 7 months and became market leader in February 1980. Our new slogan, naturally, was: 'You're Number One at Budget.'

7

This Image Business...

One of the things people ask of innovators in business is: where do you get your ideas? That, and how did you know it would work?

The short answers are that our customers provide most of our new ideas, and market research tells us if it would work or not — except I don't allow market research to over-ride my intuition.

In April 1985 Brian Sweeney and Associates, in association with the Budget advertising agency, D'Arcy-MacManus and Masius, researched the proposed Freedom Cheques campaign.

The idea of Freedom Cheques arose, like most of our new ideas, from a customer's suggestion: Hans Tholstrup, the adventurer, rang me one day and said, 'Have you thought about making a facility available to all the four-wheel drive clubs in Australia? I'm an example: I take four-wheel drives everywhere. What I really want is a book of coupons so I can drop into Cairns and rip out three coupons and have the four-wheel drive for three days — and then I fly to Darwin and I want one for five days and I rip out five more coupons.' I told Hans we hadn't thought about it, but we would.

We kicked the idea around and thought, why limit it to four-wheel drives? Why not include everything from Range Rovers to sports cars to Commodores? People could buy a book of Freedom Cheques for $450, present them at any of Budget's 300 offices around Australia and get the vehicle they wanted. We were already well-established in recreational and special-purpose vehicle-hire by then. It suited our operation: what about our customers?

Research results weren't encouraging.

Sweeney and Associates did a series of group discussions with potential users who were shown a draft Freedom Cheques commercial. 'The shortcomings far outweigh the benefits,' they reported. Potential customers said 'The idea is great for Budget's cash flow,' and 'There's no way I'd fork out $450 up front — I can't afford it.' They were suspicious: 'They wouldn't have an RX-7 or BMW at Noosa.' They were dismissive: 'At least you can cash travellers cheques in — with these, you're lumbered with them.'

Basically, people thought 'Of course you're offered 21 different sorts of cars with the Freedom Cheques, but when you present your cheque you'll be told "we only have Commodores left."' However, I knew intuitively the idea would work. After 20 years in the industry, constantly keeping close to the customer and with the cross-pollination I get from people pumping ideas into me from inside and outside the industry, I can quickly identify what will go and what won't. I doubt that anyone in the world in my industry has had as much to do with the public as I have. So we did it. And it was a roaring success and we later developed a second stage, a slight variation.

I use research to test what customers think of the existing service and what things we could do better. We do a very thorough consumer survey religiously every six months to stay in touch with who our customers are and what they want. Are they first-time renters? How many times a year do they rent a car? Do they use Plan-Ahead? How many are women? I also use research to find out what people think of me, so I don't lose touch, I'm particularly sensitive to whether people think I'm 'getting too big for my boots'.

Breaking the airport monopoly was a public relations success, with very helpful spin-offs through all the newspaper stories and editorials reinforcing the image of Budget as the battling underdog. Becoming market leader was also partly a function of that image. In 1967 when we analysed the market, where we stood and how we could create a positive image for Budget, our research boiled down to three fairly obvious conclusions. First: all rental cars were similar and most companies used them for the same length of time, about twelve months. Second, standards of service were generally high, although they differed slightly (and significantly) from company to company, and we had the edge. Third: rental rates varied but were comparable between companies. What could Budget offer that our competitors couldn't? Me, and I was cheaper than an actor.

I've never been psychoanalysed, but Ric Otton, the chief executive of our advertising agency D'arcy Macmanus and Masius and a mate of mine, has an adman's analysis of my image.

'Bob's success as the Budget company presenter is an enigma. A businessman with an American accent, sounding a little cocky, isn't automatically a formula for success in Australia. But from an advertising point of view, anything which is different is usually an asset, and his accent was different. It was also potentially dangerous because of the negative associations. It's interesting — people now identify the accent as Bob Ansett's, not as American: you have to probe before they say, "Yeah, that's an American accent."

'People had sympathy for him because of his fights against the airport monopoly and the Government. Now he's transformed himself from a battler to a winner. His television personality has evolved from being an angry young salesman-entrepreneur, a businessman-spruiker, into a high-level business statesman. Somehow it comes across that he's not really out to make a quid — he's out to provide a service and beat the shit out of the competition. He's created the impression that he's an achiever for achievement's sake. People believe he wants to succeed, to do something worth while, not just to selfishly accumulate wealth. Material things have never been a great part of his life and I think that's subtle part of his charm.

'There's no hidden agenda. He's gutsy. He exposes himself. He has no secrets about what he wants: it's all on the table. The only part of his persona I've ever seen Bob hide is his shyness. It's extraordinary the way he carries the public mantle together with parts of him which are very shy and private. That's the only inconsistency I've seen in Bob. He's a very shy person.'

D'arcy Macmanus and Masius had been the Liberal Party's agency when I signed them up in 1979 and their experience in the political arena honed their aggression, political savvy and speed of response. 'The skills and techniques and attitudes we learnt in the political arena with the Liberal Party crossed over very easily into the Budget battle,' Ric said. On April Fool's Day 1981 Hertz ran the ad

> WHY TRAVEL BUDGET CLASS
> WHEN IT COSTS NO MORE
> TO TRAVEL HERTZ CLASS?

The copy ended: 'Why take a chance when it costs no more to travel like a winner?' Forty-eight hours later the same newspapers carried our response:

> HERTZ LOSES $3.9 MILLION
> (IS THAT WHAT THEY MEAN BY HERTZ CLASS?)

The copy said Hertz had 'more front than Raquel Welch,' they were subsidised by TAA. No-one could lose $3.9 million in a year's trading and 'still pretend to be good at the business they're in...Hertz class? Perhaps you mean outclassed?' It was almost too easy.

One of the best profiles of the image the Budget organisation projects, and the way my role in it is incorporated into that image was provided by a research report from Brian Sweeney and Associates which the Hertz ad agency Scali, McCabe, Sloves commissioned to get an unbiased outside analysis from looking at and overviewing the history of car rental advertising in Australia. I would like to be able to quote from it, but Hertz has flatly refused to consider letting me use the words they own under copy right law.

The researchers found that Hertz did not have a clear identity in their advertising and in the public mind.

The name 'Budget' on the other hand was identified as having implications of economy and therefore consumer benefit.

Second was the underdog syndrome. I had personally locked myself into the company and surrounded myself with an underdog image. The report did not state whether the association was getting more dilute as time passed or not, but the possibility was mentioned. Of on-camera advertising, they singled out the following points as successes in presentation: impact, sparking off the Australian sense of fair play, and saying something meaningful in every commercial.

But they didn't find that I'm universally liked. Bob Ansett polarises attitudes, they found. A lot of people liked me, but some did not. Whether they did or not, they all recognised that I had brought genuine market competitiveness to the industry.

Car renters felt that I had taken on my father and I had won, and that I gave the impression I would stand behind the service. The result was an appeal that worked with blue-collar workers, self-made business people and entrepreneurs. In weighing up the positives and negatives — my American accent alienated some people, but we knew that already — they concluded the positives tipped the balance, and I was doing a good job.

None of my television, radio and newspaper advertisements, none of the free advertising afforded by the thousands of news stories written about me and Budget over the years, none of the hundred or so speeches I give in person a year to organisations like the Hunter Valley Tourist Association or the Mt Eliza Staff College would do any good for Budget if the service wasn't right. If people book a Commodore and get a Datsun, if they are given a car with smudged windows and dirty ashtrays, and above all, if the rental office's staff don't care about them, you'll have created a customer all right — a customer for your competitors.

I'm not unaware that my being to Budget 'what the lion is to MGM' — a phrase I read in a report by Quantum Market Research — does have risks. And some personal costs in time and lack of privacy. Once when Josie and I were soaking up the sun on Surfers Paradise beach, enjoying a few days alone, a stranger came up and asked, 'How are the 'Roos going, Bob?' Josie winced.

When we made a promise that we would wipe $5 off the bill if a Budget phone rang five times before it was answered it worked for Budget in two ways, both with the public and within the company. For the public, there was nothing to lose: if the phone was answered quickly, they'd be pleased and the Budget image would be enhanced. If it wasn't, they would win $5 off. When they telephoned, they had the reward of a bit of fun, a small gamble which they couldn't lose. Within Budget, the bet was saying to staff: we're all betting we're as good as we say we are — don't you be the one to let us down.

If I say Budget managers, including myself, spend a day each month on the rental desk, we've got to be there — if the constant air travellers didn't see one after a year, they'd get cynical.

As I personally front the campaigns and make promises and state what I believe in, my credibility is always on the line. If I did a cosy backroom deal with the government or a competitor, if I accepted an anti-competitive deal, people wouldn't trust me.

Customers evaluate car rental companies on four specifics: they want the car they ordered, mechanically faultless and spotlessly clean — and if there is a problem they want it fixed quickly. Most companies do these things well most of the time. Because of my visibility and our effective advertising most first-time car renters come to Budget — about 30 per cent of our customers are first-time renters — which means we are constantly expanding our market share so long as we do it right for each of those new customers. It's an enormous benefit — even though television advertising is expensive, it's worth it.

Some of our advertising is intangible. When a customer comes in for a Commodore and sees a Porsche in the yard, or a yellow Rolls Royce, he thinks 'Wow, this company's got class!' He talks about it. There's a market for the Rolls — but it's very thin and it isn't enough to cover the costs of the car: they're part of the company's marketing and presentation costs and although you can't quantify them under traditional accountancy principles, or at all, I think they're worth it. The 'image' business is intangible — but at Budget it does bring tangible benefits. Many of our new marketing ideas come from people like Hans Tholstrup getting in touch with me and telling me their needs; and I don't just mean celebrities like Hans.

When I was working in the Box Hill office in suburban Melbourne a lady came in and said she rented a car every three weeks to do the family shopping in one hit at the

Chadstone shopping plaza, 12 kilometres from her home. She said she only needed the car for six hours, and it was unfair that she had to take it for 24 hours. If she could get a car for half a day she'd make the trip every two weeks instead of every three. That was the genesis of our half-day rate.

The very successful 'flat rate' campaign after we got on to the airports came from customers asking for it. We got into leisure vehicles — campervans, four-wheel drives, sports cars, cars with tent-trailers and the romance cars, the Porsches, through conversations with customers. It's called staying in touch. Because of it, and Australia's vastness, one Australian in every 5 has now hired a rental car — when I started in 1965 it was one in 33 — and we have the biggest car rental market per capita in the world.

Although our advertising has been aggressive and combative we haven't been afraid to admit our mistakes — even to advertise them. We introduced a new commission scheme for travel agents, a flat payment of $10 — regardless of rental period or the car. Nice and simple. The agents had been confused and irritated by commissions calculated on percentages for six different vehicle groups and a variety of rates — card rate, corporate rate, card rate plus the extras and so on. We didn't think travel agents should need a direct line to an IBM computer just to work out their commission. The trouble was the $10 flat rate meant the agents would only use Budget for a one-day rental: if they had a seven-day rental they'd make more from our competitors even if they got dizzy working out how much. In September 1980 we changed to a new flat rate: $5 a day for the agent, irrespective of the duration, the type of car or the location. That added the vital element for the agent — incentive — and it kept the scheme simple. We announced it in *Inside Tourism* with an ad saying 'The old adage "you learn by your mistakes" rings true yet again...At Budget our philosophy is that if you're in a big business and you make a mistake, you've got to be big enough to own up to it. We believe we've rectified our mistake and in the process developed a scheme that's simply a better way of doing business. Just another way of how Budget can drive your dollar further.'

We keep testing for the 'tall poppy syndrome' to see whether people think I'm getting too big for my boots, but it hasn't happened yet. In 1985 the communications researcher Hugh Mackay published a report on big business in Australia, a qualitative analysis of public perceptions of big business, based on 13 discussion groups in Sydney, Melbourne, Brisbane and Bathurst. The question who are the big business leaders threw up the names of entrepreneurs associated with big sporting events like Alan Bond and Kerry Packer, press barons like Packer and Rupert Murdoch and those in the news because of company takeovers and takeover attempts, Robert Holmes a Court, John Spalvins, John Elliott.

Mackay wrote: 'Two other names were prominent in these discussions: Dick Smith and Bob Ansett. Dick Smith is regarded as one of "yesterday's heroes". He is seen as a shining example of an aggressive, hard-working entrepreneur with the kind of flair which is typical of private enterprise at its best. However, his sell-out to Woolworths appears to be widely known. He is now likely to be regarded, quite simply, as "rich"'.

'Bob Ansett, on the other hand, is perhaps the most visible current example of a business hero. He is seen as the epitome of the self-made man: energetic, single-minded and successful. His personality is indistinguishable from the image and reputation of his company. He is seen as running a company which is vital and growing and which is still well short of the size that would make it a bureaucratic institution. In his own way Bob Ansett has certainly captured the imagination of the Australian community as, for previous generations, his father may have done. Indeed, the fact that he has shown "the old Ansett flair" without any obvious backing from his father is regarded as a particularly attractive factor in Bob Ansett's success.'

Interestingly, Mackay found that people are worried by business leaders who keep a low profile and avoid personal publicity. They don't like the air of mystery and secrecy surrounding big business leadership. They want to know more about the men who wield power in business. Conversely, they think most well-known big businessmen have deliberately sought publicity for themselves because 'there must be something in it for them'. I seem to be an exception. Obviously, I'm not secret and mysterious. And though it's true that I've deliberately sought publicity

WILLIAM PIERCE STUDIOS

My mother, Grace Ansett, *née* Nichol, and my father, Reginald (later Sir Reginald) Ansett

'Hanging out' at the pool is an Australian habit Californian youth shares. At The Shadow Mountain Club, a favourite hangout during Vista High School days.

Dale Soderstrom, my closest friend

Me, paratrooper with the US Army, in Korean War days — but they wanted football sprigs, not a gun, from me. *Below:* Playing American football at Camp Zama, Japan, in 1955. We won.

US ARMY PHOTO

U S ARMY PHOTO

Army All-star gridiron shot in Japan before the 'Ricebowl' Game

Dale and me carousing in Yokohama:
I thought Montgomery Clift was pretty cool then, hence the cigarette in hand. But I've never smoked

The dangers of political prophecy!
I said I'd push a golfball a mile down a street if . .

Above: The Press ran this with the line:
LOST HIS BET, MOVING TO AUSTRALIA
Left to right: Peter and Muriel Kemmsies with their children Don (7), Jeanne (2) and Tom (5); me and Karen with Timothy (2), Ronald (6) and Sherrie (4).
Below: Aboard ship, the lights of Los Angeles receding as I left the country I'd known as home, a broke 31-year-old family man

TRIBUNE, SAN DIEGO

The first Budget headquarters, La Trobe Street, Melbourne, 1965 . . .

The controversial Adelaide state HQ!

The Peel Street headquarters, North Melbourne, in the early 1970s; . . .

And Bedford Street, North Melbourne, today

PHOTO: ALEX BAUER

Right: The early canny Scot promotion: a mere 'shilling a mile' dinna ye ken? *Middle below:* Christening the Budget-sponsored Formula-1 racing car are driver John McCormack, Joanne Southward and me. We lost! *Middle below right:* In the early 1970s, it was still mini-this and mini-that. *Bottom:* The Budgettes, our own song-and-dance team in front of a mural of the headlines our promotions and progress made.

PHOTO: BRIAN

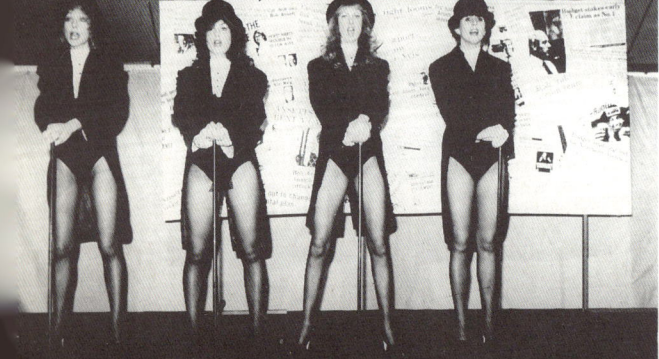

Me, Josie and Katie Cooksey, fleet co-ordinator, beside *The Budget Bird* which flew around the country collecting signatures calling for an end to Avis's airport monopoly.
Below: Behind the fence in 1977. We used this image to dramatise Budget's exclusion from airports on press and TV.

The Victorian Football League tradition has the players entering the field of play through a paper banner. Here the 'Roos are about to break through.

The Team Trot: Budget sponsorship for this annual capital-city event was an easy decision, as it promotes teamwork, achievement and fitness, cornerstones of Budget philosophy.

...nishing the Frankston-to-Melbourne Big M Marathon in 4 hours 39 minutes 30 seconds. I lost two ...e nails and Josie's opinion of my sense of humour.

PHOTO: MALCOLM CROSS

Josie Ansett today
Top right: Josie Chadwick marries me, Dalkeith, Perth 1975
Bottom right: Celebrating buying Budget, 1974. Quite a night!

COURTESY: NEWS LTD

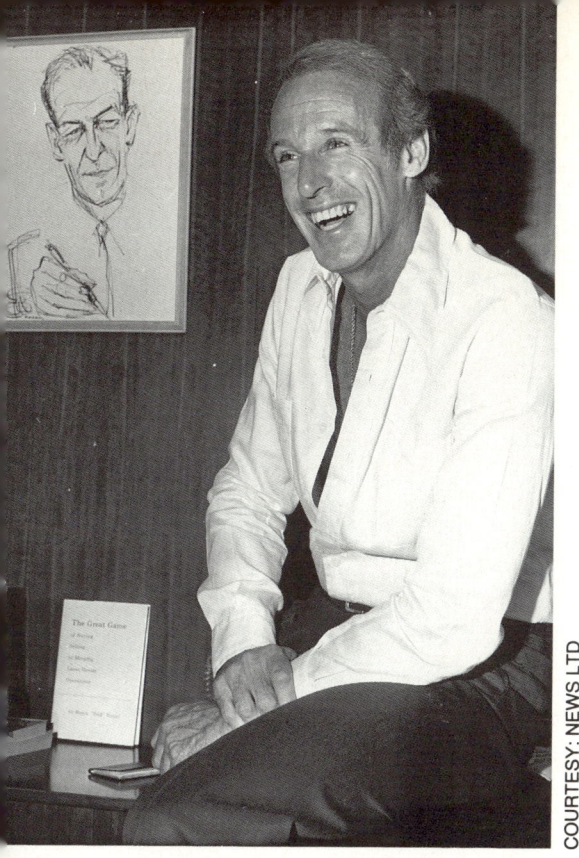

Me in front of a portrait of my father, a photograph used during the airport concession battle

I take out sole citizenship status, right down to the bowyangs

COURTESY: NEWS LTD

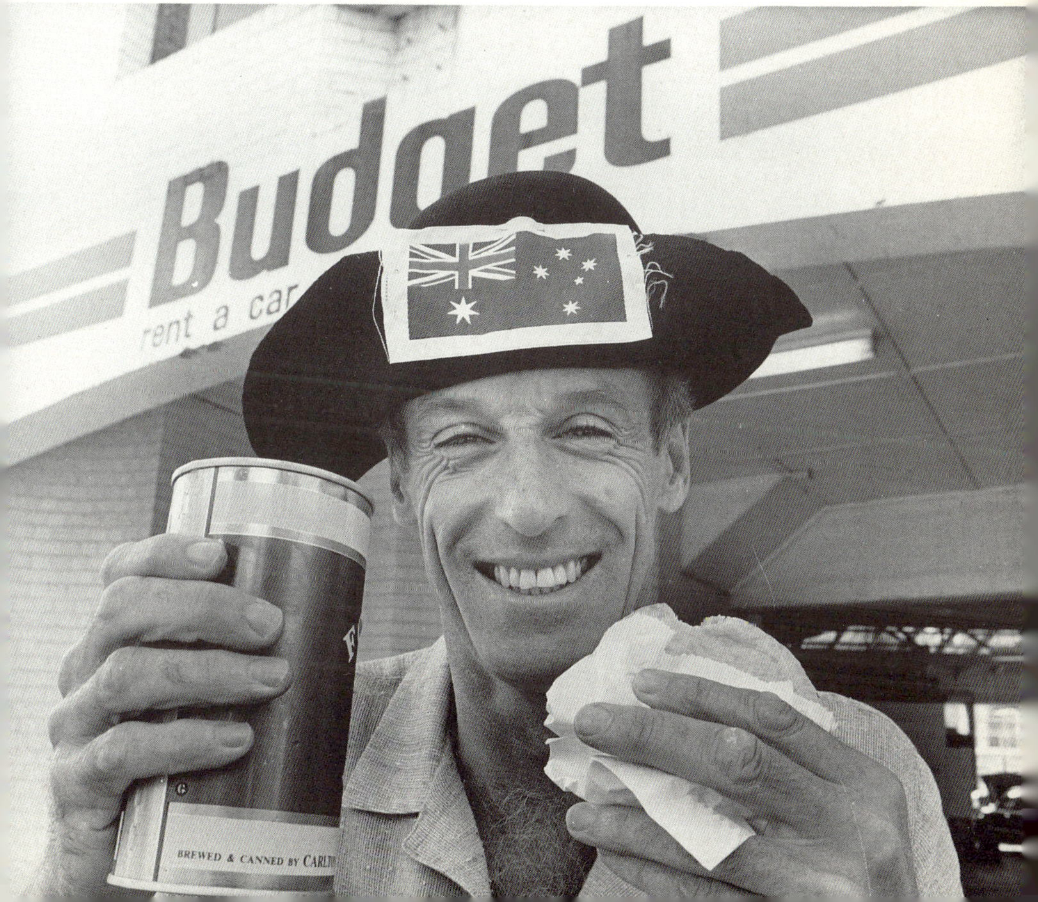

My children:
From left: Tim (7), Sherrie (9) and Ron (11)

Ron Ansett

Sherrie Crosswell

Tim Ansett

PHOTO: MALCOLM CROSS

ove: John Ansett
right: Morris Belzberg, President of Budget
nt A Car International
ht: Eric McIllree
ow: Reunion in California: Dan Fleming *(ob-
red, sitting at the end of the table)* organised this
nderful reunion dinner with my old classmates
le in the glasses to my right).

PHOTO: MALCOLM CROSS

Left: A cherished dream: Budget opens in Japan, 1985.
Above: My office: people are often surprised that it is not grander.
Below: With the North Melbourne VFL coach John Kennedy and his assistant, former star full-back David Dench, discussing a draw. Manager Ron Joseph seated, in raincoat. Looking for a Grand Final win as always.

COURTESY INSIDE FOOTBALL; PHOTO: JOHN LAMB

because there is 'something in it' for me I've also been completely open about what 'it' is. In the 1970s, it was an end to the airport monopoly. In the 1980s, it is an end to the two-airline policy. It offends the deeply-ingrained Australian sense of the fair go to see a big business ganging up with the biggest business of all, the Federal Government, to tell a competitor with runs on the board: you can't play in this ball park. There's also a personality factor. Ric Otton says: 'Bob's remarkably "unpowerful" — he doesn't exude power either as a television personality or in real life.' I don't think I remind people of their headmasters or a big capitalist.

In advertising, perception is reality: the way people see you is what matters. Would I have been as effective as the chief Budget presenter and advertising voice had I not inherited one of the best-known names in Australia? Would Budget have become the biggest car rental company in Australia if I had remained as Bob Campbell and kept my relationship with Sir Reginald Ansett a family secret?

I don't know — although I do know I couldn't have kept the secret. Ric Otton has said elsewhere: 'I think he [me] could have done it as Bob Campbell. To me his biggest contribution to marketing has been his style, his capacity to fight — that's much more important than his relationship and his fights with his father. Perhaps the Ansett name is a bonus of 5 per cent. And of course it made it easier in the personal sense to become famous. Many business people don't want to become public figures, but because he came from a famous family, the decision to become famous himself was less difficult.

If I was running for parliament, Otton was also asked, and he was my advertising man, what would he do with me?

'It would be a crusade. If Bob were to get into politics it would only be as a crusader. In his advertising and his speeches, his motivation transcends marketing. He's carrying a torch and I think he always will. If he ever did cross into politics he would have an enormous start. Being a crusader is even more relevant to politics than it is to commerce. And though it is considered dangerous in politics, it is not if you're good at it. And I think he's very good at it. John F. Kennedy was a crusader. Ronald

Reagan's a crusader. I think what Bob stands for has wide popular support.'

This is Ric's creative psychoanalysis of me, but I'm not a frustrated politician. I certainly don't want to be an Australian Barry Goldwater or Ronald Reagan. I'm not a member of any political party. I'm more effective politically in fighting government market regulation as Budget chief executive than I would be in looking for preselection, serving an apprenticeship on the backbench and perhaps never becoming a leader in government. My business philosophy, the Budget philosophy, is relevant to politics and government, but it's rooted in my own experience in the competitive private sector.

8

The Budget Culture

My chairman was quite right in saying I believe fervently in the 'Can Do' and 'Perception is Reality' slogans. I've talked about them to hundreds of organisations willing to pay up to $2000 to hear a 45-minute speech on them. I donate the fee to charity, but giving the talks is one of the most important parts of my job; letting people know what Budget and Bob Ansett are about is crucial in a high-profile service industry. Even though nearly every Australian knows the names 'Ansett' and 'Budget', not every Australian is aware of the Budget culture, how it works and why it works. Groups all around Australia from the Screen Printers Association in Surfers Paradise to the Children's Protection Society in Ballarat to the Ipswich Club in Queensland have heard my descriptions of the Budget philosophy and the Budget culture.

It's not magic.

The principles of the Budget philosophy are first, create a customer; second, create a positive corporate environment which rewards achievement; and third, create service to the customer. Profit flows from doing those three things. That sounds simple, yet businesses still go broke. How come?

You've got to get the order right. Short-term greed overwhelms the creative aspect in many businesses. Managers take short cuts and rip the customer off, thinking 'We won't see him again, so let's grab him for all we can.' It's a potent impulse to go for the immediate dollar, but it costs you dearly in the end. If you make an extra $20 a customer for a few months it looks great, but if the cost is that those customers never come back, you're broke.

We Australians are not very service-oriented people — certainly much less so than the Americans or Japanese — and that seems to be, for historical reasons, part of the national character; perhaps it's part of the admirable Aussie determination not to grovel to anyone. But it makes running a customer-oriented business more difficult. You can talk about how essential it is to give fast, cheerful and efficient service, you can give orders, you can publish company manuals — but it doesn't mean a thing unless the person behind the counter gives the customer an impression of cheerfulness, professionalism and efficiency.

Hotels are a good example. When a new international hotel opens in an Australian capital city everyone's enthusiastic, service is first class and it's a pleasure to stay there. Then a couple of years down the track the shine's gone off, the service gets tired and it becomes a very ordinary experience to stay there.

To maintain that initial enthusiasm, company culture is very important. When a person joins an organisation with positive enthusiasm, it's infectious — people absorb enthusiasm and enjoy the fun — or they become isolated, the odd-person out, and invariably they don't stay long. The Budget culture is ingrained and it seems to envelope almost everyone who joins us. It's difficult for people who don't become part of it, because they quickly become ostracised, and that takes all the fun out of their work. We have had very competent and efficient people in Budget who haven't made it, because skill, competence and efficiency aren't enough. If you don't have the attitude that everything's possible and achievable you won't make it in Budget. It's tough: track record is irrelevant. Yesterday doesn't count.

The prerequisites for everyone working in service industries are to have a cheerful disposition and enthusiasm. If those factors are right, you can build the skills and the disciplines by training and leadership. But if you don't have cheerful staff, who are optimistic and enthusiastic, you are in dire trouble and your staff are in the wrong jobs.

'Can-Do' enthusiam is bolstered when people identify with the company and its goals. I encourage this by letting every employee know about what's going on. I write to every employee each month, constantly reminding everyone of the basics. In February 1986, for example, I reminded everyone: 'If glass doors have finger marks on them, pick up a chamois and clean them. If the rental counter is dirty, Mr Sheen it. Vacuum the floor once or twice a day and keep fresh flowers in the office. Perception is reality and the most important perception is the first impression.' I also identify the top performers each month and send every employee a birthday card. Trivial? Attention to details like these has made Budget the top service company in Australia.

Customers write me more than 100 letters a week, some with complaints about service, many saying 'thank you' for efficient, friendly service, others suggesting ideas for new Budget businesses or services. When a customer identifies a staff member who has given good service, I send him or her an Achievement Award — and a cheque for $50. Customers' letters, which are another benefit of my high profile, are also an informal monitoring facility: often they're early warning signs on a branch or individual's performance. When a customer's had inadequate service, I write back expressing concern, apologise, and either offer an appropriate refund or a Freedom Cheque or two. This often secures a complaining individual or company as a Budget customer.

If you read and absorbed *The Power of Positive Thinking*, or went to a Dale Carnegie course it might open up your mind to possibilities that you didn't know existed. But you've got to *experience* the power of positive thinking, and find your own evidence that it works.

Budget does work. Every time we set ourselves a company objective, there's a general confidence throughout the company that it will be achieved. Staff expect it to be achieved. When our 'Number one in '81' campaign goal was achieved a year ahead of schedule, no-one here passed out with amazement. Of course we felt good about it, but not surprised.

One source of this confidence is our track record of setting realistic goals and achieving them. Goals must be achievable: 'Budget will be the biggest company in Australia by 1988' wouldn't get our team motivated, because they know it's unrealistic. However, if I said 'Our objective in the next 25 years is to be the biggest company in Australia', that's achievable.

I give managers considerable space. Every time we have a management change on the Gold Coast, the new manager wants to go into Coolangatta in a big way, instead of just operating at Coolangatta Airport. On the surface it looks right: Coolangatta's a big part of the coast with a big tourist volume. But if we go into Coolangatta we duplicate our airport cost structure. It's happened I think six times: each new manager believes the idea can work: 'it only failed last time because it was done badly' or 'The site was wrong: with this great new location it'll work.' Each time we go in and twelve months later it peters out. My theory is that if the new manager takes the idea as his own, he's committed to it and his chances of success are much higher than for an idea suggested by headquarters. The Coolangatta failures have cost us $30,000 or $40,000, but that's the cost of the learning curve. I believe the cost would have been much greater if I'd vetoed the idea. The cost would be in the loss of the entrepreneurial flair which Budget lives off.

The same thing happens whenever a new international hotel opens: Budget and our competitors approach the hotel for exclusive representation, to have our brochures distributed throughout the hotel's rooms. In exchange, the hotel asks for a couple of cars. The managers always think these deals will generate massive volumes of business — sometimes we even go to such lengths as putting a Budget rental desk in the hotel lobby. But with the exception of the Wrest Point casino hotel, the Regent Hotel in Melbourne and perhaps the Surfers Paradise casino hotel, the world-wide experience is that the volume of business generated by a rental desk in a hotel lobby is never enough to justify the cost. I counsel managers against it, but they continue to believe they have found an exception to the rule, and I continue to let them go for it.

Everyone's got to have a go initially — though two errors of judgment by the same manager is over the limit. In most cases I can limit the losses so the cost to Budget isn't exhorbitant — and sometimes when you tell a manager it's been tried before and it hasn't worked, that gives them extra motivation and it does work when they try it.

In 1985 Ron Ansett, the Budget W.A. manager, wanted to try using people to drive Budget cars from the east coast to Perth in preparation for the Perth summer. We'd tried it before — potentially it's a low-cost way of repositioning unused cars from Melbourne and Sydney when the demand in Perth is high — but we'd got the wrong sort of drivers, guys who were trying to beat the aeroplanes across, running into kangaroos and wrecking cars. Ron's idea was to give them seven days to take the cars across and encourage them to stop and see the sights. We sent 150 cars to Perth at low cost and reversed the cycle at the end of the summer. It worked.

MBA teachers and students have changed in their attitude to entrepreneurs. Years ago the professors would be reluctant to expose their students — some of the best and brightest up-and-coming executives in Australia — to the entrepreneurs, because they were aware that the entrepreneur challenged the theories they were teaching, whereas now they think it's useful for up-and-comers to hear about our intuition and common sense. The change is apparent to me from my talks to them over the years. At the Australian Business College in Mt Eliza, where my father lived, they would invite me to make the last address at the closing dinner. After all the cost-price theory, macro-economics, codes of practice, statistical market modelling, Maslow's hierarchy of needs, sampling error and the rest, I'd come along and inflict an hour-long dissertation on my relatively simple business philosophies. The reader cannot begin to know the kick I got to be rated the most interesting speaker.

9

In the Air

It hasn't happened yet, but whether it's 'Ansett buys Ansett' or 'Ansett buys TAA' or 'Budget Air Express Gets off the ground', journalists will be writing about my airline in a few years, and passengers flying it.

I'm pretty good at breaking down barriers to corporate competition and I love doing it. The two-airline policy is one of the last major industrial barriers in Australia today and all Australians will benefit from breaking it.

The government should not, I believe, own a domestic airline. When Ben Chifley's Government set up TAA in 1946, a lot of remote areas of this vast continent — the population then was only 7.5 million — weren't properly serviced, and some were not serviced at all. Chifley's Labor Government accepted the logic dictated by the tyranny of distance that if Australians wanted country-wide air services, including unprofitable routes, then a Government airline would have to provide them. But that's no longer the case.

TAA has pulled out of almost all remote areas with the exception of a few in northern Queensland. Neither TAA nor Ansett really provide any sort of remote-area services, third-level operators do. Ben Chifley's argument no longer holds; I hope to convince his successors in the Hawke Government of this and that they should sell TAA. The creation of TAA put my father's business at risk, in much the same way that his purchase of Avis put mine at risk 30 years later. Reg brought his influence to bear on the leading Liberal and Country Party politicians, and on the Democratic Labor Party senators. He contributed money. He was extraordinarily influential — he called the markers in when he had to.

Logically, the sale of TAA would also mean the end of the two-airline policy, the creation of the Menzies Government in 1952 — a Government with which my father had considerable clout. Well before my father took over Australian National Airways and Queensland Airways in 1957, he was concerned that ANA was failing because for six years it was competing on a head-to-head basis with a government-owned airline which didn't have the disciplines of profit, the commercial stimulus that an airline operating in a competitive market has. He was always looking ahead, he was very persuasive and he got the Liberal Government to introduce a two-airline policy that protected *one* private operator.

But the circumstances of 1957 don't exist today. The airline industry has operated in a vacuum since the 1950s. If he was still alive today and was the aggressive entrepreneur that he was in his most productive years, my father would not be content with this two-airline policy any longer, because it's inhibiting. Ansett can't get any larger than it is; TAA can't get any larger, because the government restricts their purchases, equipment and capacity. So what are you fighting for? You're just holding the status quo. No entrepreneur likes to operate in that environment.

Many corporations, not only Budget, would run TAA far more effectively than the present management structure under the jurisdiction of the Government. The argument for continuation of the two-airline policy anyway is no longer valid. It should be scrapped completely by the Government selling TAA and tearing up the agreement — which is what Sir Peter Abeles said he was prepared to do when he became joint managing director of Ansett. However, I notice he's not so aggressive on that point today, having been down the track five years and seen the benefit to Ansett: he's lost his enthusiasm. He's asked rhetorically: 'Why would the Government want to sell TAA?' It's funny how his attitude's changed, but that tends to happen when you get to be party to a monopoly or duopoly.

My father fell into the same trap. Although he was an

architect of the two-airline policy and its beneficiary, he was also its victim. His leading edge was dulled by a system which precluded him from really improving his market share. In the last years of his career the fight had gone out of him because of that environment. He was defensive. His energy was aimed at protecting the status quo.

It was a tragedy, because he had great skills. He could have done anything. He tried to break out of the mould — but he ended up going into other industries with restrictions on competition — television and the finance industry, the latter of which was very damaging to him and in the end cost him control of his company. Likewise with Avis: he fought aggressively to maintain its Government-established monopoly. He was a hungry street fighter for 40 years but by the 1970s he had lost the entrepreneurial fire which made him what he was. It's a pattern in the careers of even the greatest industrialists — they fight to get to the top but once there they look for protection to stop others doing what they have done. It's extraordinary. Will it happen to me? I doubt it. I've always operated in an uncontrolled, highly competitive and volatile environment and I'm moving into other areas like that. So I don't think I'll fall into that trap. Besides, I like to fight with my back to the wall, and I think that's the essence of the Budget ethos.

Like so much legislation, the Civil Aviation Agreement Act should have had a sunset clause; it shouldn't have been written to go on in perpetuity. Things change in the world. Do I want to destroy the two-airline agreement because my father was one of its creators? No: I want it torn up because it's irrelevant and damaging to tourist growth, because air travellers are paying more for it than they need to. I guess that in acquiring an airline I may be subconsciously motivated by a desire to surpass my father's achievements, but the only time I've done that consciously was when he bought Avis. (Ansett Transport Industries sold Avis poorer but wiser in 1981.)

Late in 1985 Ansett Airlines decided to review their arrangements with Avis, which still exclusively serviced the airline's customers. They came to us and Hertz and Thrifty and said, 'We'd like to see what you have to offer compared to Avis.' After a couple of months it was clear

Avis was being given the chance to beat whatever we came up with so I said 'I quit, what's the point?' I didn't like the way the negotiations were conducted. At that time TAA approached me and asked me to appear in their ads. They caught me at the right moment.

Early in 1986 I appeared in TAA advertisements, smiling under the words 'Ansett flies TAA'. Peter Abeles, who's a pretty emotional guy, I'm told — I think a lot of his decisions are based on emotional rather than commercial factors — took great offence. He fumed for two weeks. Then Ansett gave us one month's notice to quit our facilities in the Ansett-owned terminals at Sydney, Brisbane and Wynyard airports. Here we go again, I thought.

My natural reaction in situations like that is to attack. But I was a bit inhibited because Stan Hamley, the Budget chairman and 36 per cent shareholder, shares offices with Sir Arthur George, who's an Ansett director and a friend of Peter Abeles. Stan has a fairly close relationship with the Ansett organisation because of his association with Arthur George. My relationship with Abeles has always been cool — I've only met him twice; maybe he resents my outspokenness — but I didn't want to jeopardise Stan's position by jumping straight into what could have been an ugly and aggressive fight.

So I was prepared to talk compromise. Ansett said they would withdraw the eviction notice if I signed an undertaking not to specifically criticise the Ansett organisation or its executives without justification.

Even though it was clear to me that the eviction notice was punishment for my having the audacity to do a commercial for TAA — a commercial which didn't mention Ansett Transport Industries, or Budget — I wasn't bothered about agreeing to withhold 'unjustified' criticism of Ansett. Given Stan's position I was prepared to hold that fire and maintain the status quo.

I didn't stand still. I drew up a shopping list of actions we could take against Ansett — the most important of which was a High Court case to have the two-airline agreement declared unconstitutional under the much-litigated section 92 of the Constitution, which says that 'trade, commerce and intercourse between the States shall be absolutely free'. The High Court struck down Ben Chifley's legislation to nationalise the banks on the grounds that a government monopoly of banking was inconsistent with the 'absolute freedom' specified there. The argument that the airline duopoly is also inconsistent has legs, according to our lawyers.

We also prepared a press advertising campaign featuring a picture of Sir Peter Abeles smoking a cigar, with the headline:

ABELES ATTACKS BUDGET:
ANSETT PASSENGERS TO PAY

Another says:

ANSETT REDUCES SERVICES AT THREE AIRPORTS

Ansett was portrayed as using its privileged position under the two-airline agreement to attack Budget in a petulant way. If it wasn't for Stan's relationship with Arthur George the campaign would have been well under way by March 1986; I held fire and the moment passed.

If I were to take over TAA, my first job would be to establish a customer-oriented culture within the company. There are a lot of people in any business that have skills and ability, but the environment doesn't exist for them to take charge, take risks and grow. So they become middle level bureaucrats. The thing is to change the environment, to get people to take pride in the organisation, to clearly understand the potential that they as individuals have and the business has. A large percentage of the people in TAA would relish that opportunity. Many of them would turn into extremely creative and effective employees.

In the first year I would be meeting all the people and holding meetings with staff at all levels, working behind counters with them and quickly changing the culture of the organisation. It wouldn't take long to know whether the skills were there or whether they needed to be augmented with specific people, not necessarily from Budget, to help in re-establishing the direction of TAA. TAA, remarkably, does have a lot of people that believe in it and would like to have the shackles removed, to be able to compete. I could give them the leadership they need to make it possible for them to do the things they would like to do as individuals. I would immediately take action to eliminate the restrictions imposed upon both airlines. If there were to be 65 airlines in Australia it wouldn't worry me in the least.

The sale of TAA to me or to anyone else should be contingent on the tearing up of the two-airline agreement. Legally, Ansett could insist that the phase-out period of three years be adhered to, but I think it could be done quicker than that.

How would I establish the competitive Can Do culture in TAA? I already have a small example. Morale in TAA apparently lifted 100 per cent when they saw the advertisement I did for them. After being kicked around by Ansett for so many years, all of a sudden they were on the attack, and it felt good, they were holding their heads high. It was the first time that anyone had a real go on TAA's behalf in years. My father used to keep them constantly on the defensive — he was a street fighter. Abeles and Murdoch did the same thing. At last, for a period, they fought back. I saw the results on the aeroplanes: the staff were all smiles. I picked up my ticket and they had it made out in advance and said 'I bet Budget can't do it that fast!' Those very tangible changes happened because of the ad.

When I get complaints from Budget customers I write and apologise. Budget people know that the managing director writes to customers, and no-one wants the managing director apologising for their performance — they know I'm prejudiced towards the customer. That's another stimulus. The same thing would apply in TAA or any other business I acquire.

Creating the culture is partly creating in the mind of every employee the idea that when people ask who they work for and they say 'TAA' or 'East-West' they should be proud and feel good about it. It's those things, the intangibles, that are so important. If people feel good about working for the company, and they show a caring attitude to customers, there's no problem that can't be solved. We've had some difficult ones in Budget: a Dutch family arrived in Melbourne in the Christmas week, having hired a campervan to tour Australia. They had five kids — and the campervan wasn't there because the customer who was supposed to bring it back hadn't. We explained the situation — and checked the family into a hotel to keep their spirits up till they got their campervan. We showed we cared. If we had an uncaring person on the rental desk who said: 'the goddamn company stuffed it up again' that customer will think: 'That's the last time I'm going to deal with that company, and I'll tell all my mates and they'll never have anything to do with it.' But if we genuinely care and we're pleasant and seem to be going to great lengths to fix the problem, the customer will accept the inconvenience for a few hours and not think the company's the pits. If a plane's a few hours late and you explain why and listen to the traveller's problem and make helpful suggestions you're a mile ahead of the counter clerk who says brusquely 'The plane's got a malfunction and we'll call you.' People won't accept that. These are not big things. They are very small things but they make all the difference.

Budget evolved in an environment dominated by the sheer will to survive. The odds were stacked against us from the moment we started. Nothing has changed — we're still fighting for survival. That creates an environment that differs from your average business. If an outside employment psychologist examined the Budget executives he or she would find common strands in their personalities. They are people who are not satisfied with the status quo. They may not be orthodox business managers. At Budget we're probably not as good managers as we would like to be. Our style has its weaknesses. For example, the company's profit given the turnover: turnover of $150 million to $165 million turning in $2 million wouldn't be acceptable to many boards or owners, private and public. But it's very hard to be able to achieve both objectives, expansion through aggressive entrepreneurial market-hunting and sound traditional administration. Many of the Budget executives have been able to bridge that gap. Many of them haven't and never will. But we are large enough now that we can bring in people at a level just below them who concentrate more on the traditional role of management. That's probably the compromise that we'll continue to make. I don't want to take away the key people or dilute their entrepreneurial drive. That's something that would need to happen with TAA. There would need to be a team of people who have no limitations to their horizons — lateral thinkers. These would be people who ask every day when they come to work, 'Why do we do it this way? Why? Why? Why?' until we get everyone in the company thinking like that. They would need to have confidence that they won't lose their jobs or be severely chastened because they did something wrong. We would make mistakes. We would offer new services, and some of them wouldn't be cost-effective. We would probe and try to create a different attitude to the airline industry from the one that exists now. Once people see that my airline is having a go, even though it makes mistakes, the organisation will gather confidence and momentum and that will filter into the psyches of the employees and working will become an enjoyable adventure.

In Budget, people in the field know that if things aren't going right they come straight through to me and they know I'll support them within certain parameters. They won't be inhibited from having a go. That's an attitudinal thing that has to be built into an environment. Strangely, it doesn't take a long time. I believe in twelve months I could have a whole new culture in TAA by personally creating new rules to play the game by.

That's one avenue.

The second is to start from scratch. People's Express did that in the U.S. and it has really challenged the established operators. People's Express passengers buy their tickets on the plane. If you want a meal you pay for it. If you want coffee you pay for it. They're selling just the basic service — getting from A to B — and not the sizzle. After only about six years' operation, People's Express is one of the most successful airlines in the world today. I wouldn't want to ape what Ansett and TAA are doing. I wouldn't necessarily be looking to have a national network to begin with. I'd be interested in having large aircraft with lots of seats flying down the eastern seaboard with a shuttle service — like the New York-Washington D.C. shuttle: people walk on, get ticketed inflight, and receive no frills. I wouldn't do it specifically to improve our car-rental business: maybe a smaller percentage of passengers on Budget Air Express would use Budget Rent-a-Car than the ones who use Ansett and TAA. The airline and the car rental business have different objectives

— but there is some overflow that would make them compatible. Of course Budget took its first step into aviation with our Air Services Division two years ago. It acts as a broker: if you want a jet to take six people from Sydney to Alice Springs, Budget Air Services will acquire the aircraft, negotiate the price and meet your needs. We call it 'travel by demand.' It's growing rapidly.

The third avenue is to do something with East-West Airlines. East-West initially started a section 92 challenge to the two-airline agreement in 1981. At that time Stan Hamley and I negotiated a scheme for a reverse takeover of East-West: East-West would buy Budget and we would be the majority shareholder. But when it went to the AGC board, still dominated by Bank of New South Wales executives, they vetoed it, fearful that I would become aggressively critical of the two-airline policy. The bank itself operated in a not dissimilar restricted environment. It was a political decision, not a commercial one. I don't have a lot of admiration for a lot of the boards of public companies.

East-West dropped its suit — I believe there was some understanding that East-West would be the third airline when the two-airline policy finally died — but then developed a number of routes which are quasi-competitive with Ansett and TAA, Melbourne to Sydney via Albury, Sydney to Brisbane via Maroochydore and to Perth via Yulara (at Ayers Rock) and The Two objected to this, particularly the Yulara route. East-West mounted another challenge under section 92 to see whether the two-airline policy was legal and we had, and still have, an interest in that. At one stage we looked at joint action with East-West. We also investigated a separate attack, but that was a dead-end, the legal position being that because Budget was not actually *flying* aeroplanes we did not have 'standing' to bring an action. These things take a long time. There are all sorts of possibilities, including deals, that we have to consider. Under the present Act if the government decided to terminate it this year, which it could do, there's a three-year wind-down period before another operator can come into the marketplace. We're looking at 1990.

We started expansion overseas when we were still a fleabite company struggling to survive in the downtown discount market. The three near countries with substantial tourists and domestic population, Papua New Guinea, Fiji and New Zealand, were the most strategically important.

In 1969 I went to Papua New Guinea and negotiated the franchise with the Steamships Trading Company, longtime rivals to the famous Burns Philp and Co. It's been a steady performer ever since.

Fiji followed, then New Zealand, where we entered a franchise agreement with Dominion Rent-a-Car. This later struck trouble. Dominion got into financial difficulties and went into receivership in 1983; we bought it from the receiver and operated it as a wholly-owned subsidiary. Two companies trading in New Zealand had from July 1971 used the name 'Budget Rent-a-Car' for a tiny Auckland outfit — simply to block us or Budget International from penetrating the New Zealand market. We went to court in 1984 to challenge their right to the name and flew Morris Belzberg, the U.S. Budget President, to Auckland to give evidence. In his judgment Mr Justice Vautier said 'I am satisfied that the principal reason [for Avis N.Z.'s use of the Budget name] was and continues to be simply to seek by this means to block Budget U.S. and Budget Australia from extending their business into New Zealand and that this objective was connived at and indeed actively supported by Avis U.S... A plainer case of the deliberate pirating of the name of an internationally known business can, I think, hardly be imagined.' The judge didn't mince words about Avis New Zealand's credibility. He said David Coxhead, the managing director, had 'continually sought to evade' questions, the trading figures given for Coxhead's 'Budget' operation were 'deliberately contrived to present a false picture' and their overall evidence was 'quite unreliable'. Because Coxhead's 'Budget' used our earlier logo and uniforms, travellers were confused. As Barry O'Connell, our New Zealand manager then said, they were wearing our regalia, using a van and paper with the Budget logo, and trying to look travellers in the eye and say 'We're not *that* Budget — we're another Budget.' If you believed that, you'd believe anything. The judge said Avis U.S., a shareholder in the Avis N.Z. companies, had conspired with them to injure me and Morris. His judgment put an end to it.

I've had more than my fair share of trouble over business names — I can understand Morris Belzberg's irritation at not being able to use the Budget name in Australia because Eric McIlree had registered it in 1965, though that was legitimate: Eric registered the name with the same intent, but turned over management to an independent and competed with Avis.

In 1967 Brian Measey, who had a small car-rental business in Darwin, saw the name Budget on my La Trobe Street office and when he returned to Darwin thoughtfully registered it — doing to me what Eric had done to Budget U.S. We started an action in the Northern Territory Supreme Court to stop Measey's exploitation of our national reputation. John Ansett and I went to see Measey in Darwin, thinking we could settle before the case went to court. Brian, a wide-open Territory character, told us: 'Things are different up here in the Territory, we don't have a great respect for the law here. I'll give you an example — one night a drunk came in and said he wanted a car and I' — here he opened his desk and pulled out a handgun — 'showed him this and said, "Piss off mate."' It was just done for effect — but he certainly impressed on us that Darwin was different!

Though I was quite close to my younger brother John after my return from California, and he was a Budget director from 1974, his career was, well, chequered.

John got away from the wild Calfornians years before I did and returned to Australia and Reg in 1950 when he was 14, but he didn't settle down. He says Dad got sick of him at Mt Eliza and sent him to board at Brighton Grammar.

He had looked forward to life with Reg. 'At 15 I saw myself in an MG sports car,' he said. 'I got the shock of my life when I got a bicycle as a Christmas present that first year. I'd been driving a car in Vista, and now here I was back home with my rich father, getting a bicycle. I sold it three months later to the gardener for £20.' His stepmother Joan was upset about the sale, but Reg said, "It's his bike, he can sell it if he wants to."

'Life was much more restricted for me at Mt Eliza than

it was in Vista, because my father's house was a 40-hectare estate. The only other kids around were the caretaker's kids, and I wasn't allowed to spend too much time with them.'

John, a bright student, much better than me, matriculated and decided to go to law school, with Reg's encouragement, although his real interest was literature: he dreamed of being a writer. But he failed English, the only subject he cared about, and found to his amazement that he was getting honours in his legal subjects. 'It was incomprehensible to me: it amused me,' he said of his newly discovered gift for legal learning.

His success pleased Reg as much as it amazed John. He was much more interested in a girl called Cynthia, whom he had known since he was 15, than he was in the mysteries of case law. John was tempted to quit law school and get married, but Reg insisted he finish the course and finally set John up in a flat with Cynthia on condition that he finished his degree. 'I had to finish,' John said, 'one way or another he was going to make me finish. I guess he was right, although sometimes I think I would have had a better life had I not been a lawyer.' He completed an honours degree and worked at the firm Maurice Cohen and Co. for ten years, mostly on accident cases, representing both insurance companies and accident victims. 'I loved it for a while, but after ten years it was driving me batty handling other people's problems — I had enough of my own.' When one of the partners embezzled trust money John was shocked. He saw impending disgrace and worried that he might be personally liable for the money his partner had embezzled. He phoned Reg, who told him, 'Get a bottle of whisky and go home.' John thought Dad's main concern was the damage the incident might cause his own image. 'He didn't want it hitting the newspapers in a way that would affect him.'

John quit the law firm in 1970 with about $10,000 and started gambling heavily — horses, cards, two-up. 'The big danger is betting SP, because you can keep getting set without the cash,' he said. A bet of $1000 was big for him, but on heavy days he would turn over $20,000; after 18 months of this all his savings were gone. He worked briefly at the Law Institute 'investigating other lawyers', then for the Gas and Fuel Corporation, a job he found deadly dull. He relieved the boredom through tutoring in law at Monash University, drinking and gambling and a series of love affairs. By March 1975 Cynthia had had enough, found him a flat and kicked him out. The next month the Gas and Fuel Corporation sacked him.

He hitch-hiked to Gympie, 50 kilometres north-west of Noosa in Queensland, stayed with a friend, applied for the dole, then landed a temporary labouring job with the local council under one of the Whitlam Government's special schemes for the unemployed. The job ended three months later; he couldn't find work in Queensland and returned to Melbourne, met his second wife Judy, worked as a labourer on the railways for a year, then, with Judy's encouragement, became a partner at Lloyd P. Goode and Co.

The return to the law didn't work. 'My habits hadn't changed. I didn't do what I should have done, settle down and work hard.' It lasted a year.

John worked briefly at Budget in 1979, threw it in and went to Perth, where he couldn't find work. He came back to Melbourne and landed a labouring job with Barker Green and Parke at the Footscray fruit markets, starting at midnight. There he struck a problem: he was working under the name 'John Smith' because he'd got sick and tired of people asking, 'Are you any relation of Reg Ansett?' Barker Green and Parke paid wages into their employees' bank accounts — and of course John didn't have an account as 'John Smith.'

He went to a Footscray bank, which naturally required proof of identity. How about a driver's licence? John said he'd just come down from Queensland and he hadn't brought his Queensland licence. The banker said, 'You've got to prove who you are.' John said, 'How can I? I don't have any credit cards.' The banker had a flash of inspiration. A letter from Barker Green and Parke would do it, he said. John got the letter, and the bank account, and a subsequent market identity card with his picture on it, which confirmed his identity as John Smith. He liked working with his hands and enjoyed the bent characters on the midnight shift. Once at 3 a.m. a Mildura orange grower who had been to school with him recognised him and said 'John Ansett!' John sidled over and explained quickly that he was using a different name, he didn't want to be called Ansett — but nobody had overheard. Later, a Chinese wholesaler said 'I hear you're John Ansett', but John made a joke about it — 'Me? You're crazy' — and passed it off. I sympathise with his difficulties, having lived under two names myself. Josie, too, likes to escape into anonymity by using her maiden name Chadwick, and my daughter-secretary Sherrie was teased at school. The kids called her 'Whisky TAA'.

John worked at the markets for a year, then as a trades assistant on the Altona refinery, then was unemployed for 7 months; Judy, who was working as a music teacher, supported him.

John was too proud to ask me for help. We had been quite close since I returned to Australia. I borrowed $500 from him in my first weeks back in Melbourne, and returned the favour in 1972 when he needed $500 quickly to pay off a gambling debt. But my mother called and said, 'Robert, John's in trouble, he has no money, it's putting strain on his marriage and he needs a job.' I gave him a choice: wash cars or be clerk. He said, 'I think I'm a bit old to wash cars,' and went to work as a clerk. While he was doing this, the thought occurred to him that if he was working at a desk doing paperwork, why not work as a lawyer? We needed a corporate lawyer. 'That was the only way I could practice law again', he said. 'I've got only one client, Bob and Budget. It's a very satisfactory arrangement. We trust each other. I wouldn't fit into too many large organisations. I don't work normal hours and I don't like paperwork. I like making quick decisions and having a battle. I'm here for the rest of my working life, unless Bob sacks me. I've no ambition to go anywhere else. I'm not an ambitious person.'

Business names is not the only problem we have struck in New Zealand. In doing battle there I have really had some fun with a familiar issue which has quickened the street-fighter instincts in all involved at Budget. The two international airports are Auckland and Christchurch, and both are controlled by city authorities, the Auckland Regional Authority and the Christchurch City Council. Both have lengthy contracts with Hertz and Avis. We alleged collusion, based on the extraordinary similarities in the two bids. We took them to court and the trial judge found collusion, but under N.Z. trade practices law he wasn't able to rule in our favour. We appealed in 1985 and lost. We have now appealed to the Privy Council in London.

We went public about being excluded from the airports — the 'freedom of choice' issue again — noting that if collusion had occurred, civic ratepayers were being unfairly deprived of income. As I write, the battle rages on. I'm very glad to have my old colleague Duncan Leitch, a veteran from Budget Australia's airport concession war days, as Budget New Zealand's managing director.

The fight seems to show that history repeats itself in commerce too. We were filming a television commercial about New Zealand's scenic beauty and the services provided by Budget N.Z., pitched at the Australian traveller. The first ten seconds were to show an Air New Zealand aircraft landing at Auckland Airport; I would be filmed outside the terminal encouraging Australians to come in and sample the country's wonders. But we were booted off the airport and banned from filming. We got hold of a panel van and filmed the thing surreptitiously out of the back of it; I just stood around with my hands in my pockets until the crew drove up, shot, then beat it. There was no time for retakes. Duncan Leitch and I reacted with the reflexes of seasoned response-advertisers. We had big ads in the New Zealand dailies the next morning, opening with:

WANTED:

AIRPORT WITH 3200 METRE RUNWAY AND
TERMINAL IN THE VICINITY OF AUCKLAND

There were 60 telexes and telegrams offering us airports on our desks the next day. The South Australian Tourist Corporation was quick off the mark — they offered us Adelaide!

We moved into Vanuatu, Noumea, the Solomon Islands, the Cook Islands, Guam, Tahiti, Singapore and Malaysia. We had a hiccup in Malaysia; we chose the wrong operator and they folded after a year; the next operator, who is very good, started in 1985.

Japan was the big move. The Americans had tried to get into Japan, without success, off and on for years. I think it was lack of patience on their part; the Americans tend to see an opportunity, come in and realise it — or they don't and they go away. It was a very difficult market. It took us two years to find the right Japanese company to go with. After several false starts, we almost went with a company called Autorama, but it didn't work because Autorama was setting up a network of Ford dealerships and wasn't ready to take on car rentals. When that fell apart we had to start from scratch again. We tried the Shell Oil Company in Japan, department stores, nothing worked till we came across Orient Leasing.

The negotiations with Orient Leasing took 9 months. For me it was a fascinating insight into a culture I already knew something about from my time in Japan with the army, and of course through my first wife. But I hadn't negotiated a business deal in Japan. In Japan everything works from the ground up. I couldn't just sit down with the President of Orient Leasing and say 'Look I've got a fantastic deal you guys should be interested in.' In Japan you start with the lower echelons, the people who will actually make the concept work. I started out talking to the car-leasing operatives — I couldn't get access to the top executives till I'd persuaded the operatives it could work. That took about six months. Then we went to the finance guys, the next level up, and talked with them. Once they were satisfied — another two months — I finally got to talk to Orient Leasing's second-in-command, Mr Yamagishi, and we started the nitty-gritty negotiating, hard gutsy stuff, telephone calls and telexes, trips back and forth.

Halfway through these negotiations a couple of Budget senior executives and I were taken out to a small quasi-private nightclub. On the way there one of the Japanese executives told me this was the favourite nightclub of the Orient Leasing President, Mr Miyauchi, and he'd be there and he'd like to say hello. Sure enough, Mr Miyauchi arrived and we had a few drinks — there was no talk of business, it was just a 'Bob and Yoshi' meeting, an informal chat. Then he left and I didn't see him again until months later when the deal was ready for signing. Now he deals with me all the time.

It's an interesting system. Once a deal is done with a Japanese company you can be relatively sure it's going to work, because they exhaustively consider all possible avenues of failure before they sign: their negotiating process is one of covering all the risks. But by involving all levels in negotiating the deal, you get them committed to it. When you have people who've looked at a new project in detail and they're all satisfied 'yes, we can do that' they want to make it go because their reputations are on the line. Once the President signs the final deal, his reputation too is at stake. But if you try to legislate from above, people can say 'I'm not on board yet, I don't think it will work' and if it doesn't work they can say, 'I told you so.'

I try to apply the lessons I learnt from the Japanese in Budget. If a manager tells me, 'I reckon I can rent a bunch of Porsches up here, there's a risk, but I'd like you to back me', I know damn well it's going to work because the guy's committed. Whereas if I tell him 'I want you to take a half-dozen Porches' the chances of success aren't as great. If you can subtly plant the seed of an idea, mentioning it casually so the guy gets to thinking about it, develops it and then comes to me for approval as if it were his idea — as by now it is — your chances of success go up dramatically.

Japan is not Australia. Nevertheless, within Budget we have attitudes towards people that reflect the Japanese way. Japanese corporations are famous for their paternalism. We're paternalistic in Budget with our ideas of a pleasing work environment, our exercise programs, our encouragement for people to quit smoking: it builds a sense of belonging, confidence and commitment.

The Japanese senior operating manager, Mr Saito, visited Australia for several weeks in 1985. He had a look around and absorbed our way of doing business. On the day he left for Tokyo he had a few drinks in the boardroom with me and after he loosened up a bit he told me: 'It's remarkable — the Japanese have a very strong work ethic, perhaps the strongest in the world. Australians have a reputation for just the opposite, and justly so. If you meet a Japanese and ask what he does, he'll say "I work for Toyota" or "I work for Sanyo". They never say "mechanic" or "electrician". They just identify with the company. You've got that in Budget. But you've also got something in your company that I've never seen in a Japanese company: this absolute commitment to winning. Win! Win! Win! We've got the work ethic, but we haven't got that extra commitment to winning. How the hell do you get that?'

I told him the story about how I drive to work each morning manufacturing a provocation, thinking of some false claim of market share that Hertz or Avis has made, some statement which implies they're doing better than Budget, so I get to the office with steam coming out of my ears, wanting to win in the market place. He said 'Okay, my competitor in Japan is Toyota Rent-a-Car and every day from now I'm going to start the day with the idea that I'm going to beat hell out of Toyota.' He went back to try to work that extra dimension of the Budget Australia culture into Budget Japan. We all learn from one another.

We've challenged the Japanese Budget people to use the slogan 'Number One in '91'. Budget Japan will probably be bigger than Budget Australia by 1991 or 1992. (As I write, in fact, there's a possibility that Budget Japan will acquire Budget U.S. through our partners Orient Leasing. How about that!)

Right now we are trying to finalise arrangements in Korea, Thailand and Bali, and we're trying hard to find the right route into China. China is really a long-term investment. It won't produce immediate results, but it's important that we get our flag flying there so we've got our foot in the door to a potentially huge market. Right now the Chinese Government requires people to hire cars with drivers — rent-a-car in the Western sense is ideologically unsound, because if you're a bourgeois tourist and you drive your own rented car you're depriving a Chinese citizen of a job. Ultimately the Chinese will drop that requirement — and we want to be there on the ground floor to grow with the industry and perhaps influence the direction it follows. We're trying to negotiate a deal with one of the State-owned taxi companies. They could set aside part of their fleet under the Budget banner, so that as soon as the Government lifts the requirement that cars must be hired with drivers, we will be ready to go. If we had 1000 cars in China by 1989 I'd be delighted. If that happened it could jump to 10,000 cars in a few years. Next to Japan, China has the biggest potential of any country we operate in. There's no doubt Australia has a good image in Japan, probably better than the Americans have, which we must use to our advantage — I'd love to be the television presenter in Japan for Budget.

If you want to get rich quick there are probably better places to spend your buck than Japan and China. But if you want a long-term successful business and you're prepared to invest time and money and you have the patience to nurture it, both in China and Japan, you'll ultimately end up successful. When something catches on in Japan it really goes. The opportunities in China, of course, are also potentially immense.

10
Thoughts of an Early-Morning Jogger

The question I'm asked most often is what motivates the motivator? What motivates Robert Graham Ansett? People are curious about what keeps me running when I've established a substantial business and I obviously don't have to work six days a week to keep a roof over my head. People think 'you've climbed your mountain, you're on top — why don't you sit back and enjoy the view?' The short answer is that I don't enjoy sitting back: I thrive on challenges. I want to test myself constantly.

It's a curious thing about human nature — and this is universal, it applies just as much in Japan or the United States as it does in Australia — that business people tend to limit their horizons. They box themselves in. Inside the box is everything they're familiar with, the organisational structure, the market, the people and their own tested skills. They can move confidently within the box, but they're fearful of going outside it. I think it's like the territorial instinct — an animal is confident in its own territory and will fight any intruder, but it's reluctant to venture outside. Many business people want to escape from the box, but they don't know what their first step should be and they're scared of taking it.

If you take a first step and it doesn't work, you should not throw up your arms and never venture out again. You should go back inside your territory and await your next chance, pick your time, assess your advantages, and try a different strategy. When Dale Soderstrom and I hit the

Canadian border and the border officials stopped us because we didn't have enough money, we just drove to the next crossing and changed our story. The thought never crossed our minds that we wouldn't make Anchorage. There are very few obstacles in life you can't get around. Very few.

I see the Budget history as a series of plateaux. I had to fight to reach each of those plateaux, developing new skills, trying new strategies, always testing myself. The first plateau was financial survival in the limited cut-rate downtown market, fighting Eric McIlree's idea that Budget was just a weapon to protect Avis from attack at the bottom of the market. The next plateau was providing a whole range of services, expansion of the network — Eric would have been satisfied for Budget to get 5 per cent of the market, and there were constant arguments about going in to new locations, Canberra or parts of Tasmania or the North-West. Sometimes I wore him down. Sometimes I'd just go ahead and do it without telling him. It was a war of attrition. When I reached the point where I wanted control over my own destiny and I failed to establish Ansett Rent-a-Car, I did reach a compromise with McIlree. I had broader rein, less interference and a salary based partly on results. After he died I had to fight Avis managers to get control of the company, another plateau. For four years I did nothing but publicly proclaim the unfairness of the airport monopoly. When the monopoly was broken, Budget had to win against ATI and TAA subsidiaries again on the airport tenders. Having won on the tender, we then had to win on performance at the airports, or we would have gone broke. A series of plateaux, a series of fights to reach the next one: when you're fighting competitors like ATI and TAA and the government is thinking of a two-rent-a-car policy along with the two-airline policy, you don't have to think about how to motivate yourself.

Relaxing once you've reached a goal is an understandable human reaction, but it's not mine. Simply holding the ground you've won is positively destructive. The rot sets in. You've got to keep your people on the edge of their chairs, attacking all the time, and you can't do it if you're not on the balls of your feet yourself.

My adrenalin's pumping early. If I'm not woken by a

call from a radio interviewer or afternoon newspaper journalist — I often spend my first conscious minutes in bed trying to talk lucidly about a Federal Budget or the future of the Victorian railways or the two-airline agreement — I get up at 6.15 to a beakfast of toasted muesli and tea. Sometimes I'll have a swim in my tiny backyard pool. When I'm training for the marathon, as I am now, I'll usually run 10 kilometres.

The drive from my North Carlton home to our North Melbourne offices takes less than 10 minutes; while I'm driving with the radio tuned to the news, I'm thinking blackly about Avis and Hertz to tune me up competitively. If I need a quick check about some detail of the day's schedule, I can reach my daughter and personal secretary, Sherrie Crosswell, on the car telephone. (Sherrie, who organises my schedule, protects me from dead-time, filters my calls and schedules my callers, is the best secretary I've worked with — and I've worked with very good ones.)

I arrive at 7.30. That gives me 30 minutes before the telephones start going and I'm into the routine of coping with people, problems and opportunities. I use it to scan seven morning newspapers, noting particularly any items about the car-rental or airline industries, economic developments, trends or opportunities. I'll frequently make calls to heads of various arms of the organisation such as John Stevens, our Queensland manager, or Peter Burmeister, the Thrifty managing director, just to hear about the way things are going. I don't believe in chief executives only making contact with managers when they've got a specific problem: you don't get the full picture that way. If they're not in, I'll have a chat to the rental desk: it's surprising how often useful information comes from these random chats.

Although I understand most people have 'low points' during the work day — some find around mid-afternoon that their energy level's at its lowest, or it takes them an hour in the morning to get going — I honestly don't. Partly, perhaps, it's a function of the way I see my role: when a Budget division chief or a branch manager wants to call or see me, it's usually with a problem. They expect energy from me, and I'm there to energise them, charge them up and head them in the right direction. I couldn't do that if my energy-level was down: even if you give good advice about how to solve a problem, if you do it in a tone of voice and body language suggesting you're not on top of it, you're not doing your job as corporate leader.

Sherrie's schedule shapes most days. On days when I'm involved in shooting a television commercial (it mightn't seem like it, but those few seconds I appear in the commercials can take a whole day to shoot, especially if it's an outdoor location), I stay in touch and get things moving on any urgent problem or opportunity that's arisen by telephone. Having one in the Porsche has been a real boon.

I often go home for lunch with Josie. If I haven't had a run in the morning, I'll do it at lunchtime. Running relaxes me and gives me time to think about longer-term plans: it's literally the only time of the day I'm guaranteed no interruptions.

Most meetings are scheduled for afternoons, except the Saturday morning board meetings. They're fairly quick and informal: we circulate reports and an agenda 24 hours before so everyone's familiar with the facts and we don't waste time chasing red herrings or arguing about irrelevancies. Budget executives know I don't what to hear, 'We're renting a fairly high percentage of campervans on Freedom Cheques;' I want to know *exactly* what the percentage is. We make decisions on the spot. When a new financial manager joined us from another big transport company, he presented new proposals to an executive meeting. When he had finished and we'd heard comments around the table, I said: 'All right. Let's do it.' He looked at me open-mouthed. After the meeting he told me: 'I'd heard you did things quickly at Budget — but it would have taken nine months to get action at my old job, and you did it in 20 minutes!'

It is common for me to spend half my day dealing with information-flow: calls from journalists, speeches, replies to the 20 or 30 letters from customers I get every day, and information within the company. Sherrie acknowledges receipt of complaints and sets the investigation up on my behalf. I reply to complaints personally when I have all the facts.

While we are eager to please the public, no-one can please all of the people all of the time. Recently, a letter arrived complaining about Budget's advertising Porsches for rent in *Playboy* from a woman in a Melbourne suburb. Others from the same suburb, then still more from Queensland and New South Wales arrived, all the writers saying they had always thought Budget to be a responsible company, and expressing disapproval of our 'association with a pornographic magazine'. A national watchdog group, it seemed. I replied that *Playboy's* readership had a high proportion of relatively affluent males in their twenties and thirties who were the target audience for a sports-car rental service, and if the letter writers could suggest another way of reaching that market, we would explore it.

On Sunday afternoons I do the monthly staff letters, which often involve a restatement of the fundamentals of our business and need more time to think out clearly and carefully.

Sunday mornings are for running and relaxation. In the afternoons I quietly handle the matters requiring sustained reflection: broad planning, major investment opportunities. As I write, I'm conscious of the irritating vogue for video investment invitations, the filmed prospectus. Sometimes I watch five or six of these on a Sunday afternoon, and they all remind me how efficient the printed word is for conveying complex matters, especially money matters.

I've been lucky in important ways too. I think I'm the only father I know in Australia of California who hasn't had major problems, drugs, anti-social behaviour, unsavoury associations, anorexia nervosa or the like, with his children. Ron is a bit of a playboy, but a responsible executive: I think he's a bit like I was once. Sherrie chose her path, super-secretary and early marriage. Her husband, VFL star Brent Crosswell, is also a friend of mine, a bonus not every parent gets. They've made me a grandfather, which is wonderful. Tim is in the U.S. gaining experience as I write. Quieter and shyer than the others, he reminds me of my own shyness, concealed by the confident person who presents himself to the cameras and microphones. All three have close continuing relationships with their mother, with Josie and with me.

Josie, fortunately for me, has been caught up in business as an adventure. Her realism and sense of humour have been tonics for me. She has introduced me to things

I've really enjoyed that I might have missed altogether in a life without her; she has an eye for the fundamentals.

If I'm going to North Melbourne Football Club after work I find the same demands on my energy that I get in the office: club officials bring me the problems I can help with as President and I need the same high-level 'Can Do' energy there as well. (I spend winter Saturday afternoons watching the 'Roos play. Josie seldom misses a game; I never do. If we are in Perth or Hobart, Tokyo or Texas and the VFL season is on, we get back home *Friday*.

I usually have dinner at home with Josie. I avoid home business entertainment and working dinners, except for overseas business guests two or three times a year. Twelve hours a day is enough, unless there's a crisis on, and when I come home I shut the door to the office completely. We eat finely cooked meals *à la* Josie. The accent these days is on fresh vegetables and white meat. The marbled steaks I learned to love in the United States no longer have the same appeal — though I still enjoy red meat at restaurants. Josie supports and encourages me in shutting the living room door to business. I don't worry over problems at home: being able to completely turn off from business is one of the essentials to business success — though I don't mean I haven't had flashes of inspiration over coffee by the swimming pool.

Some challenges, like the fight to get Budget on the airports, are thrown at you by events beyond your control, but I also create my own tests. For example, I make at least a hundred speeches a year. Business people tend to underestimate the value of public speaking, but I think effective communication, being able to explain exactly what you want to do, and to carry others along with you, is fundamental to success in business. I try to get a feel for the audience. I'm not nervous before I speak, but I'm alert; all my senses are engaged. I look at the people, try to get a feel for what they're interested in, sensing from snippets of conversation at the official table what they'll relate to. You can't repeat the same speech over and over again: you owe it to your audience to be topical and interesting.

In 1982 I had to speak to old boys of Wesley College at Leonda, a Melbourne reception centre. I got there about 8 o'clock for dinner. I was due to speak at 9.30, but we didn't get the first course till 9. I knew I had a difficult audience — I had never been to an old boys' dinner before, but I saw immediately that old boys include 20-year-olds and real old boys in their 70s. By 9.30 the tables were awash with nostalgia and pitchers of beer and one of the old boys was singing the school song standing on a table. By 10, the headmaster's speech could hardly be heard above the roar of conversation. No-one listened to a word he said. I was furiously re-thinking my speech, figuring if I didn't get their attention I might as well save my breath. My opening line was: 'The first thing I want to do is apologise for interrupting your evening.' That got them quiet. I told some real-life stories. When we started in Melbourne, I said, I discovered much to my chagrin that some of our best customers were bank robbers — anyone planning a bank robbery would hire a Budget car. In fact the great train robbers in Melbourne had Budget cars. That wasn't the market segment I was aiming for, but what a great endorsement: if you're planning a robbery, the one thing you've got to have is reliable wheels.

I told them about the night I went to Sydney and saw the rental agreements being written by our manager, Norman Curran. I saw something I've never seen in any other rental office — every car was rented to a lady, all of whom listed their occupation as 'home duties.' I took Norm aside and said: 'How are you getting these housewives — how do you do it?' Just then a very attractive, vivacious woman drove by blowing the horn, waving and yelling, 'Hi Normie.' Then the penny dropped: Norm's customers were all prostitutes. It wasn't exactly the market I was looking for either, but it was a market.

The old boys loved it: I think that was my most successful night ever. (Not all people operating beyond the law have the sense to hire Budget cars. The French Secret Service agents who bombed the Greenpeace ship *Rainbow Warrior* in Waitemata Harbour, Auckland on 10 July 1985, killing the ship's engineer, went to Avis.)

Actually, although people have used Budget cars in hold-ups we do a lot of business with police forces which need unmarked cars for surveillance — sometimes they need a different car every night, so a car rental company is an obvious source. Heroin and marijuana have been found in our cars. We've also had suicides in our cars, depressed people who put a hose over the exhaust, feed it through a window and die from the carbon monoxide. There was one terrible case near Coolgardie in Western Australia. A guy suicided with a hose and when our manager found the car a week later in 40 degree heat the body had exploded — there was nothing left to conduct an autopsy on. The manager never got over it and left the company shortly afterwards.

Sometimes accidents look like suicides, a car goes into a tree at high speed and we find the guy had just left his wife and children and was depressed. The accident rate for rental cars is higher than the rate generally — in our case it's one accident for every 236 rentals, including dented fenders and minor scrapings. No doubt the rate's higher because the renters are driving unfamiliar cars in unfamiliar territory. We counsel drivers and warn them of road hazards, particularly kangaroos. We have a lot of collisions with kangaroos. North American visitors often get into trouble because they're used to driving on the right side of the road: on the superb American highway system you can hardly ever get into trouble by drifting on to the wrong side of the road — but with our single-lane major roads it's easy.

Talking to live audiences like the U.S. Budget Convention, where there are a thousand rent-a-car professionals, or to a meeting of 30-odd licensees who have a problem with some aspect of corporate performance, constantly hones my communication skills: no two audiences are alike. I don't believe anyone can do this 'naturally': it's a skill you've got to work at, always testing your ability to size up an audience and talk in a way they can relate to. There's nothing more satisfying when you know you've done it well: you see it in the way people laugh and smile and applaud. It's great. (I rate myself on a scale of 1 to 10 after each speech.)

Another test and challenge often undervalued in business is media interviews. Done well, this looks easier than it is. When I'm questioned by television or radio or newspaper journalists my fundamental rule is: be candid. I've never said anything untruthful to the press. And I always try to give them a story. You've got to give something of yourself, some time and energy, and you've got to be prepared. You've got to think carefully about what you want to say and make sure you express it clearly: if you're not clear you'll bore people, or you'll be misunderstood, or both. Whether it's in the board room or on Channel 9 or on the telephone to a journalist from *The Age*, boring people or being misunderstood is bad for your image and it's bad for business. That's not a great insight — but people often ignore it.

If you get the kind of media exposure I have had for more than 20 years — I now have a regular spot on Michael Schildberger's radio show in Melbourne, on top of all my other appearances — people expect a certain standard of performance. I have to be consistent with the Budget philosophy, consistent with my own public image, clear, truthful and, above all, interesting.

The time I spend in the witness box during Budget's courtroom battles tests and hones my skills of presentation, consistency and clarity. During the crucial trade practices action against ATI, I was in the box for six straight days, and the cross-examination, the attempts to destroy my credibility, were merciless. Testing yourself against Queen's Counsel skilled in cross-examination is really telling; I've always thought of it as a crucible for tempering my skills as the chief Budget mouthpiece.

I test the odds in a variety of ways. In the 1960s, before American Express and Diners Club credit cards became as common as cash, I got into the habit of never carrying cash; I never had any money — literally, not as much as a 20 cent piece. (The first time Josie and I crossed Sydney Harbour Bridge together I had no money for the toll, after I offered my Diner's Club card, she paid.) At restaurants — this was before I was appearing regularly on television — I would produce my Budget business card and ask to sign an IOU for the bill. I was just pushing, trying to see how far I could go, but the restaurants always accepted my IOUs. No one ever said no. It astonished me that people would do that. At airports if I wanted a newspaper I'd wander around till I found one left on a chair. If anyone recognised me they must have thought it strange that the head of Budget, Reg Ansett's son, was scrounging 20-cent newspapers. Nowadays the airlines are pretty good, they supply you with newspapers, so I don't have a problem. And I don't push restaurants any more: I acquired an American Express card a few years ago.

I suppose the same part of my psyche, the need to buck the system, explains another of my habits. I never park my Porsche on street meters or in car parks: I take my chances in the yellow-line areas. I like to play the odds, test my luck with the parking inspectors. And I have amazing luck: every time I'm looking for a parking spot someone will pull out from the kerb in front of me, right where I want to park. A parking spot materialises every time — in the loading zone. And nine times out of ten I'm not booked — it's a better system than taking the time to find empty street space or paying the car park fees. It's quicker. It's cheaper. (But I never push my luck on the meters: if you're parked on an expired meter the grey ghosts or brown bombers will get you every time.)

I drive a Porsche. I like beautifully engineered sports cars — actually, Josie talked me into it a few years ago. She has a passion for Porsches and she reckoned I'd earned the right to have my own car instead of taking whatever was available from the Budget fleet as I did for nearly 20 years. As I rarely travel with more than one other person, it made sense. The manual shift put the fun back into driving at a time when I'd grown bored with it.

I drive myself because I've only once been in a chauffeur-driven car and it made me feel uncomfortable. For the same reason, I never take taxis. I think I've caught a taxi no more than a dozen times in my whole life, mostly in Japan, never in California. I may have caught a taxi a half-dozen times in the last 20 years in Australia. It's not that I'm biased against taxis — after all, I drove cabs myself in Alaska — it's just the lack of control. I don't mind driving a cab, but I really don't like being a passenger. (I would never buy a Rolls Royce — I'd be embarrassed to be seen behind the wheel.)

That sense of control also relates to my attitudes to smoking. Although there's an old picture of me with Dale Soderstrom, both with cigarettes in our hands, that night I had had a few drinks and somebody at the bar said 'You're a dead replica for Montgomery Clift, but you need a cigarette in your hand to give it the Montgomery Clift look', so I had the cigarette for the picture, but I never took a puff. It was funny. Although I had some friends who smoked, and Dale was a heavy smoker later, most of us thought in those experimental years at high school and afterwards that sport was very important and smoking would effect our lungs. None of us was slow to sink all the beer or Jack Daniels we wanted, but smoking, even in the days before the Surgeon General's report about smoking and lung cancer, seemed to us to be bad for lung capacity and stamina on the football field. We weren't wowsers: we just wanted to do well at sport. I never sampled marijuana or cocaine either, perhaps because for our generation drugs weren't part of the scene. I'd be surprised if any of my high school friends even sampled drugs, though I wouldn't be surprised if Pete Kemmsies had a couple of marijuana joints.

When we were packing to leave our Peel Street head office in 1982 I glanced up at the ceiling and noticed, for the first time, that it had turned nicotine yellow. We were moving to a beautiful new building, the present Budget headquarters in Bedford Street North Melbourne, which won an archictectural award for the best-designed building in Victoria in 1982. What a pity it would be if our light, pleasing work environment got to look nicotine yellow too, I thought. A large part is open floor space, and some Budget non-smokers had mentioned they were bothered by smoke. I've always been sensitive to the issue — a habit which causes lung cancer has never seemed to me attractive. No doubt I could have banned smoking in the building, but an authoritarian ban would have caused resentment and it wouldn't fit the Budget philosophy of encouraging and rewarding performance. I offered an incentive: a $250 bonus to quit smoking for six months. I also banned smoking in open areas and created a section where those who want to can take a break and have a smoke. Smoking in the private offices is permitted, though it's not encouraged. We don't police the quit-smoking bonus: if people pledge to quit and say six months later that they haven't smoked, that's good enough.

There's one problem: some people have quit smoking, then gone back on, then quit again. Some have earned three bonuses like this — and I've created an incentive for people to quit, then take up the habit again! I'll have to find a way to limit multiple bonuses. But quite a few people have given up smoking for good. We've paid out between $8,000 and $10,000 over the years, and I think the scheme will go on indefinitely; now it's part of the

Budget psyche. I guess heavy smokers might decide not to apply for Budget jobs — but we don't have a fetish about it, it's all positive reinforcement for quitting.

We have another get-fit incentive: if any overweight executives want to staple their stomachs like David Lange, the New Zealand Prime Minister, has done, I'll pay for it — though so far there haven't been any takers!

Although I still enjoy Jack Daniels, a bottle of wine with dinner, a few beers once in a while, I don't go on binges as I did in Vista and San Diego — partly because I got away from the hell-raisers I grew up with, partly because I'm older, partly because I don't have the time. I'm not being parochial when I say I particularly enjoy Victorian reds, but my favourite wine is Penfolds Grange Hermitage.

The headquarters building itself complements the Budget image, light, open and brightly coloured. If anything's damaged we repair it straight away so that everyone can have a physical sense of pride in the building they work in. You can't be self-motivated in a dreary environment. There's no lift, so everyone walks up the stairs — the building itself expresses our belief in physical fitness. Private offices have glass doors. That came about because one of the senior executives had a habit of closing his door when he was having confidential discussions with the people reporting to him. I said I didn't like it, the open-door policy literally meant open doors, but he said he had a problem with that, sometimes he needed to keep talks confidential. So we compromised on glass doors — people could still see in. The trouble was the glass doors were so clean they were invisible and after a few people walked into my doors I had the slogan 'Perception Is Reality' put on my door to make sure they perceived the reality of the door before they banged their noses on it. The board room door reads 'Customer Service Centre'.

It's rare to have Budget people off sick, and I've never had a day off sick myself. I think the problem with people taking a day off with a cold or flu is psychological — they're not enjoying their work, they're in the wrong job — rather than physical. If you're not motivated you'll take a day off with a sniffle, but if you are motivated and you enjoy your work it'll take a heart attack to keep you away.

When I became President of North Melbourne Football Club, they had a fitness scheme going for their gold pass holders and supporters. I looked at it and thought it could go well beyond that and we could involve some of the Budget men and women. So they modified the program and all our executives went along for workouts. One hour of jogging, weightlifting, calisthenics and sprinting from 7 a.m. each Monday, Wednesday and Friday under the expert eye of Max Ryan, North's head trainer. Each person began with a measurement of heart rate and body fat, both continuously monitored so no one over-exerted themselves. Of course there was a tremendous difference in fitness levels — some could run ten laps without breathing heavily; others would run a couple of laps, then walk one until gradually they built up their stamina. A few dropped out. I did hear indirectly of a few complaints about it, but nobody complained to me.

That program and the Budget fun runs have increased the energy level in the corporation and the sick days have diminished while productivity has increased. We also got a bonus we hadn't expected: with everyone from different departments and different levels getting together on an equal footing for workouts, it developed a camaraderie that you don't get in an office where people are busy. On the football field they could chat and see another side of each other. It's hard to put a money value on the fitness program, but I can't remember any senior Budget executive who has got sick in the past five or six years. On salary levels of $40,000 or $50,000, if the average person takes a week's sick leave in a year, we could easily save $50,000 or $60,000 in five years. Before the program, some of the managers noticeably flattened out around mid-afternoon. That doesn't happen any more. Of the Budget workforce of 1300, about 1200 take part in some Budget-subsidised fitness program.

The year I turned 50 I set myself the personal goal of running a marathon. I wanted to finish the 1983 Big M Marathon from Frankston to Melbourne, a distance of 42.165 kilometres. I'd done a lot of running in my gridiron years, but I'd never been a long-distance runner. After some fun runs of 10 kilometres and one of 17 kilometres I was ready to try the marathon. Training took a lot of time — I was running at least 50 kilometres a week for four months, most of them with Josie. My goal was to finish in less than 4 hours 30 minutes. On a hot October morning Josie and I and four other inrepid Budget runners lined up with 7000 others for the start. We covered the first 10 kilometres in 50 minutes — 10 minutes ahead of target. After some hills between the 15 and 25 kilometre marks, we dropped back, reaching the 25 kilometre mark in 2 hours 30 minutes, dead on time. But it wasn't the easy fun the first 10 kilometres had been; my left knee was tightening and my two big toenails were hurting. At 30 kilometres I did a television interview explaining how I was running well within myself and I'd finish in just over 4 hours, but my feet were on fire, I figured I'd lose my two big toenails and my knee was still tightening. We had run for 3 hours, right on schedule. At 37 kilometres I hit the famous marathon wall: every step was pain, every cell was drained of energy. All I could do was shuffle. It took an hour to cover the last 7 kilometres, but I moved into high gear for the finish with the applauding crowd, the television cameras and the pretty girls who hung gold medals around our necks. All the Budget six finished. When Josie finished only 1 minute later she asked 'When did you finish?' I was chatting over a beer, looking quite settled in, and I said breezily: 'Oh, I've been here a long time.' She didn't find out how close she was until she saw a picture of the finish and the time-clock some while later — and of course I still haven't heard the last of it!

We immediately went to Surfers Paradise for a few days rest and recreation. My feet were a soggy pulp; I lost both big toenails. In Surfers we planned an attack on the next Big M marathon, with the idea of knocking 30 minutes off our times. It didn't happen — both our schedules were too tight in 1984 to afford the training time — but Budget took over the marathon sponsorship in 1986, and we'll break the four-hour mark this year.

I got involved with North Melbourne Football Club, the 'Roos, in a small way in 1974. I became a gold pass member, went to a half-dozen matches a season, then a few more as I gradually got hooked. At the end of 1979 the North President, Lloyd Holyoake retired and Ron

Joseph, North's general manager talked the presidency over with various club directors, invited me to the club to meet Holyoake, and offered me the presidency. I was a bit surprised, but I'd been an admirer of Ron Barassi for years — Barassi coached North into the grand final every year from 1974 to 1978, and I'd previously been a bit of a Carlton supporter when Barassi was coaching Carlton. I liked his style — though I thought he'd lost form when he started doing ads for Hertz.

Ron's approach to me was endorsed by Alan Aylett, a great player who had been North's President in the mid-1970s and was then President of the Victorian Football League. They saw me as the club front man, a guy who could make speeches and publicly represent the club and who might be useful when it came to looking for commercial sponsors. They weren't suggesting I take part in running the club. 'We want you as the figurehead. Administration and football and everything else would be left to the experts — because you are a yank who doesn't know anything about Australian Rules football,' Ron said bluntly. I liked the idea of a new challenge and I thought football was a good outside interest for a businessman to have, because it is an intense, physically competitive environment. I need a good fight at least once every couple of weeks and football would give it to me, help me stay hyped up and sane. But *active* president, as I saw it, not figurehead was my style and a job condition North accepted.

But nothing in my career had prepared me for my experience at North. When they win games that they're not expected to, I get enormous satisfaction; when they lose games they're expected to win, I feel distraught. Football's an equaliser: it doesn't matter what you are off the field, how well your career's going — you have little influence on football. Once the players run on to the field it's out of your hands, there's nothing you can do about it. If they lose you just have to accept it; I hadn't had that experience before. Australian football is a very emotional game. There's something else I like about it: in business it's hard to keep contact with a broad spectrum of friends and associates. Because of time pressures I found myself, against my will, spending most of my time with a fairly narrow range of people. Football's been good for me in that way, and I've developed a rapport with players, coaches and club officials quite different to the relationships I have in business.

I suppose it doesn't hurt my image or Budget's to be involved with a Victorian Football League Club in a city like Melbourne which lives off Australian Rules through the winter and stays interested for much of the spring, summer and autumn, but that wasn't a factor in my decision.

I told Ron Joseph and the others that I'd take the job provided we could reduce the club committee of twelve, which seemed to me too unwieldy, to a board of directors of six. I wouldn't campaign for the presidency, but if they got this change through the annual meeting and they invited me and there were no challengers, I'd do it. I was one of several businessmen then coming into VFL clubs, later followed by Alan Bond at Richmond and John Elliott at Carlton. Some think this change hasn't been for the good, but people with business contacts can be helpful in

WEGTOONS PTY LTD AND THE HERALD & WEEKLY TIMES LTD

getting corporate sponsors. I approached Qantas to succeed Budget as North Melbourne sponsor, arguing that it was logical The Flying Kangaroo should sponsor North, the mud-splattered Kangaroos, and because Qantas wanted to improve its community involvement and visibility in Melbourne — it was seen too much as a Sydney-based company, they felt. They did it and they're delighted with the sponsorship.

In 1981 I was subconsciously pushing myself to the limit, seeing how much I could take on before I fell in a heap. Budget was really humming, growing quickly, I was North's president, and the club was taking more time than I'd bargained for. I became President of the Melbourne Chamber of Commerce, I was Vice Chairman of the Moomba Committee, Melbourne's annual street festival. I was on the Vicfit committee to encourage Victorians not to be 'Norms'. I was President of the Victorian Congress of Employers' Associations, on the Tourist Advisory Council and two government transport committees. I was working 14 hours a day six days a week — though I still, religiously you might say, kept Sundays free. By 1982 I realised I'd reached my limit — I found myself taking short cuts just to squeeze everything in to the available time. I stopped playing handball and I backed off to get things back into balance.

When I wrote to Dale Soderstrom while I was nursing my aching feet in Surfers, I said optimistically: 'We are already planning the 1984 season with a view to winning.' North had finished on top of the ladder in 1983, so it was a bitter disappointment when they lost the second semi-final and then the preliminary final. But worse was to follow. In 1984 we started with two shattering defeats by 10-goal margins. The North board, all the players and officials, came to my office and I told them: 'I don't know about anybody else, but I'm going to tough this out. I'm going to have to make some hard decisions to get this place running right'. Ron Joseph, who had left as general manager, drove home that night thinking 'I can't leave him standing there copping all the flak. Football clubs are bastards of institutions! I'm going to stand beside him'. He came straight back as general manager. It was a hard year. We finished second last. But Ron and I and the others were working away while the team was getting beaten to make sure 1985 didn't go the same way.

There are useful parallels between football and business. In both, if you feel like a loser, you can rest assured you're going to be one. A football coach has to build into the players' psyches a confidence in themselves, a feeling that they're good enough to win. He has to impose discipline in training and in matches. He has to pull a ruckman or a full forward into line if he gets so carried away about his own performance that he's hurting the teamwork. He has to know when to kick backsides and when to stroke an ego. He has to know how to come down hard on players performing below their potential — but not so hard that he damages their confidence and depresses them. A coach has to be tough but fair — a bit like my old Standard Oil boss Red Hostetter. It's a fine line.

Part of my job is to be coach of the corporate team. North's coach John Kennedy is perhaps the best coach I've seen, measured over a long period. Ron Barassi was spectacularly good as captain-coach and in his first four years at North, but I think he lost some of his old touch five or six years ago. Kennedy coaches as he used to play — a dour, tenacious guy who never lets up. As a player you always knew he'd give 100 per cent till the final siren, and that's what he asks of his players now. Kennedy tells the team: 'The high fliers are spectacular and crowds love them, but watch them in the last quarter when it counts. They've dissipated their energy and the marks go to the man in front, not the guys who like to climb up their backs to take the mark from behind.' For any ball player, for any athlete, attitude counts above everything. Players who don't have great natural skills are often the most successful because they work harder. If you've got a player with both the natural skills and the commitment, you've got a rare commodity, a champion. The players you want are those you can count on to do something special when the game looks lost. North's captain, ruck-rover Wayne Schimmelbusch, is that kind of player. He doesn't have the greatest skills in the game, but he's got a heart bigger than any footballer I've seen. When the game is over he's completely exhausted, he can hardly talk, whether the game is a grand final or an ordinary home-and-away.

A star like Schimmelbusch doesn't develop if his coach

sits on him and tries to mould every kick, every handball, every tackle, to the coach's style. The coach has to know what's good and what isn't, what works and what doesn't — but he's got to give each individual the space to grow and to develop his own style. In Budget, though it's true the company is centred around me and more people report to me than management textbooks recommend, I'm also a delegator: I give people an area of responsibility and leave them alone. I don't interfere. (Of course I don't interfere in Kennedy's coaching at North, either. I played a bit of Australian Rules during inter-company matches but I couldn't adapt from American football. The styles are too different: I never kicked a ball in my years of American football, and the American style of tackling, driving a player into the ground, is a rules violation in Aussie rules.)

It's not my style to get involved in detailed supervising of everything my executives do. You can't be an effective leader if you try to dot every 'I' and cross every 'T'. I think that's what destroyed Ronald Reagan's predecessor as President of the United States, Jimmy Carter. When I heard that Carter went as far as drawing up the roster for the White House tennis courts I knew he was finished. Carter was immensely energetic, a workaholic, and he was highly intelligent, but his concentration on detail destroyed him. Reagan seems to have a lower energy level, he doesn't work the hours Carter did, but because he paints on a broad canvas and leaves the details to others, he's a much more effective chief executive.

I confess that's not the only reason I don't worry over every detail. The other reason is that I couldn't do it. I don't have an enormous attention span. I can bring to bear a great deal of energy and concentration on an issue for about an hour: then I turn it over to someone else and say, 'Okay, take it over, run with it, and bring it back to me for final endorsement.' If I have to pore over one issue for an entire afternoon, I lose interest.

I see a lot of people in business and the professions who have more talent than me, but who become obsessed with what they're doing, become too narrow in their interests, focus on one specific issue, lose the balance in their lives, and in so doing lose perspective. I've somehow got the capacity — probably it's my genetic inheritance from my father — to use my energy productively, spread it around over the issues that count rather than burning it up on one. I think that, plus my confidence in myself, is what saves me.

Because I only interfere when things go wrong, I need, and I think I have, a good intuition for something going off the rails. Intuition is gained through experience, knowledge of your business and confidence in yourself. It's a great business talent. I supplement my intuition with a mental checklist which takes me about an hour a week to run through: if everything checks out I'm confident things are going well, there are no hidden disasters; and if something is going wrong, I'll be able to catch it quickly enough to get it back on the rails.

At the end of each day I get a list telling me how many cars are on rent, how many are idle and how many are in workshops in each of our rental offices around Australia. If a State or a branch has an abnormal number of cars idle or in the workshop I watch the next day and if the situation's still the same we start taking action.

I also look at accounts receivable. We average about 55 days to collect accounts receivable; that is, collect cash from people who owe us money on the Budget credit card. About half our total income comes in this way — so each week I check it. If the average blows out to 56 or 57 days, it could be due to invoice errors, or charges sent to the wrong accounts, or a shift in the economy means people are paying more slowly. Whatever the reason, we take action.

The third main checklist item is the daily cash-in, cash-out position against the forecast. If we're getting in less than the forecast, or paying out more, I call someone to account.

I also get monthly reports on the number of accidents our cars are involved in and the seriousness of the accidents. Rental officers have to make some intuitive judgments about whether people are qualified to rent a Budget car. If they have a recognised credit card (and a driver's licence, of course) they're qualified. The exceptions are if they're under 21 or look like they've been drinking.

If a person doesn't have a credit card and wants to pay cash we're running more risk — but if they're listed in the telephone book under their own name, that indication of stability is enough and they're qualified. If they're not listed, we ask for two personal referees, one preferably an employer. There's also the visual, intuitive check of the rental officer: if a loud-mouth comes in carrying a can of beer he might not be a good risk. This intuitive judgment is part of the rental officers' skills, and they're pretty good at it. But sometimes, if they're between seasons and there are a lot of cars sitting around, there's a temptation to take a risk and rent them knowing you're taking a chance on a no-hoper. You pay for it in bad debt, bad accidents and sometimes cars stolen or lost. We have had 67 cars taken and never returned in 21 years. And our licencees have about 23. About 0.5 per cent of our cars are missing — the same rate as 20 years ago.

Patterns change: we had a very high rate of theft of Commodore cars a few years ago when a few clever people found out you could break into a Commodore easily. General Motors improved security after submissions from us and others, and now there's a significant drop in the rate of stolen Commodores. There are the novices who take the cars out and try to resell them. We always get those back. Then there are those who are stupid enough to think they can just take out a car and keep it forever, and invariably they get caught.

It's important that you present a car with no dents on it — if people get a car with dents on it and it's grubby, they think there's no point in looking after it: good presentation helps security as well as customer relations.

I don't believe an entrepreneur can have a mistake-free record. If you're error free you're probably not adventurous enough. I made my biggest mistake in 1982 when Budget bought a 70 per cent share of the Waste Equipment Company; we bought about 16 of these huge compactor trucks and had more than $2 million tied up in the company, a huge investment for us. The idea was to lease them to Cleanaway and others. The concept was good, and the market was strong — and then the recession hit, the market dropped and we were stuck with these massive units sitting around doing nothing. The Waste Equipment founder was a good entreprenuer, but he wasn't a good manager. We ended up buying him out — which we should have done in the first place, and put in our own managers. The whole exercise cost us about $1 million.

Earlier, I made a bad mistake when I bought Budget from Avis and had to relocate our accounting department from Sydney to Melbourne; I hired a credit manager who was a disaster, our liquidity was drying up in a period of quick company growth and our accounts receivable were in a god-almighty mess. I was lucky to have AGC in the company at the time: they were able to pump some more money in temporarily, though my equity dropped from 45 per cent to 30 per cent. It took me about a year to sort it all out. The credit manager had all the credentials, but he couldn't do the job: it was an error of judgment on my part.

I've made lots of mistakes, of course, but they haven't had a serious impact — although if I'd made them all at once, they would have. Even the million-dollar mistake had little emotional impact on me — because when you start an enterprise from nothing, what's the worst that can happen? You lose it all — so you're back where you started. So what? I had a pretty good run and a bit of excitement. I have a pretty good time now that I've got something; I also had a pretty good time when I didn't have anything. I don't sit around worrying about what is the worst that can happen. I *know* what it would be like: it would be like 1965.

11

Around the Next Bend

My broad goal over the next five years is to have Budget securely positioned in the top 100 companies in Australia. In 1984 we were the 450th company; in 1985 we jumped over 100 companies to 349th. In 1986 we were ranked 295th. Each time the leapfrog gets tougher because the numbers get bigger. But we'll do it by sticking to the knitting — doing the things we've done well in the past. We're not going to diversify for the sake of diversification. And I'm going to make sure that no matter what directions we take the public perception of Budget will remain as it has always been — that of an innovative company that takes on the establishment and is very sensitive to consumer interests. That image has to be sustained *at all costs*.

When we get an airline, it will not be as part of a regulated system. Budget will not be part of a two-airline system, or a three-airline system, or any government-shielded deal. There are two reasons for this. Budget would not operate well in a non-competitive environment: we've expanded the whole car rental market, and our share of the market, because we're good competitors and competition is the heart of Budget's dynamism. Becoming part of a duopoly would undermine the foundations of the enterprise. But in our scenario, more people would fly to more places. The second reason is that it would destroy people's perception of Budget as a customer-sensitive battler against the status quo. If we were to buy Ansett or

TAA — we would be the first car rental company in the world to take over an airline, though it's happened the other way round many times — we would work aggressively and publicly to end government regulation of airline business, although this might be at our expense in the short term.

Although running an airline is obviously a different business to running a car rental company, the two deal directly with the public and specialise in customer service. The airline business is about selling a concept of mobility, service and convenience, selling a need, and skilful marketing. Likewise with car rentals. Buying an airline is, for example, much more compatible with Budget than an airline buying a television station as my father did. It's more compatible than Thomas Nationwide Transport owning Ansett — TNT is an integrated enterprise which transported goods for business, not for the ordinary Australian. Airlines and car rental companies 20 years ago dealt with the same segment of the community — the upper socio-economic group, the top 2 or 3 per cent earners. Largely because of our success in creating customers, the car rental industry has transcended that limited market: nearly everyone now has a need, and can afford, to rent a car. That isn't true of flying — but it could be with the right sort of marketing, advertising, customer service, and pricing. Ansett and TAA are still dealing more than they should be with the top income group and business travellers.

It's essential not to spread the company too thin. I've seen that happen: and when enterprises run too fast for the players in the company to keep up with the pace, they start taking shortcuts and neglect fundamentals. That won't happen to Budget. Our immediate diversification is into car dealerships. In February 1986 we acquired a Melbourne Ford dealership, the first of the Budget dealerships in each capital city. This is a slight variation on our traditional activities. It's partly a tactical move to protect our exposed flanks. If car manufacturers change their attitude to supplying car rental companies we'll have some protection through the dealerships. It's a bit of insurance. Setting up our own advertising agency is also a possibility for similar reasons.

Now that we've done the hard work of establishing a

national brand image and a network of close to 300 offices we can select compatible industries to integrate with. Suburban Budget Rent-a-Car offices are now a bit like suburban bank branches: they don't make a great contribution to profit, but they're the shop-windows.

A week never goes by without me getting two or three recommendations to establish new businesses or take over existing ones, but it's my firm policy to concentrate only on the things we know how to do well. The chauffeur-drive division obviously fits in well; so does air services. A major part of our growth in the next five years will come from a leasing company we're forming with our Japanese franchisee, the Orient Leasing Company, the biggest leasing company in the world.

We started our car-leasing division in 1981. It's been growing at a rate of about 60 per cent a year; in 1986 it's operating 11,000-plus cars and it has the potential to quadruple in size in the next five years. Leasing is a very important division of the Budget organisation. I hired Peter Hansen from Hertz — the only executive we've ever taken from Hertz — and gave him the division with this instruction: run it as you would your own business. He has. From a meagre start he's built it up to a nationwide operation employing 70 people. We have the best people in the industry in this division. We don't simply lease cars: finance companies do that. But five years ago corporations were just beginning to recognise that their car fleets, insurance, parts and maintenance were becoming more expensive, and also to realise that they weren't experts in running car fleets — sales companies or manufacturing concerns or hotels are not geared to managing car fleets efficiently. We offer the purchasing and disposal skills of an organisation which deals with more than 20,000 cars, and of course with our buying power — Budget is the largest buyer of cars in Australia — we can get pretty good discounts from manufacturers. We recommend the type and make of cars suited to the company's needs, repair and maintenance service, insurance recommendations, advice on how to minimise tax liability. The customer pays us in effect a monthly rental which covers all the operating costs except petrol; at the end of the lease the car reverts to us and we sell it.

The new leasing company, a 50-50 joint venture with

Orient Leasing, is a good example of our diversification process. We have the brand name: if Orient Leasing were to start on its own in Australia it would have to go through the slow, expensive process of establishing a national brand name. With Budget, the new company has that from day one. For us, one of the beauties of the partnership is that Orient Leasing will guarantee the funds. It's a major public company and can acquire funds cheaper than we can — and with our insatiable appetite for capital that's important. The joint company will lease big-ticket capital items to corporations: computers, aeroplanes, all kinds of heavy equipment.

The projections I've seen are very attractive: the profit potential is far greater than in our car rental division. We're looking at a big, profitable company. And of course it's compatible with the Budget fundamental, our commitment to, our passion for, service.

Is there anything Budget wouldn't get into? I wouldn't rule out any area that has some synergy with car rental. The North Melbourne football team doesn't fit into the Budget corporate structure — that's an indulgence for the chief executive. But it's not out of the question that I'll own North Melbourne — not because of any burning ambition I have to own a football team, but because I think that North Melbourne will require private ownership to survive — and if there's going to be a private owner of that club I think it should be me because I can do it better than anyone else. It's becoming very difficult to fund the team through traditional sources, so it's either private ownership or a merger with another club — and none of us at North would do that except in absolute desperation.

I think that a National Football League in Australian Rules is not far down the track. I wouldn't be surprised if in 1987 a team from Western Australia and a South Australian team joined the Victorian Football League and the VFL became the National Football League with national television coverage. Of course there are difficulties and there will be some pain — some VFL clubs may go under — in the transition to a national competiton, but I think that's the way the game must go. I agree with my friend Ron Joseph, North's manager. 'We've got Western Australia and South Australia wanting to be part of a national competition,' Ron says, 'because all we've done over the past 20 years basically, is rape them of their top players. Sport has emerged on colour television in that time and the sportsman has become a superstar. The natural trend is to go national, bring in television and generate more corporate dollars. Australian Rules Football is a great product, and we've got to market it properly. We can all bury our heads in the sand and say 'Let's stay as we are, let's not alter Australian football in Victoria.' But if we do that in 20 years' time the game won't be what it should be — the leading sport in Australia.'

My own game plan is confined to the next 12 years: when I'm 65 I'll decide whether to continue as chief executive of Budget Transport Industries. I won't make the mistake of holding on to power in the company if I've lost my killer instinct or my drive and energy level. I might find that at 65 I still have just as much energy and need of challenge as I did at 50, but at this stage, at 53, I know that in 12 years it's something I'll have to reassess. I think Dad made a mistake by not retiring at 65 and stepping up into the chairman's job. I think the protection offered by the two-airline policy dulled his energy, so I'm in a different position in that respect. Now I sometimes find that after three or four months of really intense work I need a break. I usually take three or four days in Surfers Paradise and come back totally refreshed.

If I were 35 or 40 now, I'd be more interested in starting my own airline from scratch than in buying Ansett or TAA or East-West. At 53 I'd prefer to buy an airline and change it to fit the style of the company I manage, but I'm quite prepared to do it from scratch. Either way is fine. Nevertheless, whatever I do it has to fit into the next 10 or 12 years. I'm prepared to dedicate 10 or 12 years to charging ahead and taking on challenges — but then I've got to reassess. I think I'm a realist. I know my own strengths and weaknesses. I need to keep operating in the style I've developed, being one of the first into the office every morning, being in there on Saturday mornings, being accessible, providing moral leadership — all those things which take time, and take a toll. I can't operate any other way. Others might be able to, but I can't — so if through lack of energy I find I have to cut corners I'll know it's time for me to withdraw. I know when I'm overextended: it happened in 1982 and I shed some responsibilities as a result.

Will I continue as Budget presenter as long as I'm chief executive? It depends on public reaction. If people come to think I've lost that essential 'fighter' image or I'm not looking after the customer any more, I'll quit. There would be nothing worse than hanging on after an adverse reaction had set in. It hasn't happened so far and I don't expect it will, but if it does I'll go.

When I withdraw as chief executive I'll probably step up to the chairman's job. I know it's difficult for a new chief executive to move into an entrepreneurial company when the founder is sitting above him as chairman — Harold Geneen, the dominant founder and chief executive of ITT, went through six chief executives in quick succession after he became chairman, because no-one could live up to his standards. But it's a challenge I think I'm capable of taking on.

I expect my successor to come from within Budget and I'd be very disappointed if that didn't happen. It will probably be someone who's spent years working in Budget, studying the way I operate, absorbing the strengths and weaknesses in my management style. Because of this intimacy in our relationship it would be easier for the new chief executive working with me as chairman.

Because I'm the most visible of the Budget team, people sometimes think the company's a one-man band. It's anything but that: we have some of the best people in the world in this company. As I write there are at least half a dozen possible successors within Budget. Peter Burmeister, who now heads Thrifty and has been with Budget more than ten years is getting the experience of running his own business, totally on his own, without any interference from me. He has the skills, the aptitude and the personality to head up an organisation like Budget. We've got Duncan Leitch, now the New Zealand managing director, who has been with the company for 12 years, knows me intimately and is applying the Budget management style in his territory. We have Bob Frost, an Englishman who was Vice President of Budget International — he set up most of Europe and the Middle East for Budget International, and he certainly has the temperament and experience and he's fitted in beautifully to the tough Budget culture. John Stevens, our Queensland manager and one of my most reliable sounding-boards for marketing ideas would certainly be capable of taking over Budget if he was the one chosen.

There's another young man in Budget who's certainly got the ability, he has all the ambition in the world and so far he's moving along nicely. It's up to him to develop consistency and stamina. I'll let my son Ron speak for himself:

'I remember Dad used to drive me around on his Oroweat truck to the supermarkets. I remember water-skiing on the Colorado River and him taking me up to Los Angeles to see the Dodgers play. I remember him pushing the golfball a mile with his nose — instant celebrity! I thought it was good because he was on television.

'I washed cars at Budget when I was 10 or 12. At high school I spent most of my holidays working with the Budget mechanics. At 14 I worked in the reservations department. At 15 I rented cars to people. At 16 I relieved the Tasmania manager when he was on holidays. I'd get to work at 6 a.m., wash cars till 9, rent cars till 5, then drive a car up to Launceston or fly up and drive one down. Then I'd go to the casino till 3 a.m. I'd be back washing cars three hours later — I don't know how I did it.'

He sounds a bit like me; he's our Western Australia manager.

How can you be your own man in a company owned and run by your father? Ron said:

'You've just got to be the best at what you do. I want to run the best office in Australia and prove to you, and to myself, that I can do the job. That's why I feel I've got to be the best at what I do — because of my father. It used to worry me that some people in the company were sensitive about our relationship, but it doesn't now.

'My only ambition is to be successful at whatever I choose to do. There's no way I'm going to look 10 years ahead and say, "That's where I'm going — managing director of Budget Transport Industries". That's putting a limit on yourself.

'It can cloud your vision if you have only one objective in mind. You can miss opportunities. I got to Perth in November 1983. Budget W.A. then turned over $75,000 to

$80,000 a week and we had 400 rental cars. Now [early 1986] we're consistently turning over about $220,000 a week, and our fleet's about 900 and it will double again in the next 12 months. In 1986 we'll generate more revenue than Victoria — I'll bet you we can do it by December this year!

'I get a lot of invitations to make speeches, but I'm not ready yet to talk about successful business techniques: do people want to hear a 27-year-old guy talk about his business philosophy? I enjoy public speaking itself — when an Adelaide group asked me to talk about 'famous relations' that was fun — but there's a lot of subjects I'm not yet qualified to speak about. Business techniques and philosophy are two.

'I see weaknesses in this company, but I also see them being fixed. However, I wouldn't add anything to the basic philosophy. There are some specific areas in the company which could be improved, where we are using 5- and 10-year old systems. I'm always are pushing: there's got to be a better way.

'I'm not going to limit myself by thinking I'll be at Budget in ten years. I don't know.'

I will nominate my successor 6 or 12 months before I'm ready to give it away, so the decision's still at least a decade away and it will depend on the company's major interests and the commercial and political environment; there's no way of knowing those details 12 years in advance: by 1998 everything could be different. Although the present Budget chairman, Stan Hamley, thinks that if I fell under the proverbial bus tomorrow the changes that would have to follow would cause a lot of anguish, I see the task of handing over to the right person at the right time as a challenge. Maybe I'll phone Oceanside and ask Red Hostetter what he did.

12

Soapbox

I'm an incurable optimist and I think Australia's physical beauty, our unique sense of humour, our relaxed attitudes, our laid-back lifestyle and our clean air make it the best country in the world to live in. I also believe things are going to get worse before they get better in our country.

We've never had to fight to change the status quo. The United States went through the revolutionary war of independence in the 1770s and then the civil war between the States in the 1860s. In the lucky country we've had no violent convulsions like that, but I think the next decade will bring very high unemployment (it's high now in a country that used to pride itself on less than 1 per cent unemployment), social dislocation and suffering before the people revolt against the burden of government, particularly the burden of taxation, which of course was the main cause of the American revolutionary war. National debt will grow, interest rates will remain very high, tax burdens will weigh more and more heavily and fall disproportionately on the shrunken pool of people producing goods and services.

There will be a revolt. People will quit producing. Of late, the Federal Government's response has been to cut marginal income tax rates on one hand, and impose capital gains and fringe benefits and entertainment taxes on the other. That is not improving our situation, it is rearranging the deckchairs on the *Titanic*. I think we will suffer until we as a people take the power away from the politicians, bureaucrats and trade unions that have it. I believe it is going to be really tough in Australia for a while. But hopefully this period will be short and sharp so we can reunite as a nation and work together to fix our problems.

We are rich enough to look after people who can't look after themselves, and we should always do that. But we don't have to do that for people who are just damn lazy and don't want to do anything. I have a friend with a very attractive daughter who's just finished high school. She was going to go to university, but she's fallen in love with a no-hoper, and she's going to move in with him for a year and live on the dole and then go to university. Why should the rest of the community pay for the indulgence of this girl? That's not an unusual case: the way the system's structured, the dole is the right of anybody not in work, not the right of those who are thrown out of work or who simply cannot get a job.

Attitudes are more important than facts. In Australia we suffer from the 'tall poppy syndrome'. I think this syndrome is a product of our fear of achievers: people in the arts or business or the professions — perhaps even in sport — who are successful are seen as a rebuke to the unsuccessful. They make us feel guilty about our lack of achievement, so we cut them down: if no-one is perceived as achieving, everyone feels comfortable. I don't want to harp about the United States — we do many, many things apart from running rental car companies better than the Americans — but the American attitude to success is quite different: if a friend achieves a success, paints a fine painting, starts a successful business, invents a better mousetrap, the Americans celebrate that, thinking Goddamn it, Bob's done it, I'm gonna do it too! The success of others is an inspiration in America. But it's not written on Uluru that Australians can't achieve. Our medical scientists, architects, artists, film-makers, cartoonists and business people include an extraordinary number of world-beaters but we still don't celebrate these successes and give ourselves credit for our achievements.

In *When The Luck Runs Out*, Frederick G. Hilmer recognises the 'conscript mindset' of much of the Australian work force, as opposed to the 'volunteer mindset' that represents America. Hilmer suggests this is a legacy from

Australia's origin as a convict colony. Australians and Americans both came from the same stock, but the settlers went to America of their own accord. It was their decision. For those that came to Australia it wasn't their decision, and somehow this has permeated through generation after generation. One of the reasons for this in the last quarter of the twentieth century is that Australian businessmen have been slow to recognise the importance of work environments that provide job satisfaction, recognition of achievement and making the job as much fun as possible. Some say our climate is a factor, that devotion to the work ethic is difficult in hot climates, particularly in the tropics, but I don't think that's really a problem: there's a very strong work ethic in Singapore, for example. I don't think productivity peters out at Rockhampton because the tropic of Capricorn cuts the Queensland coast there. And I don't mean I think Australians should have a narrow obsession with the work ethic: we shouldn't try to ape America or Japan. We should keep our relaxed laid-back lifestyle, but graft on to it a pride in what we do at work. Job satisfaction is one of the great rewards of life, what some writers call 'psychic salary.' Too few of us draw a psychic salary; for a hedonistic people we are depriving ourselves of one of the main *pleasures* of life.

The problem starts with the school system. Our schools are not designed to encourage achievement, to stroke those kids who can achieve more than the rest of the class, more than all of us maybe. If Einstein was a patent clerk in Sydney instead of Switzerland, he might have felt guilty about investigating the law of relativity. We've followed the traditional English education program rather than specialising to meet the needs of today's society. There's peer pressure, but there's also teacher pressure: the teachers in the state schools seem to be very militant and concerned about their own amenities and careers rather than about their students. They don't strive to reward achievers. Their picture of business, for example, is a dreary one, rather than the exciting adventure it is in reality. When the kids leave school this is reinforced by the dole system: we must be the only country in the world where a kid can leave school and immediately go on the dole. And the fact that a young person leaving school must be paid an adult wage is just a disincentive to business to hire young people: you pay an adult award rate to a young person who's just left school, has no experience and has to be trained. And youngsters don't need as much money to get by: most of them are living at home and have to contribute something to their board, then they have their entertainment money and their car money and that's about it. When I got a job at a Standard Oil service station I was paid about $50 a week, a paltry salary even then — but it didn't matter, I got experience and learned the basic lessons which have shaped the rest of my career.

It benefits neither the kids nor the country if they emerge from school without knowing how to get a job, or start their own business or whatever it is that they want to do. Once they leave school they are subject to the industrial system, with the inordinately powerful trade unions which probably have more power in Australia today than unions have ever achieved in any country. Nothing can move, communications can't occur, businesses can't operate and governments can't govern without the support of the trade union movement. They are the de facto government, as if we didn't have enough government without them.

I understand the reasoning of union officials who want to protect their members' jobs, but I also have great empathy for the youngsters who leave school genuinely wanting to work, but ill-equipped to do it, and facing the barrier that business isn't prepared to pay them the adult award. What do they do? They look for work, they can't find it, they get frustrated and they get into the never-ending cycle of dependence on government. After a year on the dole they're older but no wiser in terms of job skills and experience, and less employable because of their demoralisation. I can empathise because of the contrast with my own experience: I was hired for every job I applied for, and it gave a great boost to my confidence. Unemployed school leavers are paying the price for the policies established because the trade unions and pliant governments fear a lower youth wage might mean older workers getting the sack. In practice it simply doesn't happen that way.

Trade union power and the government fear of union leaders are counter-productive in other ways. We now have about 700,000 people without jobs — yet there is a great shortage of skilled labour in Australia. At Budget we are looking overseas for skilled labour — but the unions are opposed to increased immigration.

They fear that immigration will add to unemployment. But historically, the greatest periods of economic growth and improved living standards have occurred during periods of high immigration. Migrants create demand, they work very hard, they don't just get jobs, they also create jobs. Historically migrants have not added to unemployment, because of the motivation, skills and money they brought with them, but we ignore that because of some unino sensitivities. In 1986 it's difficult to find car washers. One asks: what are the 700,000 people doing? What are the 25 per cent unemployed youth doing? It's the system! It's not designed to be productive. It has been influenced by well-meaning people who simply don't understand what drives an economy, what it is that creates jobs and wealth.

Part of the price of our adversarial system — unions versus management, capital versus labour — is the divisive attitudes it ingrains in the national character. We ought to be able to join together with common goals instead of tearing each other apart all the time. The Americans have softened adversarial politics: an American President has to get support from the opposition to get major legislation through Congress. President Reagan has to rely on support from Democrats; in Australia the adversarial approach colours every segment of our life. Our judicial system is becoming irrelevant to much dispute solving simply because it is so adversarial: if parties are locked in mortal litigious combat for three years, the chances of both being satisfied with the outcome are zero — which is why many contracts now use the mechanism of arbitration to solve disputes. It saves time. It saves money. It yields solutions both parties can live with. I speak as a survivor of several litigation battles.

To open a milk bar you need approval from 20 different authorities; before you can paint your house you need government approval. We have Federal, State and local governments regulating our behaviour, staffed by armies of bureaucrats. Bureaucracy is obscene and obsessive in its task of perpetuating itself. This is just what a young and vigorous country like Australia doesn't need. We're in trouble when tax consumers outnumber tax payers.

I have a suggestion: abolish the state governments and establish a two-tier system, a Federal Government and local governments, the latter consolidated to make them more efficient. This would liberate tens of thousands of public servants who now do nothing but shuffle papers all day, make local governments more responsible and responsive, and cut back the crippling burden of swollen bureaucracies which live off the wealth created by others. If we can liberate the paper-shufflers to become wealth-creators, reduce the tax burden and free the heart of our economy, the small business person, from the stifling hand of the regulator, we'll be getting somewhere. People have just about had it with taxes: I don't think they can absorb any more. (This is not, by the way, a right-wing idea: Bob Hawke suggested abolishing the states in the 1979 Boyer Lectures on the ABC, though we haven't heard anything from him about it since he became Prime Minister.)

We also need to direct our welfare system to those who need it. There should be a means test on pensions: why should the government pay a benefit to people who have created enough assets to get by on? Where's the fairness in taxing everyone to pay pensions to people who don't need them? Of course those retired people who don't have their own home or superannuation to live off should be looked after. I don't, incidentally, have any objection to the shift of pensions by way of superannuation to the corporations. I think the American system is better in that respect: social security is funded by both employer and employee over there. Social welfare programs that are inefficient and counter-productive, as ours are, are unfair to everyone: the workers who pay more than they should, the pensioners who need and deserve a pension but are unfairly resented for being a drain on the community. I have no sympathy for those who draw a pension they don't need.

Welfare payments also reinforce the idea that doing a job well is not an inherently worthwhile goal: at the moment unless you're earning around $230 or more a week, you're better off on the dole once you take into account Medicare and taxes and so on. The system tells people, particularly young people: why work?

Although I'm a believer in the invisible hand of the market, in individual initiative and in creative entrepreneurial energy as the fundamental solutions to our economic, and many of our social, problems, I'm not a simple-minded ideologue about it. I believe it's right to introduce lead-free petrol, for example: as I discovered when I was living in Los Angeles, there's nothing more basic than having breathable air, it's one of Australia's advantages over much of the industrialised world and we should do what we can to preserve it — so long as we remember that there's a cost, and eventually the public has to bear it. Regulation, sometimes imposed to benefit powerful business interests, is inherently damaging. We should, for example, abolish our liquor licensing courts: all they do is restrict the market. People should be able to buy a can of beer or a bottle of wine in a milk bar or a supermarket or anywhere else where people want to buy and sell beer or liquor. If people want to drink, they will: controlling outlets and trading hours because of a combination of the breweries and the wowser lobby is an absurdity.

But I'm not advocating work, work, work and no play. I don't think we should go the way of the Americans and cut back annual holidays to two weeks. Four weeks' annual leave, and our public holidays, are part of our way of life. That's us. That's Australia. But pay loadings on holidays should be abolished as quickly as possible; so should penalty rates for weekend and holiday work. I also wouldn't like to see Australians develop the narrow fear of missing a day's work that the Japanese have: we can balance our relaxed lifestyle by taking pride in our work. We had that attitude once: it's only in recent years, probably after World War 2, that we've had this change in attitude to the work ethic. The socialist influence has damaged the status of achievement. In the schools there's a psychological barrage against achievement and it permeates right through our society.

Until the mid-1960s, Australian business was too timid, unwilling to take risks, permeated by the old-school-tie networks. But there has been a transformation in the last 20 years. The old-school-tie networks are rapidly disappearing, and a new generation of aggressive young Turks are challenging orthodoxy.

In the 1950s, and early 1960s 10-year corporate investment plans were not unusual. That all changed: institutional investors, the AMP's and so forth, started to look aggressively at improving their return on investment. No longer do they just buy a share parcel and leave them in the assets column on their balance sheet indefinitely. Years ago Ansett Transport Industries had a number of major institutional investors loyal to ATI; they stuck with my father's company through the first takeover attempt in 1972, but the second time, in 1979, they didn't.

At the same time, corporate boards and executives were changing priorities: they were no longer prepared to support long-term investment in research and development to expand their markets. Short-term profitability became the order of the day. Companies that weren't earning acceptable profits became targets for the rapid-growth companies. There was a sudden buildup in pressure on the companies that were taking the long-term perspective, investing in research and development — that is, in the future. They became subject to takeover because they weren't producing the short-term returns their shareholders wanted. There was a drastic change in the way public companies were operated, and every time results were published which didn't live up to forecast, there was intense pressure on managers to increase profitability. The trouble with that is it's a cycle of decline: every time you decide to increase short-term profitability you're winding down your business because you're not investing in the future. That's one of the reasons I have no enthusiasm at the moment for Budget to become a public company; I don't want to maximise profits at the expense of growth. I think we are now in a new world of capitalism where it is increasingly difficult for public companies to sustain long-term growth other than through acquisitions. It's not healthy for Australia. With every acquisition there's one less company listed on the sharemarket, there's usually a shedding of labour, there's a shrinking of the tax base — hopefully we're through the worst of it now.

As for management specifics, one of the worst deficiencies of senior management is the inclination to protect themselves against threat from below. If they can't tolerate having someone below them who is as good, or better, than they are, it's self-destructive. An executive who doesn't have a second-in-command able to take his place will miss the opportunity for promotion to a bigger job. Duncan Leitch, once our general manager, now our New Zealand managing director, has always regarded it as part of his job to find a person who can replace him — so he's always being pushed from below, and he's always able to step up because there's a person competent to replace him.

Australia developed some outstanding international business entrepreneurs — Rupert Murdoch, Alan Bond and John Elliott, for example — partly, I think, because anyone who can make it in Australia can make it anywhere in the world. We have a very tough market. The toughest in the world. It's a small, thin market, only 15 million people largely congregated in widely separated cities over this huge continent, and on top of that we have extraordinary government interference in business, high taxes and old-fashioned trade unions. But if you look at the industrialised world country by country, I think Australia can hold its head pretty high. Most Australians exposed to the U.S. or the U.K. markets do well, often because they are a breath of fresh air. They're more creative. They do things less expensively. They work better with people — Australian egalitarianism has its positive side — than the Old World establishment types or the overblown, isolated corporate managers of North America.

We are, rightly, reducing trade barriers, which means Australian manufacturers will have to compete against like businesses in Australia and also against international business. They will have to be very good. The whittling away of Australian manufacturing production and capacity in the last 10 years has occurred partly because of lowering tariffs, partly because we have a system that props up workers' incomes. As a result, we have a lifestyle and standard of living which is the envy of most of the world, but there's a price to pay, and the manufacturing sector has been paying it. Its contribution to gross domestic product has shrunk alarmingly in the last 20 years, and our current account deficit reflects the result. So does our national debt.

We've dropped from being the eighth biggest trading country to twenty-third in a short time. I think we've made the mistake of trying to be all things to all people.

We have to identify niches in the world market where we have comparative advantages because of our resources, climate or skills, areas where we can do really well, and concentrate on those. The Swedes did it with the Volvo; the Swiss did it with watches — but there's nothing manufactured here for which Australia is famous around the world. We should simply get out of industries in which we're never going to be able to compete in efficiency, productivity and price, and concentrate on growth markets where we have advantages.

Which markets? That's the sixty-four-thousand dollar question. We live in the developing region of the world in the Western Pacific basin and we have a massive market, shaped like a horseshoe, from Western Canada, through Washington, Oregon, California, Mexico, South America's Pacific seaboard, New Zealand, India, all of South East Asia, Korea and China to Japan. A lot of potential customers there. We must identify products to promote and sell in this region. An Australian solar heat company is making great inroads in Japan and looking to extend to Korea and to other parts of the Pacific; that's an opportunity created by our hot climate. On the service side, Jet-Pak International Pty Ltd discovered that there's a big demand in Japan for fresh asparagus during the Japanese winter: they fly fresh asparagus to Japan every day, having worked with the Japanese to package the product in a way acceptable to the Japanese consumer. We should follow these examples and select products where we have advantages over international competitors and put all our energies into those items. We must retain enough flexibility so that if demand drops we can shift to something else, or somewhere else, or both.

Some economists fear Australia will go the way of Argentina and become what Edward Wheelwright once feared we would, the 'poor white trash of South Asia'. There's a risk, but I don't think it will happen. We have a lot of comparative advantages. We're resource rich. We're stable. There's now an awakening to the lunacy of the policy of building up inefficient protected industries to sustain employment. There's now a concerted effort to ensure we don't go the way of Argentina. We like the way of life we've established here, the sense of fun, the hedonism, the sardonic sense of humour. Given the right conditions, Australian workers are the best in the world. They compete ferociously. They work very hard, not to be 'the best', but to beat the guy across the street. In the end it's the same thing. I don't believe Australians are wedded to mediocrity and second-rateness: that's one of the myths left over from our colonial experience. In business, art, science, movie-making, literature, architecture, sport — you name it — we can do as well, we can do better, than the best in the rest of the world. I think we are in for a painful few years, but when it comes to the crunch it will be ordinary Australians who will say 'All right — let's get on with it.'

Acknowledgements

The publishers wish to thank the following for their efforts and/or use of copyright material in this book: Jane Booth of the San Diego Historical Society, Dwight G. Donatto of the Union-Tribune Publishing Co., Anthony de Bolfo of *Inside Football* and Syme Media Pty Ltd, Herald & Weekly Times Pty Ltd and the Editor of *Who's Who in Australia*, Mr Arthur Treble and the Inglewood Historical Society, and Sherrie Crosswell of Budget.

Every effort has been made to contact copyright owners. In some cases, however, it has not been possible to do so. The publishers sincerely regret any errors or omissions which may have occurred and will correct any brought to their notice.

Index

AAA Drive Yourself Pty Ltd, 84
ABC, 121
Abeles, Sir Peter, 134, 153, 155, 156, 157
abolition of state governments, 206
accidents in rented cars, 178
achievement, 147, 149, 207,
Addison, Dave, 111
Adelaide, 87, 200; office site, 83
adversarial systems in Australia, 205
advertising, 116, 134–5, 139–40, 142, 166, 175; agency, 194; beginning; 94, 95; mistakes, 143; TAA, 155; TV, 142
AGC *see* Australian Guarantee Corporation
Age, The, 123, 132
Air New Zealand, 166
airline ambitions, 197
airline policy, 152–4, 155, 157
air travel indicators, 86
Alaska, 35
Alexander, Ross, 64
ambitions, 193
Anchorage, 41–3, 44, 48
Anchorage Times, 47
Ansett Airways, 16, 18, 19, 152, 154–5, 194
Ansett, Charles John, 13,14
Ansett, Cynthia, 77, 163–4
Ansett, Elizabeth, 13
Ansett, Grace (*née* Nicol), 15, 17, 18, 21, 22, 31, 56, 165;
Ansett, Lady Joan (*née* Adams), 19, 76, 162

Ansett, John, 16, 20, 23, 24, 31, 33, 34, 77, 100, 108, 120, 162–5
Ansett, Josie (*née* Chadwick), 89–95, 108–9, 111, 118, 174, 175–6, 184
Ansett, Judy, 164–5
Ansett, Karen, 55, 58, 63, 87, 94, 95
Ansett Knitting Mills, 15
Ansett, Sir Reginald, 11, 19, 50–52, 145, 100–1, 110, 117, 118, 162–3; and McIlree, 78; airline policy, 152–4; attitude to Bob's return to Australia, 63, 76; cars, 16; flying, 17; hot-dog franchise, 55; job hopes of, 62; name, 34; office, 11; qualifications, 12; womanising, 18
Ansett, Ron, 58, 62, 151, 175, 199–200
Ansett, Sherrie *see* Crosswell, Sherrie
Ansett Transport Industries, 63, 76, 100, 110, 117, 133, 155, 172, 208
Ansett, Tim, 62, 175
Anzarett, Charles, 100
arbitration, 205
asparagus, 210
ATI *see* Ansett Transport Industries
Atkins, Bob, 111
attitudes, American, 202; Australian, 201, 202, 203, 205, 209, 210–11; and skills, 68
Auckland Regional Authority, 165–6
Australian Financial Review, 113, 120
Australian Guarantee Corporation, 106–8, 110, 160, 192
Australian National Airways, 153
Autorama, 167

216 BOB ANSETT

Avis, 79, 93, 95, 96, 111, 112, 114, 115, 121–2, 132, 134–5, 154, 162; and ATI, 154; Budget's connections with, 85–6, 88; car source for Budget 82–3; for sale, 117; name, 84; training, 80
Avis New Zealand, 161, 165
Avis U.S., 84, 161
Aylett, Alan, 185

Bacall, Lauren, 57
Bali, 169
Ballarat, 15, 16
Bank of New South Wales, 106, 160
Barassi, 135, 185, 188
Barker Green and Parke, 164
Belzeberg, Morris, 84, 111, 112, 116, 161, 162
Berry Springs, 90
Big M Marathon, 183–4
Blue Gardenia night club, 53–4j
board meetings, 174
boardroom, 182
boards of directors, 160, 208
Bond, Alan, 144, 186, 209
Bonebrake, Charlie, 29–30
bonuses, 67
Boyer Lectures, 206
Brady, Diamond Jim, 46
Brian Sweeney & Associates, 137, 138
Brighton Grammar, 162
Brisbane, 87
Brown, Nick, 91
Brown, Vic, 97
Bruce, Stanley Melbourne, 17
Bruning, Bern, 96
Buck, 47–8
Budget Rent-a-Car, early days, 79–81; first day with, 81; name, 84; in the Northern Territory, 162
Budget Airlines, 101
Budget Air Services Division, 160
Budget Bird, 113
Budget International, 11, 112, 161, 198
Budget New Zealand, 161, 166, 198
Budget U.S., 111, 161
Burge, John, 17
bureaucracy, 202, 205–6
Burmeister, Peter, 173, 198
business, enjoyment, 81; failure, 192; and football, 188; teachers, 151

Campbell, Don, 19–23
Canberra, 114
Cairns, 87
Canadian border crossing, 38
capital, 196
car, dealerships, 194; leasing; 195; purchase, 195; theft, 191
Carisbrook, 16
Carlton Football Club, 185, 186
Carnation Milk Company, 56–8, 70–1
Carnegie, Dale, 149
Carter, Jimmy, 189
cartoonists, 125–131, 186
cash sales, 85
Cec's Car Rentals, 133
Cessnock, 133
Chadwick, Reginald, 95
chairmanship, 197, 198
Chamber of Commerce, Melbourne, 187
China, 169–70
Chifley, 152, 155
Christchurch City Council, 165–6
citizenship, 135
Civil Aviation Agreement, 154–5, 157, 160
Clairemont, 59
Cleanaway, 191
cleanliness, in business, 67
climate, and work, 203
Cloverdale, 37
Cobden, 15
Collett, Pat, 94–5
Columbia, 21
commission, for travel agents, 143; on volume, 71
commitment, 86
company ratings, 193
competitiveness, 74–5, 80; of Australians, 82
computerisation, 121
Congress of Employers, Victoria, 187
conscript mindset, 202
Cook Islands, 166
Coolangatta, 150
Coolidge, Calvin, 11
Cooper, Ralph, 100–1
corporate environment, 158
courtroom work, 179
Cox, 27
Coxhead, David, 161
credit control, 192
credit risks, 190–1
credit sales, 85–6

INDEX 217

criminal customers, 177
Crosswell, Brent, 175
Crosswell, Sherrie (*née* Ansett), 62, 165, 173–4
Cullen, Peter, 114, 120–2
Curran, Norm, 100
customer, complaints, 149, 157; creation of, 73; expansion of base, 83; ideas, 137, 142–3; place of, 147; rapport with, 71–2; service, 65–6, 71, 75; unusual, 177–8
culture, of company, 69
Curtice, Cactus Jack, 56

Daily News, (Perth), 85
D'Arcy MacManus and Masius, 137, 139, 140
Darwin, 14, 89–90,111
debt, national, 201, 209–10
Dell, Frank, 62
Department of Transport, 111, 116, 121–2
Devonport, 87
Digger, 59
Disneyland, 57, 70
diversification, 193
dole system, 202–4, 206
Dominion Rent-a-Car, New Zealand, 96, 133, 161
drinking, 182
driving, 180
drugs, 181

East-West Airlines, 160
education, 203
Elliott, John, 144, 209
employee identification with company, 157
employment, small business attitude to, 73
entrepreneurs, 209

Fallout Shelter bar, 59–60
fatherhood, 175
feedback, from customers, 149
Fiji, 161
firing, 103
fitness, 182–3
Fitzroy Football Club, 15

Flat Rate, 134–5, 143
Flemming, Dan, 26–7, 49, 87–9
Florence, 91–2
flying, 59–60; RM Ansett, 15
football, American, 21, 25, 29–30, 189; army football, 52–3; college football, 56
football, Australian Rules, 15, 176, 189, 196; and business, 188
football *see also* North Melbourne Football Club
Ford, Christina, 78
Ford, Henry, 78
Ford Motor Company Australia, 194
Fort Benning, 50, 52
Fort Ord, 49, 55, 70
franchising, 133
Fraser Government, 115
Fraser, Malcolm, 122–3
Freedom Cheques, 137–8
Fresno, 31
Frost, Bob, 198
fun runs, 183

Garner, Errol, 57
Gas and Fuel Corporation, 163–4
Geneen, Harold, 198
General Motors Holden, 86
George, Sir Arthur, 155–6
Getz, Stan, 57
Gippsland, 133
Glendale, 37
goal-setting, 82, 149–50, 193
Gobbo, Justice, 119
Goldwater, Barry, 61–3, 146
Gopher Canyon, 28
government action, 201
Great Train Robbery, Melbourne, 177
Grenadis, Marshall, 28
gridiron see football, kAmerican
Guam, 166
Gunning, Sally, 49–50
Gunyong Valley, 19
Gympie, 164

half-day rate, 142–3
Halton, Charles, 115, 121
Hamilton, 16–7
Hamley, Stan, 106, 155–6, 160, 200
Hanson, Peter, 195

Harritt, Elmer, 29
Hawke, Robert J, 152, 206
hedonism, Australian, 201,210
Hertz, Heinrich R, 84
Hertz Rent-a-Car, 79, 96, 114, 122, 132, 135, 140, 195; name, 84; New Zealand, 165; sale to TAA, 120
Hewitt, Ron, 50−2
Hickey, Jim, 123
High Court, 155, 160
Hilmer, Frederick G, 202
hiring policy, 74, 148
Hobart, 87
holidays, annual, 207; public, 207
Hollywood, West, 57
Holmes a Court, Robert, 144
Holt, Harold, 78
Holyoake, Lloyd, 184
Hong Kong, 53
Hostetter, Red, 35, 44, 66−9
hot-dog sports franchise, 54−5
hotel industry, 86, 148, 195; and car rentals, 150

Iberia, 63
ideas, business, 137
image, of Budget, 138−41, 193; personal, 139−41, 143−5, 198
immigration policy, 205
Inglewood, 13
Inglewood Advertiser, 14
innovation, 137
Inside Tourism, 143
insurance, 86
intra-company communication, 149
interviews, media, 178−9
intuition, 190−1
investors, 208
Ipswich, 133
ITT, 198

Jamison, Max, 26−7
Japan, 58, 167−8
Japanese, negotiating with, 167−8
Jarman, Phil, 97
Jet-Pak International Pty Ltd, 210
Joel, Jack, 18
Johnson, Amy, 14
Johnson, Lyndon B, 61−2
Johnson, Rafer, 86
joint venturing, 196

Jones, Charlie, 115
Joseph, Ron, 185−8, 196−7

kangaroos, 178
Katransky, Alex, 96
Kays Rent-a-Car, 18, 81, 88, 96, 114, 119
Kazuko *see* Ansett, Karen
Kemmsies, Muriel, 63
Kemmsies, Peter, 60−3, 77, 87
Kennedy, John F, 61, 145, 188−9
Kennedy, Robert F, 58, 86
Kenton, Stan, 57
Kerang, 16
Kleinig, John, 124
Korean war, 49, 52,
Korea, 169
Kununurra, 90

Lager Lovers' League, 88
Lange, David, 182
Las Vegas, 49
Last Chance Saloon, 46−7
Launceston, 87
Law Institute, 163
leadership, 69; in the army, 70; in business, 68
learning, in business, 74−5
Legget, Des, 89
Leitch, Duncan, 124, 166, 198
liquor licensing, 207
Livie, Barbara, 90
Lloyd P Goode and Co, 164
lobbying, 115
Long Beach, 55
Los Angeles, 20, 56, 58, 72, 199, 207
Lowy, Frank, 98−9
Lynch, Phillip, 116

MacArthur, General, 52
Mackay, 87
Mackay, Hugh, 144
Macombo nightclub, 54
MacRobertson Miller Airlines, 89
Maher, Bill, 96, 121, 123
Malaysia, 166
management, checks, 190; mediocrity, 208−9
managers, and the public, 142; freedom of, 150, 158

manufacturing decline, 209
marathons, 183-4
market, Australian, 209; expansion, 193-4; penetration, 143; research, 137-8
Maryborough, 15-6
Maurice Cohen & Company, 163
McIlree, Eric, 77-9, 84-6, 95, 99-100, 104-5, 140, 162, 172
Measey, Brian, 162
mediocrity, Australian, 211
meetings, 174
Melbourne, arrival in, 63-4
Menzies, Sir Robert, 62, 153
Methodist Ladies' College (Ballarat), 16
Mexico, 30, 31-2
mistakes, 159, 191-2
Mitchell, Bill, 59, 60
Miyanchi, Yoshi, 167
MMA *see* MacRobertson Miller Airlines
Mobil Oil, 87, 100
Monrovia, 21, 70
Montgomery Airfield, 59
Moomba festival, 187
Morris, Peter, 115
Morris, Theo, 99
motivation, personal, 171, 173
Mt Buller, 98
Mt Eliza, 17, 18, 19, 31, 110, 151, 162-3
Murdoch, Rupert, 134, 144, 157, 209

Nettlebeck, John, 98-9
New Zealand, 165-6, 161
New York Post, 88
New York — Washington DC shuttle, 159
Newcastle, 133
news stories, 141
newspaper scanning, 173
Nicol, Grace *see* Ansett, Grace
Nicol, Melville, 16
Nicol, Stanley, 15
Nicol, Stan, 79-80
Nixon, Peter, 116, 123
Norfolk Island, 133
North Melbourne Football Club, 176, 183, 184-7, 196,
Northrop, Justice, 120
Northway Cab Company, 44-7
Noumea, 166

Oceanside, 27, 35, 44, 200
O'Connell, Barry, 161
office architecture, 182
offices, suburban, 195
Oklahoma, 43, 50
Orient Leasing, 167, 195-6
Oroweat, 59, 61-2, 72-3, 199
orthodoxy in business, 207
Otton, Ric, 139-40, 145-6
over-government, 204, 205-6, 209

Pacific Rim market, 210
Packer, Kerry, 144
Papua New Guinea, 161
Paracoda, 19-20
paratroop training, 52
parking, 180
Pascoe, Frank, 89
paternalism, in Budget, 168; in Japan, 168
pensions, 206
People's Express, 159
persistence, 11
Perth, 87-8, 91, 111, 151, 199
petitioning, 115
petrol, lead-free, 207
Phoenix Hotel, The, 64
Playboy, 175
police as customers, 177
political attitudes, 145-6
politics, adversarial, 205
Port Hedland, 88
Power of Positive Thinking, The, 149
price, 116
Prime Minister's Department, 122-3
Prince George, 39
Privy Council, 166
profit motive, 73
profit, 147-8, 196
profitability levels, 158, 208
psychic salary, 203
public speaking, 141, 147, 176-7, 178, 200

Qantas, 92-3, 187
Quantum Market Research, 141
Queensland Airways, 153
Quinlon, Skeeter, 44, 69-70

Reagan, President, 145, 146, 189

Reid, John, 105
Reinecke, Ian, 121
relaxation, 176, 197
research and development, 208
Richmond Football Club, 186
Ridgeway Military Academy, 20–1
Rigby, Paul, 88
Rockhampton, 87
Rogers, Andrew, 119
Rome, 91
Ross Aviation, 87
Rudolph, Jerry, 25, 29–33, 35, 41–2, 45
Rudolph, Margaret, 33, 41–2
running, 173–175
Ryan, Max, 183
Rylah, Sir Arthur, 78

Saito, 168
sales companies, 195
Salinas, 37
San Diego, 31, 33, 58–9, 77
San Diego Evening Tribune, 62
San Jose, 31
Santa Barbara, 37
Scali McCabe Sloves, 140
Schimmelbusch, Wayne, 189
Scotch College, Melbourne, 17
self-motivation, 169, 173
service, 147–8
service industries, 194
Seymour, 15
Shannon Airport, 114
Shellbank Holdings, 79, 96
Shell Oil Company, Japan, 167
sickness, 182
Singapore, 166
Sinatra, Frank, 57
skills, and attitude, 68
slogans, 68, 73, 82, 116, 118, 136, 147
Smith, Dick, 144
Smith, Helen, 82
Smith, Neil, 63
smog, 207
smoking, 168, 180–2
Soderstrom, Dale, 25, 28, 31–3, 35, 37–49, 52, 54–7, 68, 71, 88–91, 171–2, 180–1
solar heat, 210
Solomon Islands, 166
South Australian Tourist Commission, 166
Spalvins, John, 144

Speakes, Sheriff, Ed 27–8
staff letters, 175
Standard Oil Company, 35, 44, 68; training course, 66
Steamships Trading Company (PNG), 161
Stevens, John, 80, 199
stunts, 97
successor, 198–200
Sugami Hara swimming pool, 53
suicidal customers, 178
Surfers Paradise, 87, 197
Swinburne Technical College, 14
Sydney, 87, 92–3

TAA, 63, 120, 121–2, 132, 152, 155–6, 159, 172, 194
Tahiti, 50, 166
Takami, 54
takeovers, 208
tall poppy syndrome, 202
Tasmania, 199
taxes, 201, 206
Taylor, General Maxwell, 52
Taylor, Nev, 89
teachers, 203
telephone service, 141–2
tendering, 124–5
Texas, 112
Thailand, 169
Tholstrup, Hans, 137
Thomas Nationwide Transport, 194
Thredbo, 94
Thrifty, 96, 173, 198
Tihunga, 20
tips, 68
trade barriers, 209
Trade Practices Act, 122
Trade Practices Commission, 112, 119
Trade Practices Commission vs ATI, 124
trade unions, 202, 204
travel agent sector, 85–6
Trevino, Carmen, 41
Trourig, Terence, 101
Tokyo, 52–3
Toowoomba, 133
Tourist Advisory Council, 187
Townsend, Robert, 80
Townsville, 87
Transport, Department of, 115
Tuddenham, Des, 97

INDEX 221

Tullamarine Airport, 106
Tulsa, 43
two-airline policy *see* airline policy
two-airline agreement, 193, 197

Utah, University of, 56
unemployment, 201, 204—5

Vautier, Justice, 161
Vanuatu, 166
Vicfit, 187
visibility items, 86
Vista, 22—5
volunteer mindset, 202

Ward, Ed, 31
Waste Equipment Company, 191

Watts, 57—8, 71
Wesley College, Melbourne, 18—9, 176
Westfield Corporation, 98
Wheelwright, Edward, 210
When the Luck Runs Out, 202
White, John, 89
Whitfield, Pat, 34—5, 43, 50
Who's Who in Australia, 76—7
Williamson, David, 82
Wilson, Nigel, 132
Woolworths, 144
Wooten, Doug, 96, 123
work ethic, 202
workers, Australian, 211
Wrest Point, 199

Yamagishi, 167
young, employment disincentive, 203—4